D0773182

Household Accounts

SUSAN PORTER BENSON was a historian of American labor and gender who received her Ph.D. from Boston University. She taught at Bristol Community College in Fall River, Mass., for almost twenty-five years, at the University of Missouri at Columbia for seven years, and, at the University of Connecticut, Storrs, for the next dozen years, where she served for five years as the director of the Women's Studies Program. She was the author of *Counter Cultures: Saleswomen, Managers, and Customers in American Department Stores, 1890–1940* (University of Illinois Press, 1986), and numerous articles and chapters on gender, family, and work. In addition she was a co-editor (with Steven Brier and Roy Rosenzweig) of *Presenting the Past: Essays on History and the Public* (Temple University Press, 1986).

Household Accounts

Working-Class Family Economies in the Interwar United States

Susan Porter Benson

Afterword by David Montgomery

Cornell University Press
Ithaca & London

First published 2007 by Cornell University Press

Printed in the United States of America

Library of Congress Cataloging-in-Publication Data

Benson, Susan Porter, 1943–2005.
   Household accounts : U.S. working-class family economies, 1919–1941 /
Susan Porter Benson.
      p. cm.
   Includes bibliographical references and index.
   ISBN 978-0-8014-3723-6 (cloth : alk. paper)
    1. Households—Economic aspects—United States—History—20th century.
2. Family—Economic aspects—United States—History—20th century.
3. Working class—United States—History—20th century.   4. Consumption
(Economics)—United States—History—20th century.   5. United States—
Economic conditions—1918–1945.   I. Title.

   HC106.3.B47 2007
   339.4'7086230973—dc22

                        2006102926

Cornell University Press strives to use environmentally responsible suppliers and
materials to the fullest extent possible in the publishing of its books. Such materials
include vegetable-based, low-VOC inks and acid-free papers that are recycled, totally
chlorine-free, or partly composed of nonwood fibers. For further information, visit
our website at www.cornellpress.cornell.edu.

Cloth printing   10 9 8 7 6 5 4 3 2 1

*To Sue's students at the
Universities of Connecticut,
Missouri, and Warwick, and at
Bristol Community College,
1968–2005*

Contents

A Note on *Household Accounts* and Its Preparation

When Susan Porter Benson died in July 2006, she left her book manuscript 95 percent completed. The gaps included the absence of complete citations to a few secondary sources and the need to check over various parts: to see that a book constructed in a complex way and done over several years, often during an illness, did not repeat points and examples across chapters. It was also necessary to integrate one short section on secondhand goods into the book and to incorporate more transitional material as chapters started and ended. Sue conferred with Jean Allman and David Roediger regarding these matters shortly before her death. It was agreed that Allman and Roediger should bring these small matters to completion, enlisting the expert aid of Nancy Hewitt, Charles McGraw, and Sharon Strom, each of whom took responsibility for revising sections of the manuscript. McGraw also completed the important standardization and checking of the manuscript's footnotes. Ophelia Benson provided expert editorial assistance. Jim O'Brien meticulously prepared the index. The watchword in every case was to preserve the spirit and letter of the manuscript rather than to revise extensively. The book appears only under Sue's name, as it is in every sense her work. Sue's husband adds that this agreement brought joy to Sue, and him, in the last days of her life.

Portions of this book were revised by Sue from previously published material. Chapter 1 expands on "Living on the Margins: Working-Class Marriages and Family Survival Strategies in the United States, 1919–1941," published in *The Sex of Things: Essays on Gender and Consumption,* edited by Victoria de Grazia (University of California Press, 1996). Chapter 2 recasts "Gender, Generation, and Consumption in the United States: Working-Class Families in the Interwar Period," in *Getting and Spending: European and American Consumer Societies in the Twentieth Century,* edited by Susan Strasser, Charles McGovern, and Matthias Judt (Cambridge University Press, 1998). A small section of Chapter 4 and the material under the subheading "At Second Hand" in Chapter 5 appeared as "What Goes 'Round Comes 'Round: Second-Hand Clothing, Furniture, and Tools in Working-Class Lives in the Interwar USA," in the *Journal of Women's History* 19, 1 (Johns Hopkins University Press, 2007).

On the last day that Sue felt strong enough to discuss the manuscript and strategies for completing it, her main concern was whether or not to use the real names of the working-class women and men who are at the very center of this book, those who were interviewed, observed, and documented by U.S. Labor Department Women's Bureau agents in the 1920s and 1930s. Though nearly seventy-five years have passed and though the documents are in the public realm, Sue worried that the "subjects" of investigation had not given their permission, nor had their descendents, to be named in an academic history book decades later. In so many ways, Sue's concerns were absolutely typical of how she approached the pasts of working-class people—with the deepest respect, the most sensitive of care, and with profound empathy. Sadly, we did not reach a decision on that day and, in the end, were not sure how Sue would have chosen to handle the issues of naming and anonymity. Ultimately, we chose to leave the names as they appear in the Women's Bureau Papers and in the chapters Sue wrote. Readers should know that responsibility for that decision lies with us and not with Sue.

JEAN ALLMAN
DAVID ROEDIGER

Urbana, Illinois

Acknowledgments

The following acknowledgments, regrettably incomplete, were assembled from the author's notes.

Thanks go to the National Archives staff, where Willian Creevey was especially helpful, to the Social Welfare History Archives staff and University of Minnesota, particularly to David Klaasen, Linnea Anderson, and Mark Hammons, as well as to the staff at the Sophia Smith Collection in the Archives of Smith College.

Financial support for this study came from the Weldon Spring Foundation at the University of Missouri, the University of Missouri Research Council, the University of Connecticut Research Foundation, and two fellowships from the National Endowment for the Humanities, including one held in residence at the National Humanities Center.

Comments from respondents to conference papers improved the final version of the book. Daniel Walkowitz, Jean-Christophe Agnew, Walter Licht, Philip Scranton, and the audience at the Hagley Research Seminar, Muriel Nazzari at the 1996 Berkshire Conference, and Victoria de Grazia and Susan Strasser at the North Carolina Feminist Historians Group gave valuable advice.

Feedback from panel members and audiences at the Conference on Consumption in the Twentieth Century, sponsored by the German Historical Institute and the Smithsonian Institution in 1995, Les circulations des objets d'occasion, Istituto Universitario Europeo in Firenze in 2002, the Conference on Consumerism, Domesticity, and Middle-Class Identity, sponsored by IREX and the Hungarian Academy of Sciences in 1993, and at meetings of the American Studies Association, the Organization of American Historians, and the American Historical Association sharpened the book's arguments, as did responses by those attending talks at Western Connecticut State University, George Mason University, Tunxis Community College, University of North Carolina, University of Chicago, University of Washington, and University of Iowa.

The expertise and friendship of health care professionals, including Pamela Moore, James Watson, Herbert Ridyard, Leszek Kolodziejczak, Grant Golub, Stacy Nerenstone, Albert Puzzo, and Jeffrey Cohen made possible the completion of research.

At the University of Missouri the collegiality and criticism offered by colleagues and students including Tammy Proctor, Grace Lee, Randy McBee, Julie Willett, Steve McIntyre, Beth Ruffin McIntyre, Tani Barlow, and Sundiata Keita Cha-Jua mattered greatly.

In North Carolina Temma Kaplan, Elizabeth Kirk, Kate Bartlett, Marianne Hirsch, Katherine O'Brien O'Keeffe, Craig Monson, Ed Muir, Jing Wang, Sue Levine, Judith Bennett, Cynthia Herrup, Barbara Harris, and Nancy Hewitt provided stimulation and support.

At the University of Connecticut Shirley Roe, Altina Waller, Nina Dayton, Karen Spalding, Blanca Silvestrini, Francoise Dussart, Richard Brown, Bruce Stave, Ronald Coons, Jennifer Baszile, Frank Costigliola, Myra Marx Ferree, Diana Meyers, Marita McComiskey, Bridget Geraghty, Catherine Jacquet, Bandana Purkayastha, Angela Rola, Sheila Kucko, and Nancy Shoemaker deserve special thanks. So too does a remarkable group of graduate students there, including Rosa Carrasquillo, Joyce Hanson, Charles McGraw, Margaret Robinson, Philip Samponaro, Melissa Ladd Teed, Teresa Vergara, Sherry Zane, Leslie Frank, Jackie McNeil, Catherine Page, Sherry Obey, Richard Moss, Lindsay Hunter, Sally Milius, Elizabeth Watts, Mary Pat Mahnensmith, Amy Albert, Sandra Enos, Signe Friedrichs, Jen Heckard, and LuAnn Saunders-Kanabay.

Such far-flung and long-standing friends as Roy Rosenzweig, Deborah Kaplan, Stephen Brier, Jennifer Brier, Janet Francendese, Zofia Burr, Ardis Cameron, Susan Strasser, Kathy Peiss, Ellen Furlough, Larry Glickman, Venus Green, Daniel Horowitz, Helen Lefkowitz Horowitz, Lee Marvin,

Virginia Winstanley, Mameve Medwed, and Jayne Merkel contributed to much of my work.

How to thank old friends from Providence and Columbia? Peter Evans once wrote, "I cannot imagine how people write books alone." I agree: Jean Allman, Dave Roediger, Tina Simmons, Bruce Tucker, Barbara Melosh, Gary Kulik, Louise Lamphere, Peter Evans, Peter Bret Lamphere, John Miller, Ellen Lapowsky, Kate Dunnigan, Maureen Dunnigan, Mary Fredrickson and Clint Joiner. Evan Joiner, Megan Joiner, Natalie Kampen, Catherine Lewis, Judith Smith, Sharon Hartman Strom, Fred Weaver, Anne Fausto Sterling, and Nelson Fausto.

And thanks to all in my various families: Eunice Siegel Marcus, Jay and Sue Marcus, Lissa Marcus, Stephanie and Bruce Newell, Loraine Siegel Porter, Alvin Porter, Ed Benson, Anne Walker Benson and the far-flung Bensons: John, Lynne, Caetlin, Liz, Steve, Jasper, Iris, Andy, Barb, Tom, Jay, Nick, Sue, and Ophelia.

S.P.B.

Household Accounts

Introduction

This book surprises me. It surprises me that I chose to write it to begin with, and it surprises me the way it has turned out. Because it almost seemed to sneak up on me, its shortcomings have not evoked despair, and its small pleasures have become real delights. I suspect its surprises will ultimately turn out to be logical developments from my life and work. This introduction represents my attempt to account for the surprises, and to work my way through to the logic of which I did not originally suspect the existence.

I am surprised by this book most of all because it takes me away from my central scholarly concern with work. My teaching and research have long argued that work had a powerful shaping influence upon people's lives; this was an insight that was first impressed upon me as a child. I was dazzled by the transformation in the mothers of two friends who took jobs outside the home when my friends and I were in junior high school. Although both of their jobs were standard "pink collar" jobs—one in retail sales and one in dead-end clerical work—they seemed in remarkably short order to become different people—more self-assured, more assertive, more interesting and knowledgeable in their conversation, more insistent that my friends pull their weight around the house. I was too young to know to look for signs of the overwork and stress, which I now think must have accompanied this transformation. Indeed, these may have been carefully minimized by the small-town unrationalized contexts of their jobs.

In my own family, the mixed effects of work were all too apparent, as were the tangled connections between work and class. Both of my parents were children of Jewish immigrants from the Russian-Polish border. My mother's family had become quite wealthy through manufacturing and real estate ventures but lost much of its money during the Depression. My father's family ran a succession of small stores specializing in jewelry and home appliances; my paternal grandfather was trained in Europe as a watchmaker. Both of my parents went to college, although my mother's family sent her in style and my father worked his way through. She graduated from the University of Chicago blissfully unaware of the social ferment and urban engagement of the sociology department in which she majored, did most of the work toward a Master of Social Work and went to work for the county in which she grew up. My father overreached himself in getting a degree from the University of Pennsylvania's Wharton School; there was no niche in Depression-era corporate America for someone of his background. He held a variety of insecure, perhaps humiliating, jobs until he was saved by World War II. His dreadful eyesight kept him out of military service and he went to work as an electrician in a shipyard. Everything about the job appealed to him: the camaraderie with the other workers, especially his partner; the physical and intellectual challenges of the work itself; the opportunity to pinch-hit in other specialties and accumulate craft knowledge. My father was a born skilled worker. The only problem was that the family script had not written in that part. After the war, with a two-year-old child and a now unemployed wife to support, he entered the family business in which his father and younger brother were already engaged. Within a few years, my grandfather and uncle decamped for California after conniving to sell the business to my father at a highly inflated price.

My father and mother ran that business until they were seventy-five years old and, although they got satisfactions out of it, they were distinctly compensatory satisfactions, second best to what they would have liked. My mother had envisioned her paid career as a social worker shading off after marriage into volunteer work in the social welfare field. Instead, she labored to keep the books for the business, by and large a losing battle against my father's anarchic business principle of robbing Peter to pay Paul. She dunned their debtors; he ducked their creditors. Most of all, he built and rebuilt the store. He rewired it every few years, he built elaborate motorized displays, he rebuilt the display cases, he redid the heating system, re-modeled the storefront, moved the staircases. And when he wasn't doing that at the store, he was shoring up and rebuilding and remodeling our flimsy prefabricated house. He had a couple of cronies who helped him on his projects, as he helped them with theirs. They were decidedly "his" friends—my mother wanted little to do with an Irish American teamster and an African American migrant from the South who did odd jobs. Lumbered with work he disliked, my father found ways to continue doing the work that nourished his soul. The difference between his manual-worker self—good-humored and easy-going—and his retail-merchant self—grouchy and short-tempered—was not lost on me. As for my mother, on the other hand—thrust into an economic role she'd never intended to fulfill and lacking autonomy in her work because of my father's stubbornness and disorganization—she sniped and carped. They both coped, but also became embittered. I learned early that work was a central component of self-identity, and that its power to fulfill as well as to frustrate was great.

But work was only a part of it; the debt to my father's family and the rent on the store building which they had refused to sell him shadowed my childhood and made our lives poor and insecure. We had no pay check coming in, but the outlays to my grandparents had to be made with inexorable regularity. The house was mortgaged and re-mortgaged, always falling apart because of its shoddy construction and in a state of half-repair where my father's money and patience had run out. He jerry-rigged devices to compensate for his cash-flow problems; one of my most vivid memories is the Rube-Goldberg fuel-oil-fired water heater he contrived because, I understood only later, he could buy fuel oil on long-term credit, while the gas and electric companies insisted on monthly payments which he could not be sure of being able to meet. The water heater never really worked, and baths in a few inches of tepid water became the order of the day. There was always food on the table, and plenty of it, heavy on the meat in a way that then meant good nutrition. But leftovers were used to the last crumb, the refrigerator filled with Pyrex custard cups containing a few shards of meat, a dozen peas, at the same time that my father had every power tool in the catalogs and a huge stock of materials with which to work. My mother still put the satin bedspread with the lace overlay on their bed on the rare occasions when they had company outside the family, and through family connections bought expensive clothing at wholesale prices.

We didn't talk about being poor, but we were clearly second-class citizens at the postwar feast of abundance. More important, we were insecure. My parents felt themselves a distinct class above most of the people in our town, because they operated their own business: my father scorned steel-workers because they lacked independence and a sense of quality work—working-class republicanism made a curious reappearance in my house-hold—and my mother simply felt that they and their families were socially beneath her, lacking the refinement she thought she had. But thanks to the United Steelworkers, the fact was that the men in the local steel mills made a lot more money than my parents did, and the steelworkers had much greater security in terms of employment, income maintenance, and fringe benefits. When a strike halted their incomes, our income dried up as well; we shared their lean times to a greater extent than we benefited from their flush times. The relationship between money and class thus was very com-plicated in my early life. Both of my parents embraced class cultures that belied their actual economic position; money was a problem, but it was dealt with in ways that obscured our real insecurity.

Money, class, and work came together in complicated ways in my own life. My parents told me that I had everything I wanted, but what they never mentioned was that I had been taught not to want. Requests were belittled or put off, money gifts from relatives were confiscated and disappeared forever. I never had money of my own to spend as I wished; I had to re-quest money for each separate expenditure and, even when I got an al-lowance, had to account for how I spent it. I stole a silver dollar from my parents when I was seven or eight and refused to confess under prolonged and ruthless interrogation. I still feel some residual shame over the es-capade, but fifty years later I see it as a rebellion against their obsessive control over money. I was utterly mystified by my parents' claims of supe-riority to the people around us. They all seemed perfectly nice and decent people, with the same mix of strengths and weaknesses that I saw in my own home and in our kin networks. The distinctions that my parents drew seemed mean and petty; what seemed more obvious to me was that we were all pretty much in the same economic boat.

I spent my childhood in a rich ethnic world: a pastiche of new-immi-grant worlds in which ethnic religious and secular institutions, to say noth-ing of informal social ties, still powerfully shaped daily life. The original barriers had thinned by the 1950s, though. They had become permeable membranes which allowed us to pass from one group to another and back to our own. The public schools were the crucible in which some of us went farther, finding a less ethnically inflected identity that yet partook of the ethnicity about which we felt deeply ambivalent. We ate one another's eth-nic foods, knew the appropriate behavior for the various ethnic rites of passage we witnessed, played together, and dated as our inclinations led us.

Yet senses of difference persisted. On the one hand, there was a "we," a sense of our ambiguous and insecure position between an immigrant working class and a still-forming lower middle class. But, on the other hand, whatever sense of commonality we felt was fractured by senses of far more limited "we's"—were we Catholic or Jewish, Hungarian or Rumanian, Polish or Ukrainian, Serbian or Croatian, Greek or Italian? And those identities fractured still further. My own Russian-Jewish family scorned Hungarian Jews. Friends from Neapolitan families looked down on their village-born Sicilian neighbors. Serbs and Croats mixed it up in the alleyways behind the schools.

We were located in an especially complicated time for American ethnicity: children or grandchildren of the last of the "new immigrants" before nationality quotas cut that stream of immigration to a trickle, we grew up before the Immigration Act of 1965, at a time when immigration seemed irrevocably a thing of the past. Our solution was to make a new way for ourselves out of our ethnic pasts and the complex cultural resources of the postwar decades. My seventeen years in that environment demonstrated to me in innumerable ways that ethnicity is not unitary, that there are many different ethnicities. There was one ethnicity for church or synagogue, another for fraternal associations, another for neighborhood networks, another for daily life in school, another for serious courtship and marriage, another that shaped emotional life, another that shaped family connections. Women and men, boys and girls, those of different generations forged their own versions of ethnicity. I did not yet, of course, know this in a conscious way.

Much of what I subliminally "knew" about ethnicity was made explicit in my mind one day when my graduate seminar was discussing Robert Orsi's *The Madonna of 115th Street.* No newly discovered Stone Age tribe could have seemed more exotic to these relatively young, distinctly un-ethnic, mostly WASP midwesterners in the seminar than this Harlem Italian community. I had not foreseen this, and I listened with amazement as they talked themselves deeper and deeper into Italian essentialism, or perhaps even Italian Harlem essentialism: surely, they argued, these strange customs and the world of the domus were produced by some bizarre aspect of this small group's nature. Surely, they nervously asserted, no one else thought like this. Finally I could stand it no longer and announced that if this was the case, then why were Orsi's chapters on the domus the best description I had ever read of the inner life of my Russian-Jewish, small-town western Pennsylvania, storekeeping family? The discussion screeched to a halt as they gave one another nervous looks and silently amended their earlier judgments to Italian Harlem/Russian-Jewish Western-Pennsylvania essentialism. I had failed that day as a teacher, but something very useful happened to me as a scholar. The moment has been branded in my memory as the point at which my lived experience of ethnicity as a child fused with my life as a scholar. For all the yawning cultural and experiential chasm between my parents and the parishioners of Our Lady of Mount Carmel, they shared important ideas about the domus. Orsi borrows his notion of the domus from LeRoy Ladurie's *Montaillou:* it "was at once building and family, the unifying principle that linked man and his possessions." It "constituted a formidable reservoir of power and counterpower which could hold out with some degree of success against the external powers surrounding it."[1] Like the Harlem Italians, my parents' and their parents' memories of Europe were not of community but of family; they shared "a kind of popular arrogance" that their families were superior to all others.[2] They condemned individualism[3] and faced the world outside the domus with the complicated attitudes of "love and fear, intimacy and distance" included in the "essential and fundamental social value" of *rispetto*.[4] At last, after twenty-five years, I fully understood my mother's comment when I married a WASP—"At least you could have picked an Italian."[5]

Family, Work, and Consumption: A Glass Half Empty or Half Full?

I thus set out, over a decade ago, to write a history of working-class consumption, hoping to find both evidence of working-class immersion in a national culture of abundance and documentation of distinct racial-ethnic patterns of consumption. I found neither. The United States entered what is usually regarded as the era of mass consumption in the years between WWI and WWII, but the working-class majority tasted the joys of consumption in a very limited way. *Household Accounts: Working-Class Family Economies in the Interwar United States* argues that, at least in the interwar years, the glass of consumption was half empty rather than half full. Underemployment and unemployment ate significantly into working-class families' standard of living; insufficient and irregular income made life a difficult and often futile struggle to supply the basic necessities and the occasional luxury. When I began this project, I thought I would be able to illuminate ethnic cultures of consumption in the interwar years. As my research proceeded and evidence for such cultures failed to emerge, I at first still believed that these cultures were somehow "there," and that it was some flaw in my sources that failed to reveal them. It was not that ethnicity did not matter; it mattered deeply in people's cultural, kin, and neighborhood lives. But when it came to confronting the market, ethnicity became a kind of second-order influence; some groups, in some places, turned more to one strategy than to another, but again the difference was more one of degree than of kind, and all drew on a common array of strategies. I have now come to think that, while there were certainly tendencies for different groups to spend their money differently, most working-class people were part of a culture of earning and spending that was class-based rather than ethnically based. Let me be absolutely clear about this: I am not arguing that ethnicity did not figure in people's lives. Rather, I am arguing that in matters of getting and spending money, class outweighed ethnicity, acting as a limiting factor that constrained the more discretionary kinds of consumption that might reflect ethnic propensities. My contention is thus analogous to women's historians' argument that for African Americans considerations of race very often overshadowed those of gender. It was not that ethnicity did not matter; it mattered deeply in people's lives, as my own experience showed. But when it came to confronting the market, ethnicity acted less powerfully than class. Given the instability and insecurity of working-class people's lives during the 1920 and 1930s, they had quite limited freedom in the marketplace; their choices were constrained and the degrees of comfort and plenty compromised.

It is not possible, as I had thought when I began this project, to talk about working-class consumption in itself. Instead, I have come to see working-class consumption as but one aspect of a complicated array of working-class economic activities, including wage-earning, household production, market-replacement, reciprocity, and market activity. The key context here is the material: between 1919 and 1941, the period on which I focus here, the American working class remained distinctly marginal to the emerging world of mass consumption because of the insufficiency and irregularity of its income. Most Americans, to put it baldly, simply did not earn enough money or have a steady enough income to allow the wide range of discretionary spending usually associated with mass consumption. Instead, therefore, of talking about working-class consumption I focus on the working-class family economy, a term in which I include the range of decisions families made about earning and spending money as well as their efforts to avoid the money economy through a whole range of non-market activities. My concern is not with the absolute levels of consumption, nor with the quantitative aspects of the family budget; rather, I seek to understand a working-class culture of family consumption: how working-class families negotiated the use of family funds, how they made qualitative judgments about what they wanted and what they didn't, how they framed family strategies and how these strategies articulated with individual goals and desires.

Far from finding the 1920s a time of prosperity and plenty for working-class families, I found strong threads of continuity between the 1920s and the 1930s. The difference between the two periods was one of degree rather than of kind: the wolf may have howled at the door more persistently and loudly in the 1930s, but that howl was heard through the 1920s as well.[6] Second, I have found very limited evidence of group-specific patterns of household economy. The urban-industrial families depicted in *Household Accounts* include people who worked at manual or non-manual, non-supervisory jobs. Most worked for hourly or piecework wages or salaries, but some independent entrepreneurs in family enterprises or in small retailing, services, and construction firms are included, as are some foremen in factories. Every social historian knows that persons in these kinds of families have long lacked adequate income, but we seldom consider the flip side: the fact that consumption cannot, therefore, have been much but a trial, a constant reminder of subordinate class status. Their consumption revolved around hard choices about basic needs and provided therapeutic satisfactions only secondarily, if at all. Finally, such consumption has to be considered an aspect of the lived experience of working-class people, centering on their agency, desires, and possibilities. Topics usually central to histories of consumption—the development of a mass consumer culture, the hegemony of middle-class versions of consumption, and the expanded offerings of the marketplace—appear in my work as contributing but not controlling influences on working-class people's efforts to negotiate the marketplace.

These families were not swept up by the economy of abundance, but lived in a complex economy in which scarcity conditioned daily life and plans for the future. By no means peculiarly American, this had much in common with other economies distant in time and in space: the economy of makeshifts evoked by Judith Bennett for medieval Britain, the struggle to achieve subsistence identified by Steve Stern in late colonial Mexico, and the resourceful exploitation of market possibilities depicted by Gracia Clark in contemporary Kumasi, to cite only a few examples. Working-class families in the interwar United States may well have shared more with these distant groups than with middle-class household economies drawn deeply into the culture of abundance.[7]

My view of working-class household economies is not the only possible one and is powerfully shaped by the sources on which I rely. I use two main types of sources: first, reports on home-visit interviews with woman wage earners conducted by field agents for the Women's Bureau of the U.S. Department of Labor during the 1920s and early 1930s and, second, studies of families confronting unemployment that were assembled by settlement workers and academic social scientists during the late 1920s and the 1930s. Both bodies of evidence were compiled almost exclusively by woman researchers and were—always in the Women's Bureau studies, and often in the other studies—presented from a woman-centered point of view. The accounts are, as a whole, vivid and compelling, as close as we are likely to get to the voices of working-class women themselves. Despite their biases against working mothers and their desires to keep families together at all costs, the middle-class and elite people who tell us what their working-class informants said were arguably the most sympathetic interpreters of working-class life from the outside; their goal was less to reform working-class people than to mobilize state aid and public opinion on their behalf.[8] Perhaps due to a common gender dynamic of engagement, especially in the Women's Bureau data, the investigators tell us more than the interview schedules asked them to. Although distinctly different in education, class, ethnicity, and race—and quite often, marital status—the Women's Bureau agents and the wage-earning women whom they visited in their homes shared a pleasure in a good story about daily life, and when the agents recorded those stories we are the richer for it.[9]

It is the raw data of these studies, not the conclusions that were drawn in reports and surveys by the investigators, that have interested me most. Both types of sources are most valuable for their qualitative descriptions of family process and for their ability to show the complex ways in which family members divide and unite over issues of consumption. Included in these studies are families of many European ethnicities and of African descent, as well as a sprinkling of Latino families; Asians are almost absent. Using the bits and pieces of sources designed for other purposes, I have assembled a narrative of these contestations and alliances and suggested what constituted a working-class culture of family consumption.

Dynamics of the Working-Class Family Economy

In order to better understand what goes on within family economies, I turn to literatures on gender, the family, and the allocation of resources in Third World countries. At risk of doing violence to the range and subtlety of this last set of works and of underplaying disagreements among those working in this field, I would say that these ideas have been useful to me first because they assume that families functioned in a context of scarcity. Second, they see families as venues of serious contestation as well as unified action; Amartya Sen argues eloquently that family struggles are characterized by "cooperative conflict" in the allocation of resources. This notion focuses attention on the dynamism and variety of family process and offers a productive way to look at the often highly contradictory evidence about American working-class family process. Third, the idea of entitlements offers a social and cultural explanation for the unequal allocation of resources within the family without resorting to essentialist arguments about the personal inclinations of self-sacrificing women. It allowed me to interpret family interaction in terms of the different resources commanded by players in family dramas; divergent observations become less baffling and appear as the result of struggles in which the participants command different material and moral resources. Finally, the literature on Third-World families assumes that a nuclear family operates within a larger context of neighborhood, kin, and ethnic group.[10]

This is not to suggest that American scholars have entirely neglected the larger contexts in which families operate. Some observers of working-class life have documented the same contextualization of the family in a variety of time periods. Judith Smith's study of Italians and Jews in Providence between 1900 and 1940 demonstrates that while families worked together using child labor, women's work, consumption strategies, and male breadwinning to provide for the common good, struggles over spending and inadequate resources within families were commonplace. Carol Stack found that African American families in a Midwestern industrial city in the 1960s were caught in a web of family obligation that required the sharing of whatever resources came into the kin network and could rarely be used for individual gratification. Margaret Byington's meticulous study of working-class budgets in the steel town of Homestead depicted the strategies used by women and men to maximize their labor power for the survival of both family and kin at the turn of the twentieth century. Byington concluded that the managerial skills of housewives meant everything to family prosperity.[11] In many respects, *Household Accounts* uses this same focus on the family as a site of cooperation and conflict in managing money and sharing resources. My work, therefore, goes against the grain of much of what has been written about the history of consumption, because it focuses on families rather than individuals or market sectors, arguing that people do not function in the marketplace as autonomous individuals solely in response to marketing and desire but as part of families in which consumption is an object both of struggle and of shared aspiration.

Class and the History of "Mass Consumption"

Until the last fifteen years or so, historical work on class and consumption tended to recycle two generalizations: that the middle class was ubiquitous if amorphous and that the focus of American life has shifted decisively from production to mass consumption. More recently, scholars have begun to rethink these generalizations, but their work is as yet episodic in its coverage. It tends to focus on the major urban areas of the Northeast, where consumption habits and institutions were most fully entrenched; however, the uneven development of the United States meant that this area was neither a mirror nor an inevitable model of consumption for the rest of the nation. There is another inherent contradiction: most of the work is on the middle class and focuses on its formative years in the nineteenth and very early twentieth centuries, while studies of consumption concentrate on the twentieth century, especially the 1920s and beyond.[12] But how does this literature on middle class consumption speak to questions surrounding working-class consumption?

Crucially, much of what we know about the social history of middle-class consumption comes by default from studies of the working class. As historians have traced the development of distinctive working-class leisure patterns, for example, middle-class leisure has become that which is outside these patterns. Of course, no clear set of standards defines membership in the middle class, although occupation, level of income, and culture all contribute to middle-class identity. The three do not necessarily work in the same direction: one person may have a working-class job, a middle-class income, and a culture that combines elements of the two; another may embrace a rigid middle-class culture of respectability and yet lack the income to realize that culture in her or his life. One may, therefore, be middle-class in some but not all respects, and may enter the middle class through a variety of routes. Because only a relatively elite group, a minority of the nation's families, earned middle-class incomes at least until 1945, income remained a continuing brake on the achievement of a middle-class life even for those so inclined by occupation and culture.[13] Furthermore, life in the middle class has had strikingly different implications for Euro-Americans and African Americans as well for other racial and ethnic groups.[14] As a result, the U.S. middle class has been a group of such diverse interests and locations that it defies rigorous definition. Nonetheless, U.S.

historians tend to agree that, among Euro-Americans, something called the middle class emerged in the middle third of the nineteenth century. Supplanting but also differing from what were earlier called the "middling sort"—artisans and farmers who had sufficient skill or property to earn an independent living—the middle class recruited from that group as well as other sectors of society. Artisans who took the entrepreneurial rather than the wage-earning route, when forms of industrialization eroded craft manufacture, joined with the legions of young men who entered the growing white-collar occupations in urban areas: office clerks, salesmen, and (by the last third of the century) members of the growing managerial and professional classes.[15] Many of these new "white collar" jobs were segmented by gender and race, resembled factory assembly lines, and were subject to the same time management, piece rate wages, and lack of opportunity to "move up" to managerial positions that characterized factory work. Historians have had difficulty deciding whether these new workers were, in fact, making a transition into a new mode of working-class life or anchoring themselves in the lower middle class and middle class. White men were the most likely to benefit from this new tier of office work.[16]

The "collar line" between blue-collar and white-collar workers was never an impermeable boundary, and, during the period from the 1920s to the early 1970s, limited segments of the wage-earning blue-collar working class achieved incomes high enough to purchase many of the trappings of middle-class life. At the same time, the middle class shifted from one largely of northern and western European origin to one that included increasing numbers with roots in southern and eastern Europe. Although small numbers of African Americans, Asian Americans, and Latinos/as had incomes that would qualify them as members of the middle class and embraced cultural notions about respectability that had some resonance with white middle-class gentility, the U.S. middle class remained not just exclusionary (as racist mechanisms marginalized non-Europeans) but also dependent for its comfort and prosperity on the exploitation of peoples of color as domestic servants and manual labor workers.

At least until World War II the nation's working-class majority had limited access to the joys of consumption.[17] Families of skilled workers were likely to pursue what one might call one-dimensional consumption strategies, focusing on one type of consumption and denying themselves, often rather drastically, in other areas.[18] Consumption was, therefore, not a "mass" phenomenon but rather a "class" phenomenon, its appeals directed first and foremost to the middle and upper classes. Department stores, the central retail institution of the period from 1850 to at least 1960, sought the patronage of those prosperous enough to make frequent and multiple purchases. Working-class people headed for the bargain basement or the special sales, or bought sparingly from the main-store departments, but their dollars were a small proportion of those that swelled department-store coffers.[19] Advertisers, too, concentrated their attention on the prosperous rather than the typical. During the 1920s and 1930s, as Roland Marchand notes, advertisers' definition of a "mass audience . . . referred primarily to those Americans with higher-than-average incomes" and assumed that as much as two thirds of the nation's population was disfranchised in the marketplace.[20] Consumer credit increased dramatically during the 1920s, but the working class had very limited access to either conventional charge accounts or installment credit. Few department stores would extend conventional credit to working-class people before World War II, and we may therefore assume that working-class consumers accounted for a disproportionately small amount of consumer credit.[21] To a large extent, therefore, when we talk about mass consumption we are in fact talking about the consumption of a relatively elite population.

E. P. Thompson's much-quoted admonition to see class not "as a 'structure', nor even as a 'category', but as something that in fact happens (and can be shown to have happened) in human relationships" suggests that we can most profitably understand the middle class in relation to the working class, the group from which it was most eager to distinguish itself.[22] Although the term "mass consumption" suggests a linear progression toward broader consumption opportunities and the homogenization of standards of living and thus to some degree of shared consciousness, the diffusion of consumption opportunities worked in a less linear way. Whether ordering from catalogues or occasionally venturing into a department store, working-class people were not barred from partaking of what Kenneth Ames refers to as "the goods explosion," but as in the department store they were merely extras in a spectacle starring the middle class.[23] In some cases, middle-class consumers could afford new goods and services that were beyond the reach of the working class. In other cases, and this is the pattern that we shall see in the evolving chapters as described below, the working class increasingly purchased goods and services similar in function but inferior to those available to the working class.

The chapters that follow explore working-class consumption through the prism of the family. Chapter 1, "'Living on the Margin': Working-Class Marriages and Family Survival Strategies," examines consumption as an issue in working-class marriages, considering the evolving role of men as breadwinners and women as household managers. I argue that—contrary to popular images of women as delighted consumers—working-class wives found much more worry and struggle than pleasure and autonomy in the marketplace. Working-class husbands, by contrast, were more likely to use their earnings for personal gratification. My sources offer special insights into two-earner families, and this chapter considers them, as well as families in which women do not ordinarily earn. The gendering of household work and its relation to cash-replacement activity also figure centrally in this chapter.

Chapter 2, "'Cooperative Conflict': Gender, Generation, and Consumption in Working-Class Families," explores economic relations between parents and children in the light of changing expectations about consumption, expanding educational opportunities, and changing labor markets. As traditional expectations about filial duty eroded, parents and children negotiated new patterns of family support. Conflict ensued, but what is more impressive is the degree to which both parents and children compromised their goals in order to maintain family peace. This chapter also examines the gendered discourse about children and consumption along with the different ways in which sons and daughters related to their families. Paralleling my findings about husbands and wives, I find that daughters were far more disadvantaged as consumers than their brothers.

Chapters 3 and 4, "The Mutuality of Shared Spaces" and "What Goes 'Round, Comes 'Round: Working-Class Reciprocity," explore working-class families' market-mediated relationships with kin outside the nuclear family and with neighbors. Here I see families caught between the ethics of mutuality and reciprocity, on the one hand, and self-interest and advancement, on the other. Kin and neighbors shared space, child care, food, and other goods and services, but the sharing was increasingly mediated by cash. Because obligations were in the process of being renegotiated, expectations were not clear, and the lack of clarity produced conflict at least as often as it led to mutual satisfaction. Despite the potential for conflict, neighbors and kin still provided most of the assistance that nuclear families sought outside themselves; help from mutual benefit societies, social service agencies, or the government played a distinctly secondary role.

Chapter 5 examines working-class families' relationships with the marketplace. While I discuss working-class families' experiences with installment credit and household finance companies, I argue that these new institutions generated only a small fraction of working-class credit. Most families continued to rely on local merchants with whom they developed highly personalized credit relationships; the more rationalized systems of credit were ill-suited to families whose incomes were as irregular as those of most working-class families between the world wars. The credit they sought was for the basic necessities of life far more often than for the latest consumer delights. Moreover, most working-class families did their best to avoid relying on credit, often preferring to buy and sell in markets for second-hand goods, instead of going into debt for new consumer items. What was for middle-class consumers a mark of businesses' faith in their economic standing was for working-class families a sign of their inability to supply their needs. Credit thus became a juggling act in which different claims were constantly being balanced and rarely satisfactorily met.

1

"Living on the Margin"
Working-Class Marriages and Family Survival Strategies

"Walter Benda gave every cent he earned to his wife," a settlement worker observed approvingly, "and she planned carefully."[1] Scholars such as Susan Levine, Kathy Peiss, Elizabeth Ewen, and Judith Smith have called our attention to the diligence and creativity of working-class women who, like Mrs. Benda, acted as managers of the family fund; they have also acknowledged the limitations of that role, especially when errant husbands proved less cooperative than Walter Benda.[2] In fact, I would go even farther than these historians in revising the essentialized picture of the working-class woman as consumer. The power of this trope depends upon an assumption of a gendered division of labor within the family: male as breadwinner, woman as householder. My sources—primarily the raw data from Women's Bureau investigations of wage-earning women and their families as well as case studies of working-class families experiencing unemployment during the 1920s and 1930s—suggest a much less intense gendering of the work of keeping a family going. On the one hand, the male breadwinning ethic was far from universal among these families. Men's attitudes toward breadwinning ranged from total acceptance of the ethic through various reservations about it to outright rejection of the responsibility involved. Moreover, many women expressed a sense of obligation to earn some or all of the family support, even when husbands and/or fathers were present and earning. Similarly, some women expressed a preference for wage earning over household work, and some men saw housework as part of their responsibility. One of the most intriguing things about this material is the degree to which the Women's Bureau agents and the social-science writers did not "take in" these gender transgressions; they invariably ignored this evidence or wrote it out of their analyses. Ironically, this gives me greater confidence in making my arguments: it makes me think that the evidence they did record, even though it clashed with their world-views, is relatively trustworthy and probably only a portion of similar evidence that otherwise-oriented investigators might have recorded.

The marriages discussed in these documents differ distinctly from the companionate marriage that was so widely touted during the 1920s and 1930s.[3] I reject the use of the term "companionate" for these evolving relationships for two reasons. First, companionate marriage implies a strong and primarily romantic bond between marriage partners. In working-class relationships the affect was more of a generalized familial one based on loyalty and obligation rather than on romance or sexual attraction; indeed, family economic survival competed with and often obscured such feelings entirely. In this respect, their closest analog would be European peasant marriages in which there was a clear sense of shared responsibility and joint enterprise.[4] Second, I find the term inappropriate because companionate marriages rested on a continuing, even rigidifying, set of segregated sex roles that cast husbands as breadwinners/producers and wives as consumers. My argument about working-class partnership marriages is that they involved a definite, if subtle and partial, breaching of the boundaries between gender roles.

The fluidity that marked partnership marriages did not originate, let me emphasize, for the sake of working toward some abstract notion of gender equality; rather, the material conditions of life in the North American working class reinforced some people's willingness to improvise and to put other goals above the maintenance of dominant-culture gender constructions. Working-class people made adjustments in one aspect of their lives in order to relieve pressures and lighten burdens in other aspects of their lives. They sought to make the best of lives lived amidst great difficulty, lives conditioned by circumstances not of their own choosing. These relationships should not be idealized, just as whatever degree of gender equity there may have been in slave marriages should not be idealized. In the latter case, any gender equity came at the price of being owned as chattel property; in the case I examine, gender equity was inseparable from want and scarcity. And in both cases, adherence to dominant-culture notions of gender did not take top priority. The families discussed in this chapter negotiated a difficult set of circumstances in which expectations were not clear. Their family economies, like the ones studied by Jeanne Boydston in the early republic, were mixed economies that drew on a rich array of resources: wage-earning outside the home, wage-earning within the home, and cash-replacement activities.[5] Many of the families in this study were also immigrant ones, as was the majority of the working class at the end of World War I.[6] As such, they confronted both a new culture in the United States and a particularly volatile phase of capitalism.

The Travails of the Male Breadwinner

Because men, by and large, could earn higher wages than women, access to a man's wage was crucial to the family economy. The ideal husband earned steady wages and contributed his entire pay envelope to the family fund.[7] Many men spoke of their desire to earn a family wage, such as the Italian man who labored on the streets of Philadelphia and told the Women's Bureau agent, "I want the wage and my wife stay home."[8] That we should not take such demands for a family wage simply as expressions of male dominance is suggested by the comment of another Philadelphian, a Polish textile worker, who wished "things were so that men could earn enough to support a family then women would not have to slave at two jobs."[9] A man might want a family wage for many reasons, but this one alerts us to the fact that he might do so more out of respect for his wife's hard labor than out of a sense of his male privilege.

Even for those men inclined by culture and temperament to be model breadwinners, the labor market provided as many barriers as opportunities. The drive for efficiency and productivity if anything intensified during the 1920s and 1930s, assuring that insecurity and instability of employment would remain a part of men's occupational experience. The skilled men in my sources were thrown out of steady work by technology—printers and skilled carpenters seem to have been especially hard hit—one woman said of her father, "a cooper hasn't a job these days."[10] Semi-skilled and unskilled men found continued or increased periodic and seasonal unemployment. "Slack work"—short hours—was a repeated complaint, and workers who had long been accustomed to seasonal, usually winter, unemployment, found those seasons of unemployment stretching, as did one Italian-born laborer, from a month to three months to five months. One month of unemployment, or even three months, might be planned and saved for, but seven months of a laborer's wages couldn't stretch to cover a year.[11] In early 1933, a Washington, DC, carpenter voiced the spiraling frustrations of dealing with low pay and slack work: "One lone salary is not enough to buy a home and support a family on. . . . It was hard when I had steady work and now I just can't do it."[12] *The Immigrant Woman and Her Job*, a 1930 report of the Women's Bureau, offered a sobering view of the difficulties of male breadwinning. Of the 468 Philadelphia married women interviewed for the study, 218 accounted for their work by mentioning their husbands' difficulties in breadwinning. Nearly four out of five referred to their husbands' difficulties in securing regular work, either because their trades were seasonal, because they could not get full weeks' work, or because they were outright unemployed. Irregular work loomed much larger in these women's worldviews than did wage rates: just over a quarter mentioned the low wages earned by their husbands.[13]

Like everyone, men had multiple identities, and these identities had the potential to conflict. Union men, for example, asserted their manly independence through union activity, but that could cut two ways. If successful, it assured more regular work and higher wages, and hence enhanced a man's ability to fulfill the breadwinner role; if unsuccessful, however, it might seriously hamper his breadwinner potential. A Philadelphia taxi driver, for example, enjoyed six years of steady employment at substantial wages but then joined his fellow taxi drivers in a strike for higher wages. The strike was broken and he was blacklisted for eighteen months.[14] A Memphis man was out of work for almost a year after the 1922 railroad shopmen's strike.[15] One African American man found himself singled out from his new union fellows: when white employers realized that they would have to pay him the same wage as the union's white carpenters, they fired him and hired whites only.[16] An Oklahoma man left town during the railroad shop strike of 1922, ostensibly to find work elsewhere, but he made no contact with his wife until a week before the Women's Bureau agent visited her in May 1924.[17] Changing the point of view, then, changes the meanings of union militancy. From the vantage point of the family economy, it might mean lowered wages because of various types of discrimination, or it might be the knife that cuts the last ties of a lackadaisical breadwinner to the family. Manly assertion in a union was a gamble under the best of circumstances, but during the 1920s, at least, it does not seem to have been a winning gamble for the family.[18]

Other men rebelled against the breadwinning ethic itself instead of against their employers. The transition from bachelorhood to serious wage earning seems to have been difficult. A Women's Bureau agent noted that one recently married man "seemed to lack ambition or force";[19] another, whose wife said that he "never likes his job—always has trouble," took a more adversarial stance toward the labor market.[20] A Providence woman told the Women's Bureau agent that she had married but her husband never worked and after three months she left him; she apparently counted herself fortunate that he did not demand money from her.[21] The bachelor subculture of which George Chauncey has written so eloquently, which countered the male breadwinner role with its "alternative definition of manliness that was predicated on a rejection of family obligations," may have continued to exert a social and erotic pull on urban men even after marriage. Reluctance about breadwinning would have been an eloquent way to perpetuate the bachelor subculture's scorn for "the domesticating and moralizing influence of women."[22] Perhaps the best explanation for this phenomenon came from a southern textile worker to whom the writers of the classic history *Like a Family* gave the pseudonym of Ruth Elliot. Musing on her husband's irresponsibility and alcoholic binges, she speculated that at the root of it was the fact that

> When we were married we wasn't anything but kids. We had three babies, one right after the other, and somebody had to settle down. And it had to be me. Jesse never did settle down. It was too much of a load on him. If he had stayed single and hadn't saddled himself with a wife and kids, he would have sowed his wild oats and gotten over it. Instead, he planted a permanent garden, and it was disastrous. I know that now. But that didn't help me out a bit then.[23]

In some cases, which we might term the fair-weather breadwinners, men rebelled against the rigors of the labor market and industrial work discipline. One man, a Greek-born shoe-factory worker, took being out of work quite casually, determining "that he is doing his best and is in no way responsible, and that if he isn't able to support his family, some one else will have to do it. . . . He searches for jobs, but is not adaptable."[24] A fired streetcar man refused to work "unless he can find an easy job and so far hasn't been able to find one."[25] Other men balked at the punishing demands of the jobs available to them; a St. Joseph man who could only secure jobs that required "heavy carrying" finally decided that "he had rather stay home than break his back."[26] Wives often saw such behavior as shiftlessness, as did the ex-wife of an African American Chicagoan who claimed that her husband "would not work walking up and down the streets all day smoking cigarettes so I put him out."[27] But in a class by himself was the St.

Paul man who would work at the Armour Company only during the summer when he could play on the company baseball team and steadfastly refused the company's offer of a steady job at twenty-seven dollars a week.[28] Seen only in the light of the men's work lives, these examples might appear to suggest evidence of assertive manliness—as a rebellion against industrial time discipline and bad working conditions or as assertive union activity. From the point of view of the family, though, they meant insufficiency and uncertainty.

For less obvious reasons, other men physically distanced themselves from the breadwinning role. Desertion was a common response to a range of problematic job situations. Men who sought to escape unemployment sometimes abandoned their families. One New York woman defended her husband to a social worker: "It's only when he can't get work he runs away!"[29] Jobs that were disliked also encouraged desertion. Transference probably fashioned impatience with a less-than-ideal home life out of what began as an unwillingness to put up with a difficult work situation: one deserter had changed jobs "frequently, [being] easily dissatisfied, not a steady worker even when work is available,"[30] another "gets very excitable and quits."[31] The arbitrary authority structures in working-class jobs provided one source of irritation; a paper mill worker quit his job because the "boss kick too much,"[32] while a machinist had a habit of quitting jobs after conflict with his foremen.[33] In such cases, desertion was not always an all-or-nothing matter. Some returned "from time to time" but failed to take responsibility for family support,[34] whereas others secured jobs elsewhere and sent token amounts home—like the husband of a Kansas City woman who began "acting strange," decamped to Chicago and then Kenosha, and sent home a mere $50 in five months; still others simply disappeared.[35] A Croatian-born Kansas City wife, herself a meat-packing worker, summed up the impossibility of relying on an absent husband when the Women's Bureau agent asked if her husband helped support the family. She "shrugged shoulders and laughed and said 'Maybe—maybe not.'"[36]

Only one source, *The Immigrant Woman and Her Job,* gives us a significant amount of concrete information about the patterns of men's desertion. Going on the figures alone, though, leaves the erroneous impression that desertion, and desertion of a particularly difficult kind, was most characteristic of Jewish men. All but two of the Jewish women interviewed for this study lived in Philadelphia; sixty, or 26.9 percent, of those were or had been married. But thirteen had been either temporarily or permanently deserted, meaning that over a fifth of the Jewish women had this experience. This was in sharp contrast to an estimated 5 percent of Polish women and less than 2 percent of Italian women.[37] Things look even worse for Jewish women when we find that nine of the Jewish women were deserted either when pregnant or with children aged three or younger. It would seem, then, that Jewish men were especially heedless of their breadwinning obligations and indifferent to the welfare of their wives and children. A closer look calls into question this ethnic interpretation, however. Eight of these nine women had children in day nurseries—something that was true of only 2.6 percent of the children in all the families surveyed—and it seems likely that these women were contacted through the day nursery. Irrespective of ethnicity, then, well over half of the Philadelphia desertions where the ages of the children at time of desertion could be identified included children in the three-or-under category. It seems at least plausible that the pattern of desertion of families with young children was a more general one that resulted from the combined stresses of less female wage-earning, greater demands on men for breadwinning, and the family adjustments that come with the addition of a needy young child.

Even resident husbands typically withheld at least a portion of their wages from the family fund.[38] Most probably kept just enough for their daily expenses. A Boston plumber, for example, kept back between three and five dollars of his handsome weekly pay envelope of forty-two dollars for "fares, lunches, and smokes."[39] So widespread and generally accepted was this practice that a settlement-house worker was censorious of one wife who challenged her husband: "Mother tries to impose too great limits on father's allowance for cigarettes, carfare, lunches."[40] A Kansas City tile maker withheld even more, but he could still be counted upon to pay for the rent and groceries.[41] Expenditures on alcohol and gambling, forms of consumption that could enhance a man's position with his peers, also cut his contributions to the family fund. One Chicago meatpacker so indulged himself that his only financial contribution to the family was to buy "some food."[42] Slack work might lead a man to disengage more completely from the family economy; a Kansas City construction worker was described by his wife as someone who "does not have steady work and [is] not much help when he does."[43] Some women seemed to accept this practice, suggesting that there may have been two economies in a household: that of the male head of household and that of the rest of the family. A Rhode Island woman relied on her income from lace pulling to supplement the contributions of three of her children, but she expected nothing from her husband. Although a carpenter by trade, he had not been able to secure any work in his craft. At the time of the Women's Bureau agent's visit in 1934, he had been unable to find any carpentry work for eight years, and his liquor store job did "not pay enuf [*sic*] to give any money to family."[44] One Jewish immigrant to Philadelphia contributed nothing for rent or food, but, noted the Women's Bureau agent, "once in a while . . . buys children 'shoes for 90 cents' or gives them candy."[45]

Some husbands protected their control over their wages by not telling their wives how much they earned, a pattern that appears among African Americans as well as Euro-Americans and among wage-earners as well as the self-employed. Even though their husbands might withhold information about their pay envelopes, women used their knowledge of prevailing wages to gauge what they were earning; a Rhode Island lace homeworker told the Women's Bureau agent that "her husband doesn't tell her how much he makes but that she thinks he made $36 last week."[46] An Oklahoma African American wife of a barber remarked that he "says he don't make nothin' I don't know if he just tells me that or maybe he don't"[47] and a Polish-born meatpacker did not know how much her husband made in a metal foundry.[48] Even more extreme was a Polish woman in Philadelphia who not only did not know what her husband made but also did not know where he worked.[49]

Whatever the complicated dynamics that led a husband to withhold or contribute his wages to the family fund, they were not simply and directly related to the quality of a woman's performance as householder. A settlement worker profiled a neighborhood woman:

> She was plump and engaging, and often drunk. . . . She was a great scandal to the neighbors because her husband loved her and gave her his money and was faithful to her and never beat her. As one of her next door neighbors said, "There's Margaret next door being beaten and bullied and living right, and that Aggie Bennett with a man setting such store by her and her perfectly worthless."[50]

Perhaps Aggie's comfortable relationship with her husband reflected her attitude more than her behavior. Sociologist Mirra Komarovsky broke into a discussion of men's personal spending in the midst of a disquisition on methodology:

> Take, for instance, a question concerning the attitude of the wife to her husband's smoking. This proved revealing of marital relations in a number of cases. The expenditure for smoking is practically the only personal expenditure of the unemployed man, and it is often symbolic of marital conflicts. In happy families the typical attitude of the wife is,

"That is the only pleasure left for him. Why should I nag him about it?" In families with conflict, the wife says, "Smoking is not a necessity. There are things that the children and I need more." The actual practice connected with it, that is, how the money for smoking is allotted, what restrictive effect the wife's attitude has, may reveal the relative status of the husband.[51]

Even during the Great Depression, husbands continued to withhold some earnings from the family fund. The occasional approving note in the National Federation of Settlements' 1932 survey of unemployment about a husband who "gave every cent he earned to his wife" suggests that this was far from typical behavior.[52] Some men's contributions to the family fund were so unpredictable that for at least one woman the Depression and a husband's unemployment came as a fiscal blessing:

> Mrs. Adams doesn't know what to say about the effect of the depression because in the last five years she has been more secure than in any other period of her life. When the family applied for relief she insisted on getting the relief check herself. She also controlled the money that was coming in from the boarders and the children. Thus, for the first time in her life she knew exactly how much she had instead of just getting what was left after Mr. Adams' saloon bill was paid. She doesn't feel the humiliation of being on relief and is quite well satisfied with the present status.[53]

The Depression also revealed in high relief the meaning of pocket money for men. Guilt and shame, of course, plagued men who could no longer support or contribute to the support of their families, but these feelings were compounded by the anguish caused by their own financial dependency. Mr. Patterson, profiled by Mirra Komarovsky, felt such pangs intensely: "It is awful to him, because now 'the tables are turned,' that is, he has to ask his daughter for a little money for tobacco, etc. He would rather walk miles than ask for carfare money. His daughter would want him to have it, but he cannot bring himself to ask for it."[54] Some men linked their pennilessness to other aspects of the loss of male status: "The whole thing was wrong. . . . It was awful to have to ask her for tobacco, or to have to tell the landlady, 'My wife will come, and I will pay you,' or to have the dinner ready when she came home."[55] Men experienced a lack of pocket money as disempowering and feminizing. It meant dependency, insecurity, uncertainty, and public embarrassment, and being at someone else's beck and call—all feelings from which their status (however precarious) as breadwinners had insulated them, but which had been the staples of their wives' lives. Class as well as gender shaped their reactions: they missed not lavish consumption but small comforts such as tobacco, carfare, newspapers, and the occasional drink. If they had been women, their pocket change might have been termed pin money. The freedom to spend in these ways was a sign of a man's modest independence as a breadwinner and a workingman.

Husbands held tenaciously to their right to control their wages, and frequently deserted or threatened to do so when women tried to mobilize them to increase the family fund. One woman hesitated to insist that the family apply for relief despite the "almost unbearable" strain that managing the family's budget put on her. Her husband had already deserted twice before and threatened to do so again if she pushed the relief issue.[56] Another husband was described as "a rather selfish person." The settlement-house worker went on to say, "The fact that his family is not able to have the things necessary for good health and happiness, does not seem to distress him particularly. In fact, he threatened to leave them all many times."[57] Again, Mrs. Adams, whose husband missed his pocket change, saw the Depression as her ally; according to the caseworker, "If she had insisted on taking his wages away from him when he was earning, she is sure he would have just deserted the family and she would have been left with the two children."[58] If the loss of all support was the price of pressuring a husband either to be a better provider or to collaborate in her attempts to provide, a wife might well calculate that it was better to scrape by on what she had. Even more daunting was the prospect that a man's desertion might not just remove with him his pay envelope, but also the family assets. One Philadelphia man left the family repeatedly, but when he departed for the last time, "he sold bedding, clothing, and anything that could bring any money—and left 60 cents on table for her."[59]

Of course, not all men were voluntarily deficient in breadwinner roles. Many tried diligently to be the providers for their families, only to be thwarted by the conditions of the labor market. An unemployed man in the New York area during the mid-1930s told a sociological investigator how important it was to him that he could earn twenty-five dollars a month as a janitor and thus be the one who "kept the roof over their heads."[60] An East St. Louis sausage maker asked a Women's Bureau agent, "Don't you think Missus if I could [make] a living for my family my wife [would not] go to work?"[61] Some felt that they could adequately support their families without their wives' earning wages; often, such men were young and relatively newly married—naive, we might say, about the demands that raising a family would put on them and still in the prime of their youthful earning power.[62] In another note that prefigures a popular argument of the post–World War II period, one husband argued that his wife's meager earnings made little difference to the family budget and that both their son's and his wife's health were suffering because of her job.[63] He may well have been correct. But the most bizarre example of a man's dedication to breadwinning was that of a bigamist, convicted and in prison, who faithfully turned over his monthly earnings of nine dollars as a prison barber to his wife on her regular visits to the prison. His wife clearly considered his bigamy a minor sin in the light of his array of husbandly virtues: not only did he turn over his wages regularly, but he was a good earner, making as much as forty dollars a week when not in prison; moreover, she termed him "very kind and good hearted—never spoke a cross word to me in his life" and excused his bigamy because "whiskey got him."[64] Their marriage certificate, elaborately framed, held the place of honor on the mantel of her two-room home.

The rejection of the breadwinner role was, moreover, not invariably an act of self-indulgence or a privileging of another aspect of male identity. The African American men mentioned above found themselves in a uniquely disadvantaged position in the labor force, and one can easily imagine the succession of disappointments that led that Chicago man to abandon himself to pacing the streets, cigarettes his only consolation. Although the sharp edges of the labor market's injustices and irrationalities cut most deeply into African Americans' chances to establish a male-breadwinner family, Euro-Americans also had ample reason to become discouraged and ultimately alienated from a role they were blocked from fulfilling. The husbands who sought "easy" work and refused to break their backs might have had a lazy streak, but they might also have been mindful of the grim reality of industrial accidents and injuries. To refuse back-breaking work could mean to conserve one's potential as an earner; to take the work might be to consign oneself to the scrap heap of industrial casualties. Philadelphia women interviewed for *The Immigrant Woman and Her Job* gave vivid examples of what the workplace might do to a breadwinner: a hand destroyed by a machine, rheumatism from a humid workplace, lead poisoning from a battery factory, a back injury from heavy lifting in a sugar refinery.[65] Added to these might be at least some of the many reported as sickly: general poor health might well be the wages of a brutally demanding job for a man whose family was too hard pressed to provide optimal nutrition or good medical care. A substantial number of working-class men during the 1920s and 1930s must have faced their workdays feeling something decidedly less than hale. The evidence from working-class families, black and white, in the 1920s and 1930s, suggests that the crisis in the male breadwinner's role might not have, as Barbara Ehrenreich suggests, originated with the *Playboy* mentality of the 1950s, but in the working class of the 1930s.[66] But similar patterns have different meanings in different contexts. When working-class men distanced themselves from or rejected the breadwinning ethic, they did so primarily because of the material context of their working lives, rather than because they sought personal and material fulfillment outside a family context. When middle-class men did the same, they acted far more autonomously; they were less often pushed out of the breadwinner's role than they walked away from it. In both cases, of course, the result was an increasingly difficult life for the women and children left to fend wholly or partially for themselves.

The Good Manager

The female counterpart to the breadwinner was the good manager, a miracle worker of consumption. The world of household production having yielded much to the marketplace, women were left to make the most of very little, trying to create sufficiency out of inadequate materials. Mary Simkhovitch described the good manager:

> As spender it is she who gives the family its tone or character. Upon her interest, skill and order the family economy depends. Around her the whole machinery of the family revolves. . . . Her economic importance is far greater than that of her wealthier sisters, for, as income increases, the proportion of it controlled by the wife diminishes.[67]

Until her eldest child could enter the labor force, a mother had to rely on "her husband's wages and character, and her own strength and ability as a spender."[68] In the parlance of the social worker or reformer, the accolade of "good manager" was the highest praise, carrying the implication that the woman thus described maintained good physical, social, and emotional order in her home. A woman could be a good manager even if not supported by a male breadwinner, but these single women often lived with other adult women who helped with the support and labor of the household. One woman, who earned the rare label of "very good manager," was a mother's pension recipient living with a second pensioner who took care of both women's children while the first worked.[69]

The sources construct the good manager as a woman endowed with formidable powers, a kind of earth mother of the marketplace whose skills in stretching resources while meeting standards of respectability and cleanliness seemed almost mystical to the middle-class researchers and social service workers who observed them. A New Orleans settlement worker profiled a mother of seven, wife of a worker at a bag factory:

> In some hands $18 might not be productive of much comfort but in Hilda's it worked wonders. Their home was clean, their furniture was good and they had been able to achieve something near their ideal of right living. Besides this, incredible though it may seem, they had several hundred dollars in the bank and they prided themselves on being respectable, substantial people.[70]

Good management at this level was not only crucial to material welfare, but also a powerful contributor to class status, lifting these people into a cultural realm that might otherwise have been beyond the reach of their economic resources. Such domestic miracles were a source of pride to the women who accomplished them—a Kansas City meatpacker was described by the Women's Bureau agent as "a very close manager . . . [who] took pleasure in explaining how she managed"[71]—as well as to the husbands who were the beneficiaries of them; a Philadelphia laborer boasted that his wife was "a good manager and can squeeze every cent out of a nickel."[72]

Even the most skilled manager, however, was not independent from the material base from which she had to work. As a Philadelphia woman told a settlement worker, "I can always manage when the money is regular."[73] Another Philadelphia woman made the case at greater length: "When he's working steady I can just manage, but when he's out, things go back. First I stop on the damp wash, then on the food and then the rent goes behind. . . . You've got to have that pay envelope every week or the children don't eat."[74] A good manager's mettle was tested when unemployment or slack work struck the family. On the one hand, a good manager could continue to maximize the family's well-being in lean times, and her skills could sustain her sense of purpose and self-esteem. When Hilda's husband's work at the bag factory became irregular and then nearly dried up, the family spent its savings, dropped its insurance policies, turned off the gas and electricity, and sank into debt. As if inspired by adversity, Hilda rose to the challenge and demonstrated that good managing involved psychological as well as fiscal skills:

> Hilda has shown much courage and cooperation. She sympathizes with her husband, encourages him to look for work, and does not blame him when he is unable to find it. She economizes to an almost unbelievable degree and at the same time she keeps the house neat and attractive.[75]

The role of good manager, like the late-twentieth-century role of super-woman, took its toll; feelings of responsibility and tendencies toward self-blame and self-exploitation increased as material possibilities shrank. Of Hilda, the settlement worker observed: "But in spite of her determination the strain is telling on her. She is losing control of her emotions and says she feels so bewildered that she can't think logically."[76] Reduced to living in a tumbledown shack, a Philadelphia woman was even more ground down by the demands of managing household expenditures: "'I can just pay the rent & get food. I have to eat don't I? I can't buy any clothes,' she told the Women's Bureau agent. "The struggle for existence," the agent commented, "seemed almost too much."[77] Being a good manager, far from conferring real power and autonomy, looked a lot like a stressful paid job. Women had little authority over the material circumstances that shaped their families but had enormous responsibilities for securing their welfare. A settlement house worker heard from one woman who experienced the female equivalent of the alienation felt by Ruth Elliott's husband: "I got married when I was sixteen. I see my mistake, but it's too late now. Lookin' after a house an' a crowd of children is too much."[78] Good management was labor-intensive, requiring meticulous attention to the use of resources and time-consuming efforts to get the most out of scarce pennies.

Even more difficult was the position of the woman who could not rise to the demands of good management. A Boston wood finisher's wife never got the knack of it. A settlement worker described her as "spunky," some-one who did "her best to make both ends met. But years of experience have not taught her how to plan her income so as to get by, and she feels that the burden falls unduly on her and she is censorious."[79] Even careful tute-lage by her husband did not make one woman a good manager:

> Mike was proud of his family and brought home every bit of his money. He was sometimes annoyed that Rose did not manage better and save more. He would get pencil and paper and figure out for her what her expenses should be and urged that they try to keep within this amount and so increase their savings. Rose made an earnest effort, but she was not a very good manager and sometimes the money went for things that the little family might well have done without.

Small wonder that she succumbed to providing small treats, with four chil-dren under the age of seven. Careless manager though Rose might be, she still had her ways of coping: she occasionally "parks her children with a neighbor and gets a day's work to help along a bit." More worrisome was the settlement worker's observation that Rose seemed to be going short on food herself in order to feed the rest of the family well.[80] The good manager role was a socially constructed one; good managing was no more a "natural" female ability than steady breadwinning was a "natural" male inclination. But that fact did not lighten the weight of social expectations on those who performed badly the work society assigned to their gender.

The trope of the good manager to some degree obscures the process of economic decision-making in the family and tends to assume that good managers both made the decisions and spent the money. An Omaha couple might stand as one end of a spectrum ranging from full discussion and mutual agreement about the allocation of the family's money to arbitrary control by one of the spouses. These childless meatpackers in their late twenties earned about the same amount of money; the husband participated in all housework except sewing. The Women's Bureau agent wrote that the wife "wanted a new coat and a rug this fall but they talked it over and decided that all extra money must go into the house payments."[81] Agents occasionally reported that they interrupted couples in discussions of their finances; the woman in a St. Joseph couple, for example, told the agent, "We was just sitting here planning how we were going to hit our tax bill,"[82] and an agent found a Chicago couple with the wife's "pay envelop [sic] open before them and they were planning how to spend the money the coming week."[83] At the other pole stands a Detroit couple brought into court in 1935 by a department store and an automobile finance company for non-payment of bills. The husband testified that he had no idea what his wife had purchased at the department store, although he guessed that it might be something for one of their six children. In this extreme of non-communication, not even a court summons could provoke the husband to cross the boundary between his economic realm and that of his wife.[84]

However decisions were made, in most cases the women managed the resulting expenditures, an undertaking that amounted more to disbursing than to discretionary spending. Remarks such as "he leaves the bills and other obligations for her to handle" recur in the family case studies,[85] although the Women's Bureau data, as we shall see below, sometimes show more complicated divisions of consumption labor. But the spending role, like that of the good manager, involved more responsibility than authority. Economist Jessica Peixotto described this division of labor in the families of San Francisco typographers during the 1920s:

Occasionally the man was found to be the real purchasing agent; but here, as in most income groups, the wife had the more intimate knowledge of the way the family funds were used. It was only in the usual order of things to find that her knowledge of the man's payments for union dues, for tobacco, and for other personal expenses was vague.[86]

Husbands commonly consumed for themselves, taking their needs off the top before turning their wages into the family fund. Wives rarely had access to, influence over, or even knowledge of these expenditures. Gender dynamics, therefore, constituted an important limitation on a wife's role as the family spender. Peixotto noted further: "Most schemes of family spending are routinized . . . according to a routine which was not so much the result of a conscious budget plan as the habit of years."[87] What seemed to be a rut was in fact a response to scarcity and want, arising out of the fact that most working-class families had very little discretionary income. The typical woman householder devoted almost all the money that came into her hands to fixed expenses such as rent, basic needs such as food, and emergencies such as medical bills. Her creativity was more likely to be exercised in deciding which bills had to be paid immediately and which could be put off rather than in embellishing her family's life with consumer goods. The range for choice and initiative here was narrow; class dynamics as well as gender dynamics hedged in working-class women as they spent their family's money.

Although the pattern of family spending was routinized, it varied from family to family. Some husbands shared the discomfort and shame of not being able to make ends meet; Hilda's husband, for example, met "his bill collectors himself, not leaving them to Hilda."[88] Other husbands left such humiliations to their wives, or even exacerbated their wives' problems. In this category was a factory foreman whose wife "handle[d] the family disbursements": "He did not spend much, but what he did was not budgeted and he sometimes left his wife with a problem on her hands to pay for his purchases."[89] Husbands and wives could clash over spending; different styles could produce conflict. Some husbands felt uneasy with their wives' disbursements but hesitated to interfere in their domain; such was the case of a Toledo construction laborer: "Mr. Whalen would like to pay his back bills promptly, but most of the financial responsibility rests with the wife after he turns over his pay."[90] Male improvidence evoked contempt from wives who considered themselves savvy consumers. Thus, a St. Louis candy-factory worker watched silently while her "very garrulous" husband held forth on the economic situation that caused his unemployment, but the woman followed the Women's Bureau agent out to the gate to say that her husband "shoots craps and does not know the value of money."[91] Good managing, however vital to the family's economic survival, did not necessarily produce domestic peace.

The role of good manager, however hedged in, was not the only one available to married women. Women whose husbands, for one reason or another, failed to fulfill the breadwinner's role adequately—and this would be a very high proportion of the husbands in the working class as I have defined it—turned to other ways of making do. Neither the Women's Bureau agents nor the other observers of working-class life explicitly recognized one alternative model for the coping woman. Her prototype was a forty-year-old Philadelphia woman, a Jewish immigrant from Lithuania who had thrown her alcoholic husband out of the house six months before the Women's Bureau agent came to call. Hers was one of the few houses that appalled an agent, who termed it "frightfully dirty, terribly disorderly. The place looked more like a poor junk shop deserted than a home." All the same this woman was clearly coping well with her situation; having gotten rid of her husband, she had secured a court order compelling him to pay her ten dollars a week. She appeared even to the shocked agent "attractive & not unhappy apparently"; and she was clearly doing well as a mother to her two daughters and two sons ("two nice boys," commented the agent) and had cheerful ambitions to support the children in their goals, saying "anything they pick out, I'll help. I no need for myself."[92] Not a good manager, she was just as clearly a good mother with a capacity to be happy and to make those around her happy.

Other strategies for getting by—cutbacks, non-market transactions, domestic production, and sending children to work—will be discussed in later chapters. Yet another—the resort to private charity or public assistance—is the focus of a flourishing literature about women and the welfare state, and interested readers should turn to that literature for a discussion of this expedient. My sources shed relatively little light on this area, but that light reveals diverse approaches of women and their families to social agencies. Families resisted turning to these agencies for the predictable reasons: pride, fear, and an understanding of how limited their aid was in fact. Women questioned by the Women's Bureau about their non-wage sources of income rarely reported recourse to charities; of 848 families questioned in a study of women in slaughtering and meatpacking, only three, all in Chicago, said that they had received assistance from charities. Even allowing for the unwillingness of families to confess to seeking charitable aid, and for the reluctance of agents to press on this issue, such aid was clearly an inconsequential source of income.[93] Others viewed the social agencies as one of their many resources; an African American woman with three children, for example, regularly turned to the St. Paul United Charities whenever she was laid off from her job.[94] The wife of the baseball player mentioned above not only relied on the United Charities for relief, but also counted on the Charities visitor to provide ad hoc marriage counseling, mediating between her and her husband during their yearly off-season separations.[95]

Female Breadwinning and Consumption

Some women developed a female breadwinner ethic which complemented and sometimes replaced the male version, and the Women's Bureau's focus on wage-earning women gives such women a large part in this story. Their motivations were often complex and multivalent, and Women's Bureau agents too frequently reduced them to stock categories, oversimplifying the tangled web of strands making up the female breadwinner ethic. When an especially eloquent woman worker, an African American in the sausage department at the Omaha Cudahy plant, encountered a sympathetic and dedicated Women's Bureau agent—Caroline Manning, who commented copiously on the schedule forms of her home visits and appears to have had a special rapport with black respondents—we learn how many motivations could converge to send a woman into the labor force, and how even a strong constellation of such motivations could be undercut by ambivalence. The sausage maker offered so many reasons for her decision to earn wages that it seems to have been overdetermined. She could get steadier work than her husband; a family couldn't live on one wage; and she felt an obligation to support her children from an earlier marriage. Her reasons overlap but still express distinct motivations. The first reflects a cool assessment of the job market: since she held the key to regular income, she could best hedge the family bets by holding on to her job. The second situates the family in the larger political economy: the cost of living was too high, and wages too low, for a family to live on one wage. The third taps into her vision of motherhood: she told Manning "these are my children, not his." And yet, however deep and broad her commitment to breadwinning, she still clung to a hope that it was but a stage in her life cycle, and envisioned a life without paid work. Following Manning outside at the end of the visit, she confided her "wish to give up steady work as soon as [her two teenage] boys could support themselves."[96]

A second example shows a different but equally complex constellation of reasons for working; civic obligation opened the way to expanded consumption, satisfying work, and family responsibility. A Newark mother of two—white, native-born, forty years of age—who was married to a man earning forty dollars a week injured her finger working on a press manufacturing paper containers. Interviewed in 1923, four years after the accident, she was back at the same machine on which she had been hurt. A Women's Bureau agent reported on her reasons for working:

> Started to work because she wanted to "help win the war." Went on because she bought a player-piano & wanted to pay for it on the installment plan. Does not earn much, but likes the place where she works & thinks that she ought to help out her husband somewhat financially.[97]

Her sense of responsibility as a deputy breadwinner is clear, but it is mixed with some very different motivations. Civic duty looms large, but one wonders, given the complex of other reasons, if perhaps the war supplied this woman with the justification she'd been looking for. The job had both intrinsic and extrinsic appeal; she could have her player piano, and perhaps some other consumer goods once that was paid off, and she could have these things while enjoying her work. The engaging and unusually full accounts of the sausage maker and the press operator are reminders that women had mixed and complicated feelings about their roles as breadwinners.

This reminder is all the more important because of the Women's Bureau's habit of using a few somewhat cryptic categories to describe women's breadwinning ethics, categories that obscure as much as they reveal. In the monumental *Immigrant Women in Industry* study, for example, over two-thirds of the women's responses were tabulated as "insufficient support from husband" or "to help maintain home and support family." The distinction between the two was that the first named "conditions of men's employment" and the second "the responsibilities that the woman had to assume," although the report stipulated that "practically the only difference in the two groups is in the manner in which the question was answered, as in each the lack of adequate support from the husband was the primary cause for the woman's working."[98] A re-examination of the schedule forms, however, does allow a somewhat finer distinction to be drawn. Of the Philadelphia women interviewed, 468 were married. Of those, 309, or two-thirds, cited reasons for working—sometimes more than one—that related to their husbands. While never losing sight of the fact that these replies were filtered through the agents' preconceptions and moods, we can nonetheless hope that the agents reflected the spirit of what these wives had to say. (Other explanations, including ambitions for children, responsibilities to family members outside of the nuclear family, and consumer desires, were a small minority of the reasons given and will be dealt with in later chapters.) The most frequently cited husband-related reason for wage earning was some version of a shared sense of responsibility or joint enterprise in the family economy; over a third of the 309 wives expressed this feeling. Wives in this category seemed to have a positive desire to pitch in by earning, a sense of their own obligation in the breadwinning of the family. A quarter of the wives said that they took jobs because a husband's illness kept him from working steadily or at all. These women testify to the toll that life in the first half of the twentieth century took on working-class men. About 8 percent of the men's illnesses were related to their service in World War I, none of them permanently disabling. About 12 percent were at some point thrown out of work because of occupational injuries or illnesses. About three out of ten wives targeted the irregularity of their husbands' earnings as the reason for their wage-earning: seasonal work or short hours kept their husbands from supporting the family even though they had a trade or a long-term connection with a specific industry or occupation. Twenty of their husbands were connected with the Baldwin Locomotive Works, one of Philadelphia's premier employers of white males. Another quarter of the husbands were out-and-out unemployed, apparently without enduring connections to draw upon. No work or irregular work was mentioned more frequently than low wages, to which only one in five of these wives referred.

The Women's Bureau agent's stock phrases often obscure as much as they reveal about women's motivations for working outside the home, and the two most frequently recorded responses are frustratingly opaque. First, the agents note that many of the women expressed a general sense of personal responsibility for contributing to the family fund, an obligation typically rendered in ungendered terms. One agent captured a forty-one-year-old Serbian-born woman's emphatic belief in her responsibility: "Always worked . . . felt that she had come to this country to work and took it for granted that as long as she could get work [she] would work."[99] Other responses in this category include: "I gotta work";[100] "I suppose I have to";[101] "Feel I should."[102] Some comments indicate a feeling of permanence, of duration, in the sense of responsibility: "It's always work, I need it and have to go";[103] "I've been the foundation of this family for six years";[104] "always has done her share."[105]

Not surprisingly, the breadwinning ethic seems to have been especially prevalent among African American women (four of the six responses quoted above came from African Americans) because of their above-average rates of labor-force participation. One woman expressed this ethic clearly if in essentializing terms: it was, she told the Women's Bureau agent, a "natural thing for colored women to work after marriage."[106] That all the responses cited came from either African Americans or immigrants from central Europe suggests that these important sectors of the working class assumed the importance of female breadwinning. However, these women did not necessarily like their jobs; a forty-five-year-old Croatian woman remarked that "no woman works for fun,"[107] and a Rumanian woman nine years her junior dourly noted, "We don't work for our health."[108] The fact that these two comments were both recorded in Omaha by different Women's Bureau agents visiting meatpackers within the same week gives the historian pause. Other replies also occurred in bunches, and it's a tough question as to whether the agents' chats among themselves predisposed them to "hear" certain kinds of comments that they might otherwise have ignored, or whether they were plugging into local received wisdom. A Mexicana homeworker in San Antonio took an opposite position from the Omaha women: "Work harder feel better, don't work hard, feel tired."[109]

A second thread in the female breadwinning ethic might be called the compensatory, since a frequently recorded explanation given by women for working outside the home was that their husbands didn't or couldn't earn enough; this thread was also difficult to read from the agents' comments. Such phrases as "husband's earnings insufficient";[110] "husband does not earn enough";[111] "necessary to supplement husband's wage";[112] "husband no good job";[113] and "could not get along on husband's pay"[114] were probably infused with a wide range of affect—regret, blame, anger, despair, sympathy, resignation, intransigence, and more—but the agents rarely gave a clue to the emotional tone of the comments, collapsing a range of meanings into a single trope. Certainly some wives understood their husbands' low earnings as reflections of systemic rather than individual problems. A Kansas City woman, for example, remarked that "they don't pay the men a living wage."[115] African American women, even when they did not mention race explicitly, were especially cognizant of the difficulties men faced in securing steady work. Typical was the Muskogee, Oklahoma, laundry worker who asserted that it was "hard for men to get anything but little piddlin' jobs."[116] Other women placed the source of instability not in the labor market but in the husbands they married; many saw depending on a husband as a chancy thing indeed, a perception often borne out by experience. An African American South Carolinian stated that she had "had good luck with her husband but he died."[117] A Memphis candy worker's first husband was killed in a workplace accident, and her second husband "was taken sick" shortly after their marriage, incurring such high medical bills that the spouses were forced to separate and live with their respective parents.[118] Such were the perversities of the economy in which these families were mired that a disaster might turn out to be a windfall. A New York family of Italian immigrants had come apart at the seams after years of seasonal unemployment for the laborer husband. When things looked as if they were beyond saving, he was hit by a truck and severely injured; the eventual financial settlement allowed him to establish himself as a successful fish peddler and to reunite the scattered family. His wife, aware of the ironies of their position, remarked "I ain't wishing my husban' any harm, . . . but we could not have got up again if he hadn't been knocked down by that truck!"[119]

Wherever the blame was placed, these responses reflect a pervasive sense of the family economy as a shared enterprise, albeit one in which men typically played the primary earning role. The Women's Bureau agent clearly got this feeling at the home of a Chicago couple, describing the wife as a "vigorous energetic strong woman—has shared financial responsibility with husband almost continuously since marriage."[120] A Philadelphia restaurant worker put it more succinctly: "What my trouble is his trouble too."[121] When paid work was a scarce commodity for both men and women, it was not always possible to choose when one entered and left the labor force; dual wage-earning was a logical way to counter seasonality, slack work, and layoffs. An African American meatpacking couple in Omaha plagued by the irregularity of the husband's work described their strategy to a Women's Bureau agent: "[They] "never know when he is going to be laid off so both work as much as they can."[122] In some cases, wives spoke of their wage earning as assistance to their husbands, and men retained the responsibility for breadwinning. These women spoke of wanting to help their husbands, explicitly or implicitly recognizing the hard row that working-class men had to hoe in the labor market: "'We both old now, past 40, can't keep a job long, too old. . . . My husband no play cards or nothing like some men. A good man. I want to help him,'"[123] or, simply, "I he'p him out."[124] A Philadelphia husband saw his wife's wage earning in the same light: "She good woman. If woman not help, bad for man."[125] A frequent note was the recognition that the burden of breadwinning, especially for a large family or one saddled with heavy medical expenses, could not be borne alone. Explaining her wage earning, a Chicago Polish-born mother of four children said, "Many kids—too much for man alone."[126]

One twenty-two-year-old woman who had incurred high medical bills told the Women's Bureau agent that she felt "sorry for her husband to have so much to carry alone. We never know seems like when I'll be sick again or he may be out of a job."[127] Women thus spoke of wanting to do their share or expressed what agents often referred to as a sense of "joint" responsibility for family support: a Czech-born woman asserted that "one can't keep all" or the African American who said that her meatpacker husband "couldn't do it alone."[128] Sometimes this sense of shared responsibility was linked to a stage of the life cycle. A pregnant woman who had just quit her slaughterhouse job said she wanted "to help while able."[129] Many were conscious of employers' preference for younger workers and saw themselves as seizing a fleeting opportunity to earn. Two Omaha meatpackers, one twenty-one years old and native-born and the other thirty-eight years old and Polish-born, saw themselves as maximizing their youthful earning power.[130] Others said they worked "to get established" at turning points in their lives, such as marriage, as did a wife of a Chicago truck driver interviewed four months into her marriage;[131] moving within the United States, as did an African American migrant from Louisiana to Omaha;[132] or immigration, as did two immigrants from Germany to East St. Louis.[133] Wives' wage-earning might also be part of a family strategy of advancement: a Philadelphia woman turned to cigar-making in order to give her husband the time to "hunt up a better job." A weaver by trade, he had been laid off and for two years had worked as an elevator operator; he was now seeking a better-paying job while his wife made cigars.[134]

Married women's breadwinning responsibilities extended beyond the nuclear family. Frequently, they worked to support or contribute to the support of other relatives. African Americans and immigrants from Europe and Mexico were especially likely to fall into this category, but so did many native-born European Americans. A Women's Bureau study of married women dismissed from civil service jobs because Section 213 of the Economy Act prohibited federal employment of spouses showed that 80 of the 113 women who were studied in detail were supporting or contributing to the support of their own relatives outside their immediate families.[135] In some cases, women took on these burdens when a husband refused to do so. A Croatian-born meatpacker, for example, had to set up her aged mother and fifteen-year-old son by a previous husband in two nearby rooms when her present husband threw them out of the house.[136]

While most women saw their breadwinning as a way of satisfying family obligations, a vocal minority used it as a route to independence within marriage and autonomy in the marketplace. A Richmond woman wrote in an essay for the YWCA Industrial Commission, "I had rather work and feal [*sic*] independant [*sic*] as I do now than stop and let him have mother and sister as well as me to support."[137] She spoke for those who did not see marriage and independence as mutually exclusive. Although independence rested on waged work rather than upon property ownership or the independent practice of a skill, it partook of the same desire to be beholden to no one as did the varieties of male republicanism. Sometimes the independence these women sought was to insulate the family from dependence on others by building up savings; thus, a Kansas City Armour worker whose shipping clerk husband earned steady wages went to work because, in her words, "I could get along, but I could not save. I do not want to be dependent upon others when hard luck comes so I shall continue to work while I am young."[138] Other women spoke of a desire to be self-supporting for the sake of their own independence, irrespective of their husbands' ability to provide. An East St. Louis woman married to a factory foreman asserted, "My husband could support me but he doesn't have to."[139]

Independence also had powerful connections to consumption. By asserting that they wanted to earn their own money so that they could spend it independently, women were commenting upon the constraints they felt in administering the family fund and the uneasiness of being a financial dependent in a market economy. That wage-earning women frequently remarked that they controlled their own wages suggests that that their jobs gave them a modicum of economic autonomy that they would not otherwise have had. For these women, breadwinning was not just a way to have more money, but also a way to have "different" money—money that was entirely under their control. Of a Chattanooga bakery worker married to a steadily employed mechanic, a Women's Bureau agent reported, "She does not work regularly, just enough to make own spending money."[140] A sixty-year-old upstate New York woman had done homework on gloves for twenty years because "she thought it would be nice to work on gloves and have her own money so she wouldn't have to depend on anyone else."[141] Another agent wrote of a Providence lamp-factory worker, "she used her own money for her self [*sic*]."[142]

From women's specific comments about what they did with their earnings, it is apparent that they focused on household improvements and clothing. A Women's Bureau agent reported that one woman who worked off and on in meatpacking said that she worked "so as to have own money to buy things for self and house."[143] Such comments recur frequently in the sources. Women often spoke of devoting their earnings to their own clothing and clothing for their children.[144] A few especially revealing comments suggest that women sought autonomy in the marketplace because their husbands were stingy and did not comprehend their desire to enhance the home. One husband was described as a "selfish mortal" who not only denied his money for "personal belongings" and "nice things for the house" but also refused to allow her to adopt a child.[145] Of a Fort Dodge, Iowa, woman who had worked as a dressmaker in an overall factory and as a dime-store saleswoman, the agent wrote: "[Her barber husband doesn't] realize all the needs of the home, such as bedding etc. that must be replaced. Feels she needs more than he gives her."[146] Consumption standards, then, could be gendered; women led the push for more, and more elaborate, household goods and clothing.

But consumption was not always gendered nor was it always linked to autonomy in the thinking of these women. Many expressed their desires for a higher standard of living for the family in general, both quantitatively and qualitatively. A St. Joseph meatpacker married to a steadily employed grain-mill worker explained her reason for taking a job: "We want all the money we can get."[147] This reason was often paired with an assertion about the insufficiency of a husband's earnings. Thus, a thirty-year-old childless Kansas City wife opined, "Takes forever to get anywhere with only a man's earnings."[148] Many women earned wages in order to move from a plane of bare existence to a level where small extras and humble luxuries enhanced their lives. Mere subsistence, many argued, was not enough; thus, a childless African American wife of a Pullman porter worked, she said, "to raise standard of living,"[149] and a Kansas City Croatian woman remarked that her family could "scrape along" on her husband's seventy-five dollar monthly earnings but needed "money for extras."[150] A woman's wages could enhance a family's status, as they did for a native-born Kansas City meatpacker married to a steadily employed millwright; she maintained: "Nowadays if you want to live respectably you both have to work[;] they don't pay the men a living wage."[151] One woman connected her family's plight with censorious attitudes toward working-class consumption and married women's wage-earning, asserting a right to expanded consumption: "Shouldn't poor people have a little pleasure in life[?] [S]omething more than just food & shelter[?]"[152] These references to class—the one oblique, the other piquantly pointed—are among the very few recorded comments tying class and consumption together.

Lest we begin to imagine a direct relationship between the therapeutic ethic of consumption and women's wage earning in the interwar working class, it is useful to examine the findings of one of the few systematic studies of the reasons that married working-class women took jobs, the

Women's Bureau's 1932 study of women employed in slaughtering and meatpacking. The great majority of respondents stated that they worked for the family-oriented reasons already discussed—the insufficiency of the husband's earnings, the unsteadiness of his work, or the need to support relatives outside the immediate family. Fewer than one in four mentioned a specific spending goal for their earnings.[153] About 10 percent of the total said they were in the labor force to enable the family to purchase a home, among them an Austrian woman who asserted, "If my house was paid I would work no more."[154] About 6 percent were working to pay expenses related to the education of children, including an African American woman who was earning to "help school my little girl"[155] and a Hungarian woman whose husband told a Women's Bureau agent, "Better for child. We give them education, they give us very much thanks."[156] Just over 3 percent were working to pay medical bills—among them a Croatian wife who said, "Lady I work just for doctor,"[157] and just under 3 percent worked to buy furniture. Clearly, these women were working primarily to deal with the unpredictable—medical emergencies—and to provide investment spending for the family's future—a home, education for the children. A later chapter will develop the argument that furniture was an object of investment. Working women's consumption goals, by and large, were modest and prudent. This is not to say that these families spent nothing on the sheer enjoyment of commercialized leisure or consumer goods but rather to note how limited an appearance such expenditures make in the worldview of working wives. They may have been playing to their middle-class questioners' sensibilities, but given the willingness of the Women's Bureau agents to note foolish or profligate behavior, the sober tone of the recorded answers to this question is noteworthy.

The sources tell little about how working couples divided financial responsibility, but scattered evidence reveals some clearly negotiated divisions of labor. Some wives willingly shouldered the primary responsibility for family support, and such a situation could reflect a deep bond between the spouses. A forty-year-old food processor was dedicated to supporting an "old husband" who kept up his pretense of wage earning by doing occasional draying with his mules, who ate far more than they earned. She told the Women's Bureau agent, "He's been mighty good to me, helped me bring up my two nephews."[158] Some husbands supported only themselves and left everything else to their wives. A Keokuk, Iowa, shoe factory worker took this situation stoically according to the Women's Bureau agent, "For three years she has had the entire responsibility of her son, her self, and the house."[159] More frequently, hostility developed, as in the case of a Virginia tobacco worker whose husband refused to contribute to the family's support and tried to throw her out of the house, which she owned. She told the Women's Bureau investigator she would "burn it before she leaves it to him."[160]

Most spouses seem to have divided up expenses in a more equitable and mutually satisfying way. Typical of this type of arrangement was the family of a Missouri clothing-factory worker: "She has clothed family, given some educational advantages to children, paid insurance, kept up home furnishings and made it possible 'to live' while older husband took the responsibility of food and rent. She has a very little saved."[161] In another Missouri family, the division was different but equally amicable: the husband bought food and fuel, while the wife (who worked in a Kansas City laundry) and two children paid off the house mortgage in four years flat.[162] The wife and daughter kept five dollars a week for carfare and to pay for their clothes and to partially pay for the husband's and son's clothes. Evidence about such financial divisions of labor is tantalizingly rare; the Women's Bureau raw data describe seven situations fully, as does one case study compiled by the YWCA Industrial Commission. In six cases of the eight, the husband provided the food, and in five the rent or mortgage payment. Whenever clothes, furniture, insurance, or education were mentioned, it was always the wife's responsibility to provide them.[163] The tendency to negotiate these divisions did not appear to be linked to ethnicity; three families of central European origin and three of apparent British origin make up the seven. In the intriguing case of a Polish-surnamed couple working in meatpacking; the husband explained, "She pays for groceries and clothes. I pay for my house and the outside expenses."[164] This apparent nod to separate spheres did not, however, appear in any other case. A more typical principle of division emerges in the case of a childless Polish couple; the husband provided food and rent, while the wife's earnings went "for saving or good time."[165] Perhaps this case reflects best the spirit of other households in which the division was not so clearly specified and in which earnings allowed for more than a bare existence. The husband took care of subsistence, while the wife provided for long-term security and for something beyond the most basic needs. The addition of children to the family might well, however, wipe out the possibility for both saving and recreation and make it necessary to turn the woman's earnings to clothing, medical expenses, or education.

The Second Shift

Just as breadwinning was equivocally gendered, so too was work within the home. Housework played an important role in working-class family economies by replacing market expenditures. Laundry, cooking, house-cleaning, and child minding could all be done on a fee-for-service basis or as unpaid work by a family member. When a wife took a job, a husband's participation in housework became an important way to conserve cash by avoiding resort to the market for household services, and, thus, a way to maximize the net effect of a wife's earnings.

A vocal minority of women linked breadwinning to their dislike of housework. A feeling of being at loose ends without enough work to keep busy was common; the women who preferred paid work over housework were not idlers or slatterns but women who wanted more to occupy their time and attention. A childless St. Paul woman living in furnished rooms told the Women's Bureau agent that she had "nothing to do,"[166] and women whose families were living as boarders frequently echoed her.[167] Two women disliked housekeeping so much that they broke up their own homes and went to live with relatives. One, a Dayton woman, did so because her husband criticized the quality of her housekeeping. Primarily committed to her paying job, she simply gave up housekeeping entirely rather than try to please her husband.[168] The other, whose husband worked out of town, lived with a sister who boasted an array of appliances: electric washer, sweeper, and iron. Belying the axiom that labor-saving devices in the home raise the standards for housekeeping instead of decreasing the overall amount of time spent on housework, this woman maintained that she had ample free time to devote to wage earning.[169] Many women shifted the burden of housework to co-resident relatives; the most frequent choices were mothers[170] and children. For example, the fourteen- and sixteen-year-old daughters of one Chicago meatpacker did all the household chores except cooking.[171] Others paid neighbors or commercial firms to do their laundry, child minding, sewing, or housecleaning.

Women contrasted the satisfactions and camaraderie of their jobs with drudgery and loneliness of household work. Two South Carolina cotton-mill workers strongly preferred mill work to household work. One told the Women's Bureau agent that she liked "to work in mill better than keep house. . . . work in mill is easier than housework, less running about and not as many things to do."[172] She resisted her husband's urging that she quit her job and take in boarders instead; she used her wages to hire a "a good colored maid," clearing five dollars after paying the maid's wage, room, and board. No idler, though, she spent her evenings making clothes for her children and squeaked by on six or seven hours of sleep. Even without hiring undervalued African American labor, a Rhode Island box-factory worker expressed the same preference for factory work, although she probably relied upon her co-resident mother to do at least some of the housework.[173] A Philadelphia woman enjoyed working in the tea room at the Wanamaker department store even though she felt the strain of keeping up with her housework: "I love to be there (at work) only it's hard to be there & keep your home."[174] An Irish immigrant to Philadelphia started working because her husband was ill, but after nine years, she told the Women's Bureau agent, "[I] would rather work than stay home." Her job packing stove polish was apparently quite pleasant; she sat while she worked and the bottles she packed were small.[175]

For other women, the home was a lonely or depressing place from which wage earning offered a sociable escape. A Philadelphia radio polisher took a part-time job because "she did not want to sit home" while her children aged fifteen, thirteen, and eleven were in school.[176] A Chicago candy packer found that there was "not much to keep her home" after her two daughters died; her only other child was an eighth-grader.[177] Another Chicagoan in the same occupation, childless and married a year, went out to work because "the days at home are long and tiresome when she is alone."[178] Women in St. Paul and Memphis echoed these sentiments, the latter proudly adding that she earned as much as her husband.[179] Jessica Peixotto's observations of San Francisco typographers' wage-earning wives ("They seem to be women who, finding themselves with relatively light home responsibilities, worked outside the home because they enjoyed it or, more probably, because their standard of living urged new classes of expenditure")[180] are consistent with the evidence in the Women's Bureau raw data, although the therapeutic aspects of work and consumption loom larger for Peixotto because she was studying a more uniformly prosperous group. The pleasure that the South Carolina mill worker and the Rhode Island box-factory worker took in their work, however, suggests that liking one's work was not a luxury reserved for those with a comfortable family income to fall back on.

A significant proportion of women relied on their husbands to take an active part in housework. The received historical wisdom about the gender division of labor in families is that the tendency is greater for women to take over men's work than for men to take over women's work. On farms, women worked in the fields but men didn't work in the kitchens; on the Overland Trail, women drove wagons and hunted, but men cooked only in the direst emergencies.[181] But in many working-class families during the 1920s and 1930s, men did carry part of the burden of household work, and their willingness to do so freed up cash for other purposes. The investigators for the monumental *The Immigrant Woman and Her Job,* written by Caroline Manning, were the first to include a question about housework on their interview schedule, but the form only included a check-off about whether women did all, most, or part of the "home duties." The space for a description of those duties was more often than not left blank. Even so, agents included enough comments on about one out of ten (103 out of 1,120) of the Philadelphia schedules to allow us to sketch a very tentative picture of men's participation in housework. Over half of these men participated in child care, a quarter were simply described as being helpful around the house, seven helped with cooking, six with laundry, two each with sewing and industrial homework, and one with dishes. Given the general nature of the question, and given that it came near the end of a four-page schedule—the longest used in any Women's Bureau Bulletin for which the schedules survive—I take these helpful husbands to be an absolute minimum.

An analysis of the raw data for Manning's study also reveals that male participation in housework was skewed by ethnicity. The husbands of eastern European women were by far the most helpful around the house; nearly 40 percent of Polish-born women and over a third of the other eastern-European-born women had helpful husbands. Germans and Italians were helpful in about the same proportion as they were in the total number interviewed, while the husbands of English and Jewish immigrants were minimally helpful: only one each out of the 57 English women and the 221 Jewish women reported receiving help from their husbands. Interpreting these ethnic proportions raises an interesting chicken-and-egg question: 23 out of the 51 eastern European women whose husbands helped worked at night as office cleaners or in restaurants. These women may have chosen these occupations because they knew they could count on their husbands to pick up the slack at home, or employer discrimination or language barriers may have limited their choices to these jobs, creating the need for someone to wash supper dishes and tend children.

The Women's Bureau study *Women in Slaughtering and Meat Packing* provides the most systematic information on husbands' participation in household work. The women interviewed at home were asked, among other things, whether and from whom they received assistance with household tasks such as dishwashing, cooking, laundry, cleaning, child care, and sewing. Among the 897 women visited, 390 were married women with husbands present and healthy enough to assist in household chores. Of those husbands, 61 did some housework. Given that this question was frequently left unanswered, and given that agents specified what tasks women received help with more often than who gave that help, I take this number—fully 15 percent of the total—to be, as in *The Immigrant Woman and Her Job*, the bare minimum of men who actually pitched in. Central European husbands acquitted themselves particularly well: nearly two-thirds of all helpful husbands were of central European origin; and one in six central European husbands helped with housework.[182] The other third of helpful husbands were married to native-born women and were divided about equally between northern and western European origins and African origin; one in ten husbands of northern and western European origin and one in fifteen husbands of African descent did some housework. Three of the seven German-born wives interviewed had helpful husbands, the highest rate for any group.

Other sources provide further corroboration of the central finding that working-class men participated in housework to a notable degree. Thirteen of the forty-one households visited for the study *Industrial Accidents to Women in New Jersey, Ohio, and Wisconsin* included husbands who engaged in some form of domestic labor. On the one hand, these questionnaires did not ask specifically about housework, but on the other hand these men were under special pressure to participate in housework, since their wives had suffered some degree of disability from a workplace accident. Six husbands lost time from work to take care of their injured wives, a demonstration that circumstances could precipitate men as well as women into a caretaker role and interrupt wage-earning careers. Additional scattered instances of men doing housework appear in the raw data for other Women's Bureau reports, as well as in family studies of the depression era, even though these investigations were even less directly concerned with the issue of household help.[183]

Though working-class men participated in housework to a far greater degree than the conventional historical wisdom allows, their participation seems to have had an idiosyncratic and ad hoc character, to have been negotiated within the family rather than as community norms. Some of the men were unemployed, some on short hours, some fully employed.[184] Some men did more housework when they were unemployed or working short hours,[185] but at least two did less around the house when they were unemployed than when they were working.[186] That most of the reports of men's household work indicate in a general way that men helped around the house perhaps indicates a task-oriented willingness to pitch in and do whatever needed to be done. Specific household tasks were mentioned a total of sixty-seven times, and men's efforts seem to have been spread across the spectrum of chores. Cleaning was most often mentioned (sixteen times), followed by child care and dishwashing (fourteen times each), laundry (twelve), and cooking (ten). Men who worked in the needle trades did the family sewing,[187] but sewing becomes an exception if we exclude these craft workers. Only one other man sewed, an African American who mended his clothes after his wife suffered a hand injury in an industrial accident.[188] Another woman injured in an industrial accident went to live with her sister and brother-in-law; when the sister had a baby, her husband took over the cooking but they sent the washing out.[189] Four men married to meatpackers worked nights and took care of children and did housework during the day while their wives were at work, using a shift-work strategy similar to that used by families studied by anthropologist Louise Lamphere in Rhode Island in the 1970s and 1980s.[190] A Chicago man, for example, worked nights repairing street-railway cars; his wife trimmed pork at Armour's during the day while he looked after their three school-age children and one preschooler.[191]

As difficult as it is to estimate the amount of housework done by men, it is even more difficult to gauge how these gender transgressions were viewed by the men and women in these families. When a Hungarian wife joined her husband in the United States after he had been here some years, she was "amazed when he offered to help her with the cooking and washing ... [and] thought that such work was unsuited to a man, and would not have him give her any assistance."[192] Only one man—the Irish husband of a critically ill wife—expressed discomfort with his domestic duties. He threw himself into the heavy household work, including the laundry, but drew the line at hanging it outside where the neighbors could see him.[193] On several occasions, Women's Bureau agents found husbands preparing the evening meal when they visited the homes of women workers. The agents gave no indication that these men were in any way embarrassed at their activities, and their matter-of-fact reporting of the husbands' cooking suggests that the men themselves acted nonchalant about it.[194] In Philadelphia, an agent found a companionable work group when she called in the evening: the woman of the house was washing clothes while her husband and his brother, a boarder in the household, washed dishes.[195] Arlie Hochschild, in *The Second Shift*, found a similar matter-of-fact sharing of earning, housework, and consuming during the 1980s in the California working-class family of Carmen and Frank Delacorte. The Delacortes developed a partnership marriage in fact even though they clung to traditional gender ideology.[196] Intriguingly, Hochschild found that the labor sharing in this working-class household was less conflictual than that in the more self-consciously egalitarian middle-class households she studied, and this finding leads to the sobering possibility that joint responsibility might evolve more easily when it is linked to logistic needs rather than to nontraditional gender ideologies. During the 1920s and 1930s shared housework frequently resulted from pragmatic paid-work adaptations. A San Antonio carpenter, out of work for two years, did the housework so that his wife could earn more through her homework of fine needlework on children's dresses.[197] We are familiar with women who accomplished the housework and tended children by wage earning in the home such as taking in boarders or doing industrial homework, but some men were able to do the same. In Philadelphia, a barber, a shoe repairman, and a shopkeeper, for example, had their shops at home so that they could mind the children.[198]

Despite the many instances of gender transgressions, in most cases household work remained the woman's primary responsibility, just as wage earning tended to be the man's main responsibility. Much of the child care done by men, for example, was rather perfunctory and involved supervision of children who were in school most of the day. Nonetheless, even a small amount of assistance gave a bit of a break to overworked women. We glimpse this in the account of a Philadelphia woman who was troubled by swollen feet from standing on cement floors at her job. Her husband worked rotating shifts, and when he worked the second or third shift she could rest at the factory during her lunch period while he gave lunch to their three primary-school children.[199] Men were typically described as "helping" with housework, although in some cases they took on major household responsibilities. A woman streetcar conductor told a Women's Bureau agent that her husband was "much help in [house]work 'good as a woman.'"[200] A woman praised her cattle-driver husband because he was "good about helping with work."[201] And on the key question of how husbands came to assist with housework, the only two shreds of evidence contradict each other. One Polish-born wife had demanded that her husband take part in household chores, telling the Women's Bureau agent, "husband no help me, I quit [my job],"[202] but the husband of a Hungarian-born woman asserted his own sense of household duty when he said, "She helps me [by earning wages] so I help her."[203] Significantly, neither of these two families had children, and negotiating the household division of labor would doubtless have been more complex if children had been in the picture. Regardless, given the supposed power of gender roles, what is arresting is the fact that so few men or women expressed discomfort with gender-bending. Most common were positive statements about work-sharing, including the husband in a textile-worker couple with two primary-school children who exclaimed, "By Jes[us], I help and I am not ashamed to say so."[204]

In two respects, men's housework had an unexpected spin. First, some men exhibited contradictory behavior. One of these helpful husbands evoked the Women's Bureau agent's sternest reproach: he was "n.g."—no good. He worked irregularly, a circumstance that, according to his wife, gave him a "lot of time to drink." But the wife also told the investigator that he helped with both the laundry and the housecleaning.[205] Two other men who were similarly condemned for their drinking and lackadaisical labor-force attitudes also acquitted themselves well in doing housework.[206] The Women's Bureau investigators focused on the drinking, but the wives clearly were cognizant of the men's contributions to the housework; one might imagine that a husband who drank but scrubbed the clothes and the floors was clearly preferable to one who only drank. Similarly, a husband's irregular employment might also be less irritating if he pulled his weight in the house when not wage earning. Such was the case of an Italian textile worker whose husband worked at painting and paperhanging only five months out of the year; as the Women's Bureau agent described her, "Happy nature & sense of humor help this woman. Apparently no resentment against husband whose winter life appears so leisurely."[207]

Second, while husbands might help, their contributions to housework did not necessarily indicate a good conjugal relationship or agreement on family strategies. One Philadelphia couple separated from time to time, but the wife acknowledged that when the husband was at home he helped "a little" with the housework.[208] One woman "wishe[d] she had never married" her husband, whose "former willingness to seek work has entirely disappeared. He prepares the simple meals, and is then content to sit before his chosen window."[209] From the perspective of husbands, participation in housework did not necessarily indicate support for a wife's wage-earning activities. In fact, two of the handful of husbands who were noted as objecting to their wives' jobs helped with the housework, one of them "a lot."[210] Once again, these domestic arrangements appear to have been responses to the logistics of household survival and to have been not only unconnected to but often in contradiction with ideology.

Making Do: Satisfactions and Dissatisfactions

These interwar marriages contained the seeds of the family strategies that Louise Lamphere found in a contemporary Rhode Island industrial city among both Colombian and Portuguese immigrant households. Arlie Hochschild, writing about the 1980s, also linked similar behavior to class rather than to ethnicity. The arrangements I have discussed here were not the monopoly of any race or ethnic group, and in any event the selection of informants and the conditions under which the Women's Bureau questionnaires were administered were not systematic enough to support definitive arguments about ethnic specificity. They appear instead to have been linked to class and immigration. It might be argued that families that had been disrupted by pulling up roots and migrating to another culture could then become more flexible in all their arrangements, more willing to experiment with new roles, more willing to respond creatively to the exigencies of their situation. Under such circumstances, male dominance and patriarchal roles, even though supported by both cultures of origin and the dominant culture in the United States, might become negotiable.

It is also important to understand that household divisions of labor changed with time and circumstance. Witness the Philadelphia street laborer who worked irregularly and drank up much of what he earned; when he had a four-year stretch of unemployment, he apparently gave up drinking, helped with the housework, and looked after the children. Steadily employed for three months when the Women's Bureau agent came to call, he no longer pitched in at home (his wife spent her evenings doing laundry) but he had formed the happy habit of giving his wife all of his pay.[211] Just as families look very different in structure at various stages of the life cycle, they might look very different in their divisions of labor. Not all families, of course, moved toward a less sharply defined division of productive and reproductive labor, and we may never know why some did and some did not. For many, respectability and male self-esteem demanded that women not engage in wage work outside the home,[212] but since my sources are heavily weighted toward families where women earned wages or where unemployment had scarred the family's economic fortunes, it is not surprising that such sentiments rarely surface. It is enough, however, to know that some families did blur gender distinctions and that patterns of shared family enterprise are not peculiar to the post-women's liberation family of the last three decades of the twentieth century but can be found in significant numbers among working-class families in the 1920s and 1930s.

Taking joint responsibility for the family economy could produce mutual respect and esteem. Few put it so explicitly as an Iowa man who asserted that "he and his wife were partners and both contribute[d] their wages to the support of [the] family,"[213] or the unemployed Philadelphia hat maker, a Hungarian immigrant, who said proudly "She good woman. If woman not help, bad for man,"[214] or the Polish steelworker in the same city who explained, "'She's helping me, I'm helping her.'"[215] But many expressed more indirectly a sense of partnership that spoke of mutual pride. An Oklahoma woman whose husband was laid off a year after they were married proudly told a Women's Bureau investigator, "My husband said, he guessed we would have gone hungry if I hadn't [found a job in a food-processing plant]."[216] The husband in a more prosperous East St. Louis couple who both worked in meatpacking credited his wife for their well-being; the Women's Bureau agent noted that he said "they have a comfortable home & have gotten ahead because his wife was willing to help when she could."[217] Housework was not on this man's agenda, because his sixty-year-old mother lived with the family and took responsibility for the housework. In this household, the wife "helped" the mother-in-law just as men helped women in other households. Perhaps in this household the sense of shared enterprise included not just a husband and wife but also his mother.

In other families, a sense of economic partnership could rest on the value of a woman's non-market efforts. A San Francisco streetcar man who said, "If Mrs. B. was not such a good mother, cook, seamstress, doctor, barber, and laundress, we could never make ends meet" respected and appreciated his wife's role in cash-replacement activities.[218] Appreciation took concrete form when families made investments to ease the woman householder's work or maximize her efficiency. Even though a Wisconsin Italian family could afford only the barest necessities, the laborer husband insisted on spending over seven weeks' wages on a washing machine, justifying his action to a settlement-house worker by arguing, "With four children there are a lot of clothes to wash and the work is too hard for my wife."[219] This wife was not a wage earner. Jewish families who, Susan Glenn argues, brought to the United States an Old-World heritage of "breadwinning partnership" were able to act on that heritage in modest family enterprises where a woman could work without damage to her husband's prestige. Thus, Mollie Linker worked "side by side" with her husband in the family candy store for fifty-five years.[220] Equivalence of status, though, was probably more difficult to achieve in the small store than when both were wage earners; tellingly, Linker referred to the family business as her husband's store.

Just as a solid partnership could be built on the recognition of shared effort in family support, instability and dissolution loomed when the partners assessed one another's contributions differently. The Women's Bureau agent picked up signals of discord in the household of a Mexicana in Laredo, Texas, who had a firm sense of herself as part of a partnership, an evaluation that was not shared by her husband. She worked at homework, which she viewed as a satisfying career, saying that she "has always sewed & likes it better than everything else," especially since the manufacturer delivered her work to her and gave her the "finest samples" on which to work. Rate cuts had trimmed her earnings from fifteen to two dollars per week, a wage at which her steadily employed husband laughed derisively: "He disapproves of the work. Wife says she wants to help as she has little other work to do. Husb. [sic] claims it is no help."[221] Two Anglo homeworkers in San Antonio had husbands who were similarly unappreciative of their efforts. Caroline Manning said of one, "Husb. [sic] fusses because I.P. sews but I.P. knows they need every little bit"[222] and of the other, "Husb. [sic] fusses so much about her working it makes her nervous"—this despite the fact that her homework had entirely supported the family when he had been ill.[223]

Women sometimes fell out with their husbands because of different cultural expectations grounded in class. A Bostonian of Italian background was married to a man who had lost his job as a printer because of mechanization and feminization of the work. She linked her disappointment in the marriage, and in fact her evident depression, to her husband's shortcomings as a breadwinner:

> Mrs. DeSantis says that she thought Mr. DeSantis was "well off" when she married him and that she would be happy. Now she is discouraged and does not know what she will do when the baby [her second child] comes, for she cannot work. She says that she takes no pleasure any more in anything. Her pride will not permit her to go anywhere because she has no clothes "fit to be seen in."[224]

The class ambitions of another New Englander, Mrs. Cohen, had led her to marry a professional musician instead of the skilled laborer with whom she was in love. When the Depression dried up musicians' jobs, Mr. Cohen took a job unloading trucks at a local store. With her social ambitions dashed, "the pent-up fury of Mrs. Cohen was turned loose. Never, she said, never would she remain the wife of a common laborer. Didn't he know why she had married him? What would her friends say? What would her family think?" After considerable pain and conflict, the family eventually made a happy adjustment to their new working-class status.[225]

The refusal or inability of one partner to share in family support could produce deep disillusion about and even outright rejection of marriage as an economic partnership. A Midwestern man refused to deal with the crisis that his lowered income brought to his family, either denying its existence or expressing his annoyance at its manifestations: the lack of ready cash or the presence of insistent creditors. His wife was driven nearly to distraction by his indifference, and the two engaged in a struggle over control of the family fund.[226] A laid-off construction foreman similarly withdrew from the plight into which the loss of his job and those of two of his children had plunged his family: "Mr. Lacroix is almost unaffected. Loss of income means nothing to him. He was glad to give up the responsibility of work. He has no conception of the problems of the rest. He sleeps, smokes his pipe and listens to the radio and is interested in the present economic situation as an academic matter only."[227] Small wonder that an Italian immigrant to St. Louis, for example, questioned the worth of a husband who hadn't worked for nearly a year, who refused to do any work around the house even though she worked full-time in a garment factory, and whose major ambition—according to her—was "to look nice all the time."[228] All consumer and a failure as a producer, he was a washout as a husband. A German immigrant woman in Philadelphia was faced with a husband who drank and repeatedly deserted; she worked hard to earn enough to support the family but finally decided that she might be pursuing a losing strategy, quitting work and telling the Women's Bureau agent, "Let him see what he can do."[229] A Dayton woman, writing in response to the YWCA Industrial Commission's request for opinions about married women's wage-earning, counseled single women who hoped to leave the labor force upon their marriage:

> She may think that she will not work when she gets married but will marry a man who can support a family, but few of us ever marry the man of our dreams. And even if she were to marry a man with a fairly good salary, he may in a very short time after they are married lose his job, or become a [sic] invalid and unable to work.[230]

Even in the most promising circumstances, a woman might trust her husband but still cut the cards. A Woman's Bureau agent wrote of a Georgia clothing factory worker, "Her husband is good to her, helps with the work, etc. But she seems to feel that no husband can be absolutely depended on, so she is buying the place in her own name."[231] Marriage was a risky undertaking, although not always because of the personal failings of the partners. Indeed, given the stresses to which these marriages were subject, the need of explaining why any held together seems more pressing than explaining why some fell apart.

Wives, in any event, showed a savvy street wisdom in assessing their husbands' performance as breadwinners even to the Women's Bureau agents. Although the agents could not see beyond a husband's heavy drinking, wives were less upset by drinking in itself than by its impact on family life. The epithet of "n.g."—no good—had shifting meanings. A Lithuanian-born woman drew a fine distinction in specifying to the Women's Bureau investigator that her hard-drinking husband was "not mean" but "just no good."[232] This man's drinking—and probably that of many others—robbed the family coffers in two ways: it caused him to work irregularly and it ate up a "large part of his earnings."[233] Bad investments condemned another husband to the purgatory of n.g. The man had bought a building where he set up a store and a dance hall and failed to make a go of it, leaving his wife to hold the bag of a heavy mortgage.[234] Yet in another case, a husband's loss of the couple's life savings on a misguided business venture evoked loyalty rather than condemnation; his wife told the Women's Bureau agent, "My husband no play cards or nothing like some men. A good man."[235] Others earned the label of n.g. for reasons less clear, mostly having to do with a husband's willful failure to be a good earner.[236] One husband's problem was that he withheld almost all his own money from the family fund. His wife complained, "Husband no good—only wants moonshine and play cards."[237] Cruel or abusive behavior was a sure route to the label of n.g., but it is notable how few times this criticism is made of bad husbands.[238] Infidelity was mentioned explicitly by only one Philadelphia deserted wife, but she was less distressed by the fact that her husband had run off with another woman than that he had done so a week after their baby died.[239] By far the most frequent category of complaints about husbands was economic. Of the 80 Philadelphia husbands who fell short of expectations, being an inadequate source of support was cited in 34; another 26 were deserting husbands whose economic nonfeasance was implicit; 2 gambled; and 20 drank, an obvious drain on the family fund. A few husbands committed particularly flagrant offenses against the family economy: Philadelphia examples include a husband who stole and spent the family savings and then deserted his wife when she had a nervous breakdown from the resulting economic worries;[240] another deserted repeatedly and finally "sold bedding, clothing, and anything that could bring any money—and left sixty cents on [the] table" for his wife.[241]

Some women appear to have responded to the failure of their marriages with special verve and energy. Southern women dominate this group. One of the most haunting responses to the YWCA Industrial Commission came from Charlotte, North Carolina. A mill worker told a long tale of child-bearing and grueling housework, punctuated by episodes of work in the fields of the family farm and in textile mills and topped off by her husband's desertion when she was six months pregnant with her third child. She wrote in evident satisfaction:

> Now I work and support my three children and my self on ten and fif-teen dollars a week and send them to school. I buy my groucys [sic] and pay my house rent and buy my winter supplys [sic]. My mother takes care of my children while I work. My age is thirty-one and my childrens [sic] are ten, eight, and six. We are doing fine.[242]

Similarly, a Women's Bureau agent paraphrased a Macon, Georgia, woman's description of the life that she, her textile worker daughter, and her granddaughter lived together: "There were no men at their house, and they did not have much, but what they did have they had in peace." She added, "Meaning there were no men who had to be kept and contributed nothing."[243] A Virginia tobacco worker who was having a distinctly more difficult time getting along sounded the same note. Since she had defini-tively gotten rid of her husband, "she is more peaceful now than she has ever been."[244] For these women, desertion came almost as a blessing, rid-ding them of the burden of difficult men. In other cases, a husband's scrapes with the law or restlessness solidified their disillusion with mar-riage. Another Georgian left her husband, for example, because he moved around too much so that "they could not keep any thing or get any thing together."[245] The fact that so many expressions of disillusion with mar-riage came from southern women suggests that the recent and continuing transition from rural to industrial life and women's new access to cash wages may have allowed their discontent with marriage to surface. Two Kansas City immigrants from Central Europe, both workers in meatpack-ing, expressed the same feeling about their "n.g." husbands. One said "she was glad when he left her"[246] and the other said she got "along just as well with him gone."[247] Perhaps they too felt close to their rural backgrounds, but perhaps they just had a low threshold for irresponsible men.

What we can say is that women with access to relatively steady if low cash wages showed a special tendency to throw off chafing bonds of marriage. The preponderance of such women working in textiles and in meatpacking, fields where women frequently equaled or surpassed men's earnings, suggests that these expressions rested on a cushion of comparative—if not absolute—prosperity. Able to earn enough that they felt their power as providers, perhaps they viewed marriage as did an African American meatpacker from East St. Louis, who referred blithely to the failure of "her third and 'recent matrimonial experiment.'"[248] Marriage was worth a try; if it worked well it meant at least a trusted companion and a higher standard of living. But it was a chancy thing indeed. A settlement worker mused over neighborhood women's attitudes toward men: "I sometimes feel as though a man were merely a happy or an unhappy accident; he is so generally regarded as part of the woman's problems, along with the rent, the insurance, and the children."[249]

A few feisty women went even farther, taking the initiative to escape from a bad marriage even without a good livelihood. A fifty-year-old Polish woman told her remarkable story to a Woman's Bureau agent. The woman came alone to this country when she was twenty-eight and pregnant, fleeing from a violent alcoholic husband. Devoted to her daughter— "I crazy about that baby"—she worked at jobs that she could combine with child care, never earning more than five dollars per week. At the time of her interview, the daughter had been married for two years and had a child. She was, wrote the Women's Bureau agent, "very contented. Has lived her own life" and was happy at home—with "not one to holler at me, no boss. Come home, house quiet"—and at work—a "nice quiet place" where she was a hand presser of waists.[250] A twenty-two-year-old Italian woman left her husband who had "always mistreated her" in a northeastern Pennsylvania industrial town and came to Philadelphia with her two-year-old, her only asset the name of a stranger who might, and did, put her up.[251] Another woman who left her husband because "he didn't behave himself" had two resources on her side: first, a job as a baster that paid nineteen dollars per week, an unusually high wage for the needle trades and substantially above the Philadelphia median woman's wage of fifteen dollars and thirty-five cents, and second, a thirteen-year-old son. At the time of the Women's Bureau agent's visit, four years later, she had quit her job because her boss refused her request for a dollar raise and was living comfortably with three younger children on the wages of her son, now a clothing worker himself.[252] Fortune smiled on one woman who left her husband after ten years of marriage because she "was tired of supporting" him. Eking out a bare ten dollars a week on industrial homework when she separated from the husband, within a little over a year she had found an excellent job as a kind of executive chef for an office lunchroom that paid her sixteen or seventeen dollars for an unusually short and pleasant workweek of forty-four hours. Another woman, who proudly told the agent, "I deserted [my husband] three and a half years ago," earned twenty-one dollars sewing housedresses.[253]

Working-class marriages were deeply entangled in production and reproduction, earning and spending. The insecurity of the economic context weighed heavily on them, producing misery and anger as well as mutual support and satisfaction. The classic husband-as-breadwinner/wife-as-consumer division of labor has limited descriptive power for these families because of the structural aspects of their lives. Men had great difficulty earning a wage regular or ample enough to fulfill the breadwinner role well, and women's efforts to be good managers were thwarted by the insufficiency and irregularity of the funds they had to work with. As individual consumers, husbands and wives reacted in remarkably similar ways: both chafed under the burden of dependency, and both sought to have some money of their own as a testimony of independence. The difference, of course, was that husbands rarely experienced utter financial dependency, as all non-wage-earning wives did; most men enjoyed a modicum of independence as consumers, and relatively few women did. Husbands expanded their consumption role only at the expense of their breadwinner role, whereas women's entry into breadwinning tended to give them more consumer autonomy. But these shifting conjugal roles, with their contested obligations, expectations, and responsibilities, only tell us part of the story of working-class consumption. Husbands and wives were situated in families that incorporated multiple generations. It is, then, to questions of gender and generation that we now turn.

2

"Cooperative Conflict"
Gender, Generation, and Consumption in Working-Class Families

Relations between generations in working-class families provide a revealing window on the ways in which consumption was affecting the family economy, tempting individuals with expenditures that might not serve the family interest but still not entirely dissolving ties of mutual obligation and shared goals. During the 1920s and 1930s, the family wage remained an elusive ideal for most working-class families, and the husband/father's wages required supplements by other family members. In chapter 1 I have addressed some of the implications of wives'/mothers' wage-earning for consumption and the family economy, and here I shall concentrate on children's impact in these areas. I include in the category "children" those living with their parent(s), either unmarried or fairly recently married. By doing so, I do not mean to suggest that children's economic connections with their parents necessarily ended when they left the parental home or married, but that the nature of relationships between co-resident unmarried children and their parents is in general qualitatively different from that between married children living independently and their parents.[1]

Children's wage-earning was, of course, not new, and it continued to be regarded as a family obligation. During the interwar period, however, it took place in a context different from that of its early industrial origins. Child-labor and compulsory-education laws took away some of parents' control and delayed the age at which children could begin to make cash contributions to the family fund. This legislation, often subverted by parents and children alike, varied in provisions and enforcement in different states and was certainly not new to the 1920s. What was novel for our purposes was its intersection during the interwar years with intensified advertising, increased mass production, and the commercialization of leisure. Material dreams and aspirations expanded, and non-earning children became more expensive to maintain. Wage-earning children, even when they dutifully turned their pay envelopes over to their families, might still be a net drain on the family budget, and in any case they made increasing demands for money of their own to spend. Children—even as they remained vital contributors to the family economy—became an increasingly mixed economic blessing. The result was a pervasive confusion about generational roles that frequently erupted in conflict over the family's claims on children's wages.

Making Something of Children

The parents of the children of the interwar period were, by and large, no strangers to the money economy even in their own childhoods. As youths, those who had passed their early years in the cities and towns of the United States would have had access to the broad range of opportunities to earn money described by David Nasaw in *Children of the City: At Work and at Play*.[2] These "street trades" included retailing goods such as newspapers, scavenging for things that could be turned into cash, and providing small services such as deliveries. Such opportunities had been widely accessible to boys and to older girls, but younger girls might still have cadged a bit from the money they were given to perform errands[3] or picked up pocket change by minding neighborhood children. As these children of the 1900s and 1910s became the parents of the 1920s and 1930s, they would have carried with them complicated memories of the meanings of their efforts and their earnings—of moments of pleasure purchased with their nickels and dimes, of struggles with their parents over their money, of the satisfactions of contributing to a meager family fund.

Their own children would have the same mixed experience with the money economy, but the relations between the generations took place in a different context. High school education, especially outside the South, and especially for the youths of European ancestry, became more readily available and was therefore a more broadly shared aspiration. A steady increase in the school-leaving age kept children out of gainful employment longer and helped to make earning money on the streets more disreputable and subject to criminalization.[4] Parents responded to their complicated set of memories and current circumstances in predictably varied ways: some relied on their children's earnings to make that struggle easier; others pushed themselves harder in order to spare their children similar struggles in their own adult lives.

One sign of the degree to which parents recognized that although school attendance limited children's ability to earn their own money, children still had a need for some marketplace existence was the broad practice of giving children spending money, often in the form of a regular allowance. Few sources explore this practice, but the intriguing fact is that the two studies which tell us the most about allowances were conducted during the Depression, both by the Heller Committee for Research in Social Economics of the University of California. The first studied the household budgets of urban Mexican families, in which the adults were nearly all born in Mexico, for the year beginning in mid-1929, and found that 71 of 100 families gave spending money to their children; the second looked at the expenditures of families of streetcar men living in the East Bay Area of northern California and of families of clerks working in San Francisco in 1933. Looking only at families with dependent children, 22 of 74 streetcar men's families, and 37 of 98 clerks' families gave their children allowances.[5] The Mexican families may seem unusually generous, but it is probably the case that they were surveyed in more prosperous times than the northern California families. The authors note that money spent on movies was calculated separately and in addition to the allowance money, conjecturing that most allowance money was "spent for candy, ice cream, and chewing gum."[6] Interestingly both the Mexican families and the clerks' families typically gave children about fifty cents a week each to have at their disposal.[7]

Only one of the Women's Bureau bulletins, *The Immigrant Woman and Her Job*, asked directly about parents' hopes for their children, and that question focused specifically on education. The interviews, conducted in the first half of 1925, showed the degree to which these immigrant families planned to divert resources into educating children and foregoing their wages in the process. Over 4 in 10 who commented on their educational ambitions for their children offered an open-ended desire to educate their children, a desire that the agents recorded both in specific terms and in such shorthand as "all able," "all possible," or "as much as possible." About a quarter more specifically aspired to give their children a high-school education or at least to educate them to age 16. Just over a quarter did not plan to educate their children beyond the legal limit or eighth grade (the two tended to coincide in Pennsylvania law at the time) or were generally pessimistic about their ability to give their children much education. Barely 1 in 20 planned other types of formal education: about half business school and half collegiate. Of the three ethnic groups represented by more than 100 women—Poles, Jews, and Italians—all had a majority in the first two categories (open-ended or high school/age 16). Although there were some ethnic differences, with Jews most likely and Italians least likely to report aspiring to higher levels of education, an apparent bias in either asking or filling in this question and other problems with the data cast doubt on any conclusions about the comparative desires of different ethnic groups to educate their children. The Women's Bureau agents recorded responses in the "ambitions for children" blank for all the Jewish married women visited, for about two-thirds of the Polish women, and for less than one-third of the Italian women. Since the agents recorded negative responses as well as positive, we can only assume that they pushed this issue more energetically with some ethnic groups than with others, perhaps in accord with their own stereotypes about the relationship between ethnicity and education.

One measure of parental commitment to at least basic education was the refusal to keep daughters out of school to meet child-care needs, however pressing. The historical role of the "little mother" seems to have faded away by the 1920s. My research yielded only two instances of the "little mother," a child kept away from school and deputed by her mother to care for younger siblings while the mother went out to work. The more egregious example was that of a twelve-year-old daughter of a Georgia cotton-mill worker; she stayed home to take care of four younger siblings, the youngest two-and-a-half-years old, while her mother, father, and fourteen-year-old sister worked in the mill. The other would at first glance seem to be even more scandalous, that of the six-year-old daughter of a San Antonio homeworker. The Women's Bureau agent wrote, "little 6 y[ea]r old girl cares for 4 mo[nth] old baby. Washes diapers, h[an]dk[erchie]fs & socks. has a small tub & washboard. Was washing socks at time of visit, baby was asleep. little 4 y[ea]r old girl helped her empty a small pan of water." The scene is straight out of Jacob Riis, but a closer reading of the schedule reveals that this little mother had two siblings between the ages of six and sixteen who were presumably at school; the mother was also at home. Presumably this child would soon follow her older siblings into school; it is difficult to assess the balance between exploitation and play in this situation, but even at its worst it would suggest that the "little mother" was a figure who, in her extreme form, had departed from the working-class family scene.[8]

Very few families had ambitions to send their children to college. Among women working in slaughtering and meatpacking, three African, three Polish, and one Lithuanian had such ambitions; among Philadelphia immigrant women, three Jewish, and one each Polish, Slovak, and Scottish did. All of this probably does not mean much except that somewhat surprisingly college was as likely to be seen as a way up for those most downtrodden as it was to be a goal for those with more of a head start, economically speaking. Some of these desires partook more of fantasy than of possibility; consider, for example, the Jewish immigrant who wanted her one-year-old son to be a physician[9] and the Polish mother who planned for her eight-year-old to be a dentist.[10] Most parents were more realistic and attentive to their children's performance in the classroom, such as the Polish mother who said of her primary-school-aged son and daughter, "if they learn well we'll send them higher" than grammar school.[11] Children's own attitudes toward education also figured into the mix, such as the grammar-school daughters of a Polish immigrant who were deeply upset about missing school while the family was under quarantine because of a brother's diphtheria,[12] and the only son of German immigrants who "love[d] books" and hoped to become a priest.[13] High school apparently was becoming a default educational aim for immigrant parents during the 1920s; a German upholstery worker had sent her only child to high school, commenting that "That's as little as you can do for them."[14]

A common, and readily available, enhancement of life was to provide children with music lessons, as did a dozen Philadelphia immigrant women—6 of them Polish, 2 Jewish, and one each German, Irish, Quebecois, and Ukrainian. The most popular instrument was the violin, and the piano came second. The sums spent on these lessons were sometimes impressive: the Quebecois family spent $100 per year on music lessons for their three children,[15] while the Ukrainian family spent $8 per month teaching a son to play the violin and a daughter the piano—the mother told the agent, "That's why I work."[16]

When families expressed themselves more expansively about the future they envisioned for their children, many expressed regret that they could not do more, but few were belligerent about accounting for their inability. Two such were a Hungarian woman who told the agent that that high school cost "too much money"[17] and an Italian woman who exclaimed "high school for rich folks!"[18] An Italian family was quite determined that their six children should achieve English literacy and numeracy, but they were appalled at the curriculum of their eldest, a daughter whose continuation-school education seemed to consist mostly of dancing. The agent noted that the mother was especially disgruntled that she had to earn wages while her daughter danced away her fifteenth year in school.[19] A range of families planned to educate their sons more extensively than their daughters—two Polish, three Jewish, and one each Italian, Russian, and Lithuanian mothers and two Italian sisters who were working to educate their brothers at levels beyond which they had reached. But two Jewish mothers favored their daughters, one planning to send her twelve and fifteen-year-old daughters through business school although their seventeen-year-old brother worked in a factory,[20] and the other planning to help her daughter become a teacher though she had no ambitions for her three sons.[21]

Ambitions for children were linked to immigrants' evaluation of what it meant to be American: one Polish woman expected little of her children because "children in America [were] spoiled,[22] but a German mother insisted that her children "must be like Americans."[23] More frequently, aspirations were couched in terms of helping children to have better lives than their parents. Italian, Polish, Jewish, Lithuanian, Hungarian, and Ukrainian immigrant mothers in Philadelphia all hoped to spare their children the travails that they had experienced. It was a common litany that education would spare children the hard work that their parents had had to do.[24] Parents expressed a desire to give their children the "right start"[25] or "a good start"[26] or to see "that they should have advantages."[27] An Italian cigar-maker hoped to give "all her girls a better chance than she had," although the eldest of the three, at sixteen, was already herself a cigar worker.[28] A Jewish woman who worked in the needle trades wanted above all to educate her children and told the agent, "That's what I'm working for—we are suffering too much. We don't want they should."[29] A Polish office cleaner, wife of an alcoholic shipyard worker and mother of three children aged six and younger, expressed fierce determination to give her children the best possible education: "I [am] mad no one send me to school."[30] Virtually no parent expressed a desire to educate their children for the financial gain of the parent. The husband in a Polish meatpacking couple asserted that education was "better for child. We give them education they give us very much thanks."[31] True to his word, the couple had put their daughter through a year and a half of business school and were sending their sixteen-year-old son through high school, with two younger daughters still in grammar school. Another meatpacking couple were both working because they felt that they could not "expect [their] children to care for them when old."[32]

The generations did not always agree on what was an appropriate level of education, but the younger generation did not consistently advocate more education than the older. A fourteen-year-old Hungarian son of a mother who worked in the needle trades and a father who was too ill to work argued against his parents' desire that he attend high school and felt that he "must work so mother can stay home"; while he was still in school he was unusually helpful around the house.[33] The daughter of a deserted Jewish mother wanted to go to trades school, but her mother hoped for "something better for her."[34] Sometimes, parents maintained their faith in education despite its lack of financial payoff for the family fund; a Kansas City couple, both meatpackers, had sent a son to business school. Even though he had been unable to find a job, they were nonetheless sending their daughter to business school as well.[35] Other parents were inclined or driven by circumstance to dampen their children's ambitions; the eldest of the four children of a Ukrainian laundry worker and bakery worker wanted to go to high school, but her mother insisted that she go to work instead.[36] A Russian office cleaner married to what she called a "rotten husband" had five children aged ten and younger and opined to the Women's Bureau agent, "God bless me when my children be big enough to go to work maybe I not work so hard."[37]

Not Enough to Mother

The tension between traditional expectations and new patterns of behavior is reflected eloquently in the language used to describe children's contributions to the family fund. The most frequent and, at first glance, transparent description of the disposition of a daughter's wages in the Women's Bureau raw data is "All to mother," meaning that the mother received all the child's earnings. Depression-era studies used this trope as well. Irvin Child, writing of families headed by southern Italian immigrants during the late 1930s, noted that "Most families require that as long as a child is still living at home, regardless of his age, he must turn over all his wages to his parents."[38] Such practices were by no means observed only in immigrant families; Ruth Shonle Cavan and Katherine Howland Ranck, in a study of Chicago families of whom two-fifths were native-born, noted that "It is customary among many families in the lower middle class [their term for working class] for the adolescent children to turn all money earned over to their mother, at least during the first few years of their employment."[39] The vision of the obedient child turning her back on the temptations of the marketplace and subordinating personal interest to family welfare clearly held a peculiar power over the imagination of social scientists, government investigators, and working-class informants alike.

When "all to mother" did not apply, however, the language became more opaque. About as many women paid board as turned over their entire pay envelopes, and about half as many were described as contributors to family support to one partial degree or another. The material distinctions between these categories remained murky. Daughters described as paying board and as contributing to family support frequently paid similar amounts into the family fund, and the two labels appear to be randomly scattered through the interview forms. The difference in inflection, though small, seems to mark a crucial difference in a family's, or a daughter's, self-perception. A board-paying daughter presumably was positioned in a fee-for-service relationship to her family, while a daughter contributing to family support was cast as part of the family's collective effort. Unfortunately, the sources are virtually mute about the roots and consequences of that distinction. "All to mother" was easy to understand and articulate, at least on the surface; other patterns were more perplexing because they reflected new market-mediated daughter-parent patterns which were in flux and for which a new language had not yet emerged.

Those who gave all to mother, paid board, or contributed to family support nonetheless had one thing in common: all were characterized as substantial contributors to the family fund. In comparison, those described as providing only for their own support were a distinct minority—only about 7 percent of the total. The interwar period was, clearly, a period in which daughters' economic obligations to their families were varied and in the process of continuing negotiation, but it is notable that these negotiations resulted in apparent economic autonomy for only a small fraction of wage-earning daughters.

Partly because my sources discuss far fewer sons than daughters and partly because sons' contributions to the family economy were more simply defined and understood, a very different set of conventions for describing sons' economic relationships to the family emerges. Sons were more likely than daughters to discharge their obligations with a specific sum of money. Even during the Depression, only a handful of sons were described as turning their entire wages over to the family. In families with employed sons and daughters both, there was in fact an asymmetry in contributions.[40] In only two cases—that of Kansas City meatpacker siblings and that of two sisters and a brother in a Waterloo, Iowa, family—did daughters and sons contribute equal amounts. Given men's generally higher wages, however, the daughters almost certainly contributed a higher proportion of their income than their brothers and were left with a smaller sum to use at their own discretion.[41] More typically, a worker in a Rhode Island light-bulb factory turned her entire $16 paycheck over to her mother, while her machinist brother contributed only $12 of his $30 earnings to the family fund.[42] An Omaha packinghouse worker gave her mother $8 per week, but her clerical-worker brother, who almost certainly earned considerably more than she did, contributed only $5. Their mother told the Women's Bureau investigator, "He needs so much himself."[43]

This may well have been true; an office worker had to be more elegantly fitted out for work than a bacon packer. But in most cases sons are described by both their families and investigators in more censorious terms than daughters, and these terms target the sons' character flaws rather than seeing them in relational terms as was the case with daughters. The improvident son appears repeatedly in the Women's Bureau raw data, perhaps because the stories are told from the perspective of mothers or sisters, who may have resented male claims to autonomy in the marketplace as well as other arenas. A Richmond factory worker who turned over her whole paycheck to her mother told a Women's Bureau investigator that her brother "waste[d]" his substantial earnings, giving small and irregular amounts to the family.[44] A Providence rubber-factory worker gave her mother "practically all she makes" to compensate for two brothers who didn't "pay enough even to cover their board" and a father who was, in his wife's words, "'none too good.'"[45]

The lazy son who would or could not contribute significantly to the family also finds his place in the sources. Winnie Pankau, a meatpacker in St. Joseph, Missouri, complained that her son took after his deserting father: he was "shiftless and [didn't] keep any job long," even though she was hard put to support him and his two school-age siblings.[46] An Atlanta hat maker reported that her brother worked irregularly and did little to help her support their widowed mother and invalid sister.[47] Mirra Komarovsky, in her study of families affected by unemployment, characterized the idle twenty-two-year-old son of a former railroad engineer as "easygoing, pleasant, but lazy." He scorned a low-paying job, saying "'Hell, working all week for $7.00! There's no percentage in that.'"[48] Cavan and Ranck, in a similar study, encountered an even choosier young Chicagoan who turned down an $18-a-week job in 1934.[49] Roger Angell, in a third Depression study, noted of one son, "His chief interest seemed to be to have a good time."[50]

To be sure, we do meet noble and hard-working sons. A Nashville shirt-factory worker had worked to supplement her husband's earnings while her high-school-student son did the housework. When he graduated, he went to work and contributed his wages to the family so that his mother could keep house. A twenty-three-year-old man willingly supported his invalid mother and unemployed stepfather, even though his three siblings refused to chip in and the stepfather labeled his stepson's only pleasure—playing the guitar—a "waste of time" and forbade him to practice at home.[51] The son of a widow disabled in an industrial accident held a steady job, did all the housework, and even cut the cabbage and peeled the potatoes for soup before he went to work in the morning.[52] The point is not that all sons resisted contributing to their families, but that substantial numbers of sons—and virtually no daughters—were portrayed as shirkers. Sons, as a group, seemed less able to balance their own consumer desires and their own interests in controlling their time and effort with their families' demands for support in a way that convinced other family members that they were doing their best for the family.

Although the sources portray daughters as generally more willing to contribute to their families, a closer look reveals that they did not always represent a "profit" for the family. When a family was relatively well off, as was an Iowa household in which the father and two brothers were coopers, it might count daughters' earnings a dead loss to the family fund. The Iowa cooper told a Women's Bureau agent that he was happy to have his laid-off daughter at home: she "just spent the money when she did work."[53] But a dutiful young woman who turned over her pay envelope to her mother or willingly paid board might not have been much more help to the family's budget than this free-spending daughter or selfish sons. Mothers receiving unopened pay packets repeatedly noted that their daughters' entire wages did not fully pay the cost of their support; those collecting board payments similarly reported that they received less than the market rate and even less than the actual cost of their daughters' support. Low wages were not just a mark of women's—especially young women's—subordinate status in the workforce, but they also marked those who earned them as disappointing contributors to the family fund and as second-class consumers.

Behind the trope "All to mother" unfolded a drama that revolved as much around consumption as around duty. In only one instance was it presented purely as a matter of family discipline; parents who had immigrated from Bohemia to Iowa asserted that they "still [had] control over" their daughter and therefore over her pay envelope.[54] In cases where the family was in dire straits, the arrangement appeared to benefit the family fund; Vera Dorn, a South Carolina drug company worker, normally paid her family five dollars per week board, but when her father lost his job in 1922 she began to turn in her whole paycheck.[55] Such was increasingly the case when unemployment spiraled during the Depression.

More often during the 1920s, however, "All to mother" was less a matter of parental control or familial desperation than one of mutual benefit. Mothers and daughters in, among other places, St. Louis, Omaha, Kansas City, Chicago, Providence, and Newport (Rhode Island) acknowledged that a young woman's paycheck didn't necessarily cover her cost of living, even at home. Katherine Sawbol, a Kansas City meatpacker, noted that her mother had paid the substantial bills for her recent appendectomy and that "she gets more than she gives" to the family fund.[56] Even without the economic disaster of a serious medical problem, a St. Louis candy-maker described her situation in almost identical terms: "she gets back more than she gives in."[57] A Providence laundry worker told a Women's Bureau agent that she "probably pays for self" but, noted the agent, "Mother thinks not" because her daughter's "shoe[s] and coat[s] cost so much[:] $12 for shoes that wear away."[58]

Similarly, many families noted how little working daughters could afford to pay for board. The mother of a Chicago candy-factory worker said that she was "not making her carfare and board."[59] An Enid, Oklahoma, Woolworth employee earned only enough for clothes and spending money, leaving nothing for board; she told a Women's Bureau agent, "If I had to pay board I guess I'd have to find a job that paid more."[60] A worker in an overall factory in Petersburg, Virginia, made an almost identical comment.[61]

The fact that daughters' board payments did not fully offset their cost to their families could not help but elide the distinction between paying board and contributing to family support. A mid-1929 Cincinnati Consumers' League study argued that, far from benefiting from low-cost family board, wage-earning women were actually "skimping on expenditures for other budget items to contribute toward the family's support."[62] Working-class voices are absent from the Cincinnati study, but an Omaha mother's description of her selfless daughter suggests how much daughters might deprive themselves to contribute to family support: "No go to show. Nothing."[63]

Clothing absorbed a large proportion of wage-earning daughters' salaries and consequently became a major item of concern in discussions of family economies. Kathy Peiss has argued eloquently that clothing was for young woman wage-earners both a medium of self-expression and an entry ticket to the world of commercialized heterosociality, but in the sources I use clothing appears as much as a cause of worry as a source of satisfaction.[64] Mary Lou Corley, the only steady earner in her household of five, fretted that her "family need[ed] her help" but that it took "most of what she earn[ed] to buy her clothes."[65] Presumably, in her small mill village, the standards for dress were not extravagant. After a year in the workforce, a young Rhode Island woman could not "earn enough to pay for even her own clothes & [was] running into debt."[66] Some mothers were resigned to continuing expenditures for clothing: the mother of Kansas City meatpacking worker Rose Pestock reported ruefully of her daughter that it took "all she makes to dress—there is something every Saturday to be bought in way of [her] clothes."[67] Some mothers were less sympathetic. When an Ohio woman lost a finger in an industrial accident, her mother commandeered over half her compensation payment on the grounds that "she would only spend it for clothes."[68]

My sources do not describe the wardrobes these daughters bought but, given that they could probably afford only relatively cheap low-quality clothing that needed to be frequently replaced, it is unlikely that they were lavishly dressed. Even when they paid outlandish sums—the Providence laundry worker's twelve-dollar shoes, for example—they shopped in a context where high prices did not necessarily mean high quality. Two comments by daughters injured in industrial accidents support this interpretation. A Wisconsin woman, after only two months of disability, reported that she "needed shoes and clothes at once" when she received her compensation payment.[69] An Ohio woman went to stay with an aunt in the country a month after her accident because she needed clothes and she "thought it wouldn't matter if [she] had none in the country.[70] If these women's experiences were typical, working daughters had few enough clothes that they suffered if their wardrobes were not replenished for a month or two.

To note the importance of dress in daughters' expenditures is not to argue that sons were immune to the lure of clothing; one Atlanta man, for example, spent all his earnings on clothes, even in the face of his family's utter destitution.[71] For both women and men, clothing exerted a strong attraction, as it had since young working-class people's early-nineteenth-century promenades on New York's Bowery.[72] But three factors appeared to charge daughters' clothing expenses with greater energy in family discussions. First, because of wage-earning daughters' closer economic ties to their families and their greater willingness to yield control over their wages to their mothers, their expenditures were more closely monitored. Second, women's clothes were by and large more fragile than men's and required frequent replacements, so that they were more of a continuing nuisance than men's often more expensive but also more durable clothes.[73] Third, longstanding ideas about women's vanity and their use of earnings as "pin money" had marked their desires for clothing as a sign of self-indulgence. All in all, the spotlight on women's clothing made their bodies a contested site of consumption in a way that did not apply to men.

Dependent Consumption and Imperiled Entitlement

Daughters' meager wages reflected employers' views of them as dependents and in turn intensified their dependency in their families. In general, giving wages "all to mother" meant consigning oneself to a dependent status as a consumer. Rather than autonomously dispensing her income, the daughter had to submit to maternal scrutiny of whatever spending money she requested. But in some cases, daughters actually chose or willingly acquiesced in this dependent relationship, because it gained them access to their mothers' superior consumer acumen. The same skills of close calculation and canny bargaining that working-class women honed in the management of the family budget could be mobilized to manage their daughters' wages as well. The mother of Alice Hennings, a phonograph-factory worker in Dubuque, boasted that she could "make the money go farther than Alice can."[74] An African American laundry worker in Atlanta, about to enter Spelman Seminary, gave her check to her mother, who purchased on her behalf.[75] And Mattie Burnett, a South Carolina spinner, told a Women's Bureau agent that she preferred to let her mother buy "for her what she needs and wants—likes to do that rather than pay board and buy her own things." Burnett may have chosen this arrangement because her family was doing fairly well at the time of the interview, with two brothers in the labor force; she might have calculated that her mother would see to it that she got more than her share since she, as the first child to enter the labor force, had for some time borne the primary responsibility for the family's support.[76]

Dependent these women might be, but it was in part a calculated dependence. "All to mother" could be a consumer strategy rather than a sign of filial duty, a way to gain access to a larger share of the family fund or to tap their mothers' skills to get more for their scarce dollars. Not surprisingly, this strategy appealed most to those who earned the least. The Cincinnati Consumers' League study showed a marked tendency for women with lower earnings to give "all to mother"; three out of five who earned the least (between $10 and $15 per week) did so, but only one out of ten earning the most (from $15 to $25).[77]

When parents were censorious of wage-earning daughters, they blamed consumption desires rather than, as they did with sons, character flaws or an unwillingness to work. A Russian-born immigrant to Iowa whose husband and a daughter were unemployed, complained to the Women's Bureau agent that "My girls want clothes, clothes" and parodied their demands: "It's Mamma pay everything."[78] Daughters' drains on the family budget could loom larger than sons' deficiencies. A Kansas City meatpacker reserved her harsh words for her eighteen and nineteen-year-old daughters because they "don't make much and they want everything," while taking no notice of the role of a twenty-one-year-old son who, according to the Women's Bureau agent, "won't work."[79] A cultural lens sharply focused parents' attention on daughters as consumers and evoked especially intense responses.

Despite the strongly gendered tone of the discourse of family economies, in some respects wage-earning daughter and sons were in quite similar situations. Although unwillingness to work was almost exclusively laid at the feet of sons, inability to find work plagued both sons and daughters, who faced serious difficulties in establishing themselves as steady workers. They fell short as supplementary breadwinners because of the difficulties they faced in the labor market as entry-level workers. A young Atlantan had secured a prized job with the post office and his mother had bought him the necessary bicycle on the installment plan. When the bicycle was stolen, he lost his job and was unable to find another.[80] A nineteen-year-old woman in the same city lost job after job because of "failure to adjust."[81] An eighteen-year-old Des Moines, Iowa, man had never learned a trade and could secure only irregular work.[82] A number of mothers decided to remain in meatpacking plants and keep their daughters home to do the housework, because the mothers could, as more experienced workers, earn more.[83] Untrained and inexperienced workers certainly fared badly in the job market, but vocational education did not necessarily better a young worker's chances for success. Four Midwestern families, three in Kansas City, Kansas, and one in St. Joseph, had invested in job training for their children, but none among the two sons and a daughter who were business school graduates, nor the daughter trained as a beauty operator, were able to find positions commensurate with their skills.[84] After three years at Boston's Mechanics Arts High School, Martin O'Connor found only odd jobs for two years, and no jobs at all for two years after that.[85]

All of the foregoing examples are from the 1920s, but young workers faced even greater problems getting started during the Depression, although the difference between the two periods is one more of degree than of kind. A Salt Lake City boy eagerly quit school but found no easy berth in the labor force, bouncing around from short-term jobs in a bakery, in a garage, and as a common laborer before work dried up completely.[86] Only one of three sons of a Polish immigrant to Chicago found steady work; the other two turned to petty crime and brought the family nothing but grief.[87] Even the relatively favorable labor market of Washington, DC, offered little to either African American or European American daughters.[88] And, of course, when children lost their jobs, their families had to assume the burden of their support. In the light of these examples, we need to qualify assumptions about youth's advantage in the labor market with a perception of young people's difficulties in finding a secure berth in a labor market that increasingly prized efficiency, productivity, and low turnover. It is also worth remarking that when it was a case of inability rather than unwillingness to earn, the problem was linked both to sons and daughters.

Children's contributions to the family coffers waxed and waned according to a variety of circumstances that were not always gendered. Some families voluntarily lowered their claims to their children's wages, but in only one case does this appear to be linked to gender. The mother of an Iowa pharmaceutical employee feared the temptations of prostitution; she told the Women's Bureau agent that she never asked for her daughter's whole pay packet, because "that was the cause very often of girls getting money and clothes in other ways."[89] At the time of the interview, the daughter was not paying even her customary five dollars per week board because she was purchasing a Victrola on the installment plan. More often parents expressed a growing generalized sense of children's entitlement to their wage. Other parents were simply not comfortable taking all their children earned: a worker in a small Georgia cotton mill worried that she was unable to save anything out of her wages, but still "wanted her daughter to be able to keep some" of her own wages.[90] Depression pay cuts and unemployment gave many families no choice but to take less of a contribution from their children. A District of Columbia father reported that his daughters were earning only twelve dollars per week apiece and "they can't pay board on that"; his son, too, took a pay cut and stopped paying board.[91]

Conversely, the unemployment of other family members often led children to give their parents more of their wages. A South Carolina woman gave all that she earned when her father was out of work, but only $5 per week when he had a job.[92]

Other things being equal, in the long run children gave less of their income, either absolutely or proportionately, to the family fund. One major cause of decreased contributions was an impending marriage. Helen Griger, an Omaha packinghouse worker, contributed enough to her family to pay for her own support for the first three years she worked, but then she became engaged and her mother cut her board to three dollars per week—well below the cost of her maintenance—in order to allow her to save for her marriage. Griger remarked that she felt "very fortunate in this unusual arrangement,"[93] but it hardly seems to be unique. At least two other Omaha families and a Chicago family renounced their claims to board from a daughter who was about to be married,[94] and one St. Louis son received the same consideration from his family.[95]

Even when a marriage was not in the near future, both sons and daughters tended to retain more spending money as time passed, and they developed more sense of entitlement to their own wages.[96] One young Chicago woman dutifully turned all of her wages over to her mother during five long years of the Depression but finally began to demand some for her own use. Cavan and Ranck nicely captured both her parents' ambivalence about this development and their understanding that her contribution was something to be negotiated and not demanded: "The mother thought her daughter wanted too many clothes, but both parents agreed that she was a 'good girl' who did what they wanted her to do."[97]

Consumer credit was increasingly a factor in children's economic roles in the family and attracted sons and daughters alike. Children learned early lessons about credit from the widespread working-class tradition of buying groceries "on the book" at neighborhood stores. Sadie Tanner Mossell noted that two-earner African American families in Philadelphia relied on this custom so that their children could buy food while their parents were off at work.[98] Mossell does not comment on children's perceptions of their experience of buying "on the book," but other sources indicate that children found it an experience charged with shame. An eleven-year-old girl in a Pittsburgh family struggling with unemployment asked a settlement worker: "Miss Moore, do you like to ask people for trust? I used to be ashamed, but my mother would say, 'Go down to the store, Mary, and tell them we'll pay when your father's working.' I hated to go, but I couldn't not, could I, for then we wouldn't have had anything to eat."[99]

As they matured and began to earn their own wages, daughters and sons experimented with the installment credit which proliferated during the 1920s and 1930s. None of the studies reported systematically on consumer credit, but the very limited evidence indicates that women most often went into debt for clothes—and men for radios. Installment credit was of course a bad bet economically, taking the most from those who had the least. The Cincinnati Consumers' League study noted that one third of the lowest paid women had resorted to installment buying (virtually all of them for clothing). However, only three out of the fifty medium-level earners and none in the highest-paid group had done so. All of the installment purchases cost more than the median expenditure for the particular item by all women in the study.[100]

Installment credit could be a source of family pleasure and recreation. The radios bought by the sons surely held this potential, although the sources do not speak directly to this issue. More often, possibly because of the middle-class bias of the investigators, consumer credit was linked to family resentment or even conflict. Two St. Joseph, Missouri, sisters bought home furnishings on the installment plan; one made payments on an over-stuffed parlor set, the other on a player piano. The latter commented, "My father never made more than $15 a week so if we want anything nice we have to get [it] ourselves."[101] An Indianapolis woman desperately trying to stay out of debt while her husband was in prison was deeply upset when her nineteen-year-old daughter and eighteen-year-old son, the oldest of her nine children, freely made installment purchases.[102] An East St. Louis brother and sister had teamed up to buy a car. Their Czech-born mother was "so out of patience—she can't talk about it," although she did remark to the Women's Bureau investigator, "Children so queer in America."[103]

The worst conflicts occurred when family members found themselves burdened with debts contracted by a relative. An East St. Louis meatpacker bought herself a "nice coat," but then was laid off and unable to meet the payments. Apparently because the coat, however nice, was a necessity, her stepfather had to take over the payments. The resulting bad feelings "almost caused a rupture in the family."[104] The conflict was not, however, only intergenerational. An unscrupulous Chicago man bought himself a $75 suit in his sister's name, giving the address of the factory where she worked. Hounded on the job by the ruthless merchant, the young woman was desperately paying off the debt at $2 per week.[105] In the insecure economy of the working-class family, installment debt was not a good bet. Although it promised immediate consumer gratification, it did so at the cost of higher prices than for cash purchases and—if payments could not be maintained—at the risk of the loss of both the item purchased and all money paid in up to that point. In family economies based on close calculation and careful economizing, it was no wonder that installment debt was a source of family conflict for both sons and daughters.

The days in which children's earnings were indisputably and completely the property and gain of their families—if ever indeed there had been such a day—were clearly gone by the interwar period. Wage-earning sons and daughters were impelled both by a sense of family duty and by the desire for consumer gratification. Families dealt with the resulting conflicts in a wide variety of ways, but the emphasis was on negotiation, on giving in a little to children's individual aspirations in order not to lose their contributions entirely.

Age, class, and gender shaped working-class daughters' and sons' experiences in the labor market, the marketplace, and the family. Age, in the picture painted by my sources, is the most powerful shaper of labor-force experience. Despite the ever-higher cultural value placed on youth during the 1920s and afterward, these young people were at pains to establish themselves as steady workers. Class doubtless shaped their work lives in other respects, but what we see most clearly here are its effects on their lives and identities as consumers. The pressures to consume assaulted all Americans more relentlessly beginning in the 1920s; for working-class families, though, self-denial rather than self-fulfillment through consumption was the rule.

Most notably of all, these documents show how gender shaped different discourses and experiences of consumption. The family discourse around wage-earning and consumption cast men as individuals, attributing good or bad performance as earners and family members to strengths or defects in their character. It placed women relationally, embedding them in the family as dependents rather than showing them as autonomous persons. Men were assessed for their qualities as workers, and their faults were expressed as failures of the work ethic. Women were portrayed as consumers, with their limited ability to contribute to the family fund taken for granted because of their disadvantaged position in the workforce and their lapses couched in terms of their desires for consumer goods, especially clothing. The discourse sounds remarkably like that Jeanne Boydston has found surrounding housework in the early republic: men's work was work, and women's was a matter of duty.[106]

The experience of consumption was as gendered as the discourse, although in a strikingly different direction. Sons simply held onto more of their higher earnings and disbursed them as they liked. Women's consumption was more closely tied to the family because of the "all to mother" pattern and their lower wages. Their consumption was more directly and specifically contested, particularly around clothing, and the joys of shopping and buying receded into the background. Ironically daughters' and sons' experiences in the marketplace belied the terms of the discourse. Men were in fact the more autonomous consumers, and women were the more reliable workers and the more dependable—if limited—contributors to the family fund. Understanding both the discourse and experience of working-class consumption in the United States in the interwar period teaches us many lessons about the limits of abundance and the persisting connections between production and consumption, but perhaps it shows us most of all how intensely gender shaped this world of consumption.

Daughters and sons were subject to similar disadvantages in the labor market and to similar temptations in the marketplace, but both they and their families responded to them in gendered ways. Sons were seen primarily as producers, daughters primarily as consumers. The discourse of working-class family consumption, while saying many of the same things about daughters and sons, nonetheless emphasized women's dependency and connections to the family and men's individualism. Such discourses existed in networks of sharing and exchange extending well beyond the family, and it is to these relations of mutuality and reciprocity that we now turn.

3

The Mutuality of Shared Spaces

No longer completely bound by a family-based peasant economy, yet still incompletely subsumed into the cash market, the economy of makeshifts in the interwar United States partook of both modes. In this transitional situation, relationships between spouses and between parents and children formed the core of the working-class family economy, though they were embellished by connections with myriad others. This chapter and the next explore these broader webs of mutuality and reciprocity. Working-class people constructed such networks to deal with the demands of their daily lives: the need to compensate for the irregularity and insecurity of wages; the desire for sociability and the closeness of kin and friends in a world where the market was an often-hostile place; and the changes brought by the life cycle and by the variations in health of their members. This realm of mutual support lurked below the level of working-class institutional supports like mutual aid societies and filled both the gaps in them and the void where social provision might have been. It was the creation of working-class people on the terrain in which they had the most control over their lives, and it fit more closely than other social arrangements with the vicissitudes of their lives and the desires of their hearts. To say this is not to romanticize such reciprocity, but to point out that it was the broadest, deepest, and most flexible resource that working-class people had to draw on and that it was an arena where they engaged in a level of self-activity often denied them on the job.

Mutuality and reciprocity are distinct but deeply intertwined dimensions of working-class life. The former highlights the sharing of resources and labor, such as housing or child care, among family, friends, and neighbors as a way to stretch limited means. The latter, which will be explored in chapter 4, focuses on the exchange of goods, services and labor, as a means both of assisting others and of gaining some minimal resources for one's self or one's family. When they worked well, mutuality and reciprocity benefited all concerned both materially and emotionally. When they failed, they left disappointment and bitterness in their wake. Even at their best, they were a fragile lifeline, subject to the vicissitudes of the body—illness, childbirth, aging—and of the economy.

The sharing and exchanges of goods, services, and cash took place not just because people had strong ties of mutual obligation but also because they were poor. As such, they evoke systems of mutuality and reciprocity across a broad expanse of space and time. American working-class household economies had more in common with discussions of the economy of makeshifts undertaken by Judith Bennett for medieval Britain, the late colonial Mexican struggles to achieve subsistence identified by Steve Stern, and the inventive uses of the market captured by Gracia Clark in her work on contemporary Kumasi than they had in common with middle-class household economies deeply drawn into the culture of abundance.[1] But the working-class mutuality about which I write was not merely a remnant of old patterns, not stolidly customary, but rather a dynamic process that reinvented custom (to paraphrase Eric Hobsbawm's and Terence Ranger's notion of the invention of tradition).[2] Such a process allowed for both mutual support and individual preference, mobilized both creativity and hard work, and produced both strong bonds and deep enmities.

Similar as these patterns of mutuality may seem to those of earlier centuries or of contemporary areas on the periphery of the world economy, they still partook of the concrete circumstances of life in the interwar period of America. The people who appear in these chapters had resources specific to the regions and industries to which they linked their fortunes and, more generally, to a U.S. economy in a particular stage of economic development that was marked by intense pressures for efficiency and productivity. Much like the Italian immigrants studied by Judith Smith in Rhode Island, they had advantages, particularly in their access to cash, that their poor counterparts elsewhere lacked. Some, following the path traced by

Carol Stack for African American migrants, re-created kin and community networks that were crucial to survival. Still, many of them—immigrants and internal migrants—lacked the supports of longstanding networks of kin and friends and had to cope with the siren song of acquisitive individualism.[3] Even the most individualistic, though, might be involuntarily drawn into small dependencies on others. One such example was the W family who was desperately conserving on fuel by living in one room of their New Haven apartment and relying on heat rising from the flat below. When the family downstairs moved out, the Ws no longer benefited from the rising heat and the plumbing froze; unable to repair the pipes, they were reduced to carrying water.[4] Not having intentionally cast their lot with the departed family, they nonetheless came to rely on their very presence and sank more deeply into misery when their downstairs neighbors left.

Indeed, the most frequent and ubiquitous form of mutual assistance was the sharing of household space, though in most cases this was a self-conscious choice rather than the chance occurrence that briefly benefited the Ws. This chapter focuses on shared housing as one critical aspect of working-class mutuality. Some families shared housing as a temporary stopgap during an emergency, but many others did so as a long-term way to maximize resources. For some, house sharing was a matter of desperation when all other options were closed; for others, it was a choice for sociability and shared satisfactions. The houses of working-class families in every part of the country were full indeed, in large part because housing was one of the few places in the working-class household economy where economies of scale could be achieved. Rents or mortgage and interest payments were, by and large, fixed, although still quite flexible by today's standards. Adding contributing residents to a household lowered the cost of housing for all concerned, and adding non-paying residents stretched resources without requiring increased expenditures of scarce cash. Households were protean groupings, growing and shrinking in response to demographic, economic, and emotional needs—and often containing people outside the nuclear family. However shabby and ill-equipped they may have been, however shaky the occupants' hold on them, houses and tenements were nonetheless places where families could build a base for confronting the political economy of class.[5]

Joining Forces in Shared Spaces

Because of the tendency of households to grow and shrink over time, the reported incidence of enlarged households—that is, those that included more than the members of a nuclear family—is only the tip of the iceberg. Even when the Women's Bureau interview schedules asked for a list of all household members, agents did not always fill in that section, and many households that included only nuclear families when visited would earlier or later have included additional members. The experience of Angelina, a young Italian immigrant, illustrates this point. Angelina came to the United States at age sixteen. She lived with cousins for five years until she married, set up housekeeping with her husband, and had two children. Her husband developed tuberculosis and after five years of marriage went to Italy for his health and entered a sanitarium on his return. Angelina broke up her home and went to live with a married sister when her husband left for Italy. After three years, she left the sister's home to set up an apartment a block away where she could take in a younger sister and brother newly arrived from Italy. She continued to take her children to her married sister's to be cared for while she worked as a stitcher in a dress shop. Thirteen years in this country when she was visited by the Women's Bureau agent, she had lived with her husband and children alone for only three years.[6] We know this much about Angelina only because a particularly energetic agent interviewed her at unusual length and typed up an extended account of her life. In the terser accounts of other lives, we shall see many of the themes that emerge in Angelina's.

Despite the difficulty of capturing the fluid practice of house sharing in these narrowly focused snapshots, the incidence of enlarged households is striking. Such arrangements are ubiquitous in the sources, and a few investigations allow us to gauge their frequency roughly. The two Women's Bureau studies that most methodically collected information about household composition—those of immigrant women and of women in meatpacking and slaughtering—reported that about one in six of the approximately two thousand households visited included more than a nuclear family; a similar proportion emerged in the Bureau's visits with Texas homeworkers although the data was less systematically collected.[7] The Women's Bureau's 1920–1921 study of Georgia recorded about one expanded household in every five and the National Federation of Settlements' case studies of 150 families experiencing unemployment before the 1929 crash found about one in four, as did Gwendolyn Hughes's "Mothers in Industry" study of over 11,000 Philadelphia households.[8]

Women's Bureau agents noted these practices but did not recognize their complexity and subtleties. They spoke of the high incidence in Pennsylvania's Lehigh Valley of what they termed "cooperative households," but their description flattened out the flexibility and variability of this arrangement.[9] They also counted boarders in the households they visited, but they used this as a catchall term covering a wide range of experiences shaped by the economic power and personal inclinations of those involved. Finally, the agents paid little attention to the uses of rental property to pursue family goals.

One of the factors that might be expected to influence shared housing was the local housing stock; different cities offered different possibilities for working-class housing. *The Employment of Women in Slaughtering and Meat Packing* illustrates these local variations in housing. Only 7.9 percent of the Chicago women visited lived in single-family houses, with nearly a third (31.4 percent) in two-family houses and well over half (59.9 percent) in multifamily dwellings.[10] Outside of Chicago, however, the vast majority lived in one-family houses, ranging from 70.5 percent in East St. Louis to 88 percent in Kansas City to 96.5 percent in Omaha. Moreover, Chicago had by far the highest proportion of renters, at 70 percent, and the lowest percentage of families owning their houses free and clear, at 6.3 percent. In Omaha and Kansas City, the majority were homeowners or in the process of buying their homes.[11] Like Chicago, eastern venues such as Philadelphia and urban-industrial New England most often offered working-class families multi-family dwellings. In Philadelphia, houses that were once single-family dwellings were frequently divided into multiple units, while double- and triple-deckers in New England were purpose-built with multiple flats, providing at least ample light and ventilation.

Each type of housing had its advantages. Single-family dwellings allowed the use of marginal spaces such as cellars, attics, porches, and outbuildings. Although less flexible than single-family housing, multiple-unit dwellings allowed kin and friends to live in close proximity without directly sharing living space, making it easier to pool domestic labor such as laundry, child-minding, cooking, and housecleaning.

Homeownership, of course, allowed the greatest autonomy in the use of living space, especially when the house had more than one living unit. Josephine Z., an Italian immigrant and a Philadelphia textile worker, owned outright a two-family house, living in one unit with her blind husband, her daughter, son-in-law, and granddaughter. Her son and his family lived in the other unit. Her son-in-law and son paid the taxes, repairs, and other bills in lieu of rent.[12] A family that owned a home might also invest in converting marginal space into living space. Such was the somewhat surprising outcome in a depression-era Chicago home: although the family's daughters had married young "to escape the tyranny of a fanatical father," the father and a son-in-law later teamed up to convert the basement into an apartment where his daughter and the son-in-law lived rent-free for two years.[13] But what stands out in this data is less the flexibility of single-family-house residents and the autonomy of homeowning families than the ubiquity of shared housing in every situation. Whether single-family or multiple-unit, owned or rented, working-class housing was stretched by householders offering housing to friends and family at or below market rates; with budgets stretched thin, even a small contribution to rent or to mortgage, interest, tax, and repair bills could enhance the household's comfort and security.

A closer look at the different ways in which families in the four slaughtering and meatpacking cities surveyed used their housing shows the intersecting role of working-class needs and housing type and tenure. At first glance, the combination of single-family housing and home ownership seems to have been the key to pooling housing resources. Omaha, East St. Louis, and Kansas City all had an overwhelming majority of single-family housing, and the proportions of home ownership (including houses owned outright and mortgaged) clustered between 55 and 65 percent.[14] They also had a high proportion of co-resident kin, ranging from well over half to about three quarters of expanded households. In Chicago, by contrast, with a low proportion of single-family housing and a rate of home ownership about half that of the other three cities, households with co-resident kin were less than 40 percent of the total of expanded households.

If we add to expanded households, however, the families with rental property, the picture changes substantially. In Chicago, families with rental property were one in three of the resulting total; this total is compatible with the low incidence of homeowning because many families rented entire multiple-family dwellings, moved into one flat, and sublet the others. By contrast, in the other cities those with rental property were no more than one in eight of the combined total of expanded households and receivers of rents. It appears that Chicagoans used rental property to house kin, just as Josephine Z's family did in Philadelphia. Mary, a Polish immigrant to Chicago, and her husband rented a two-family house and sublet the upstairs flat to her parents, receiving rent from them as well as her mother's help with laundry and child care.[15] The Women's Bureau investigators rarely noted to whom the Chicagoans rented their flats, perhaps because there were so many who reported rental property or because the Chicago interviews were conducted in July of 1928, a full three months before the home visits began in other cities and before the agents had fully realized the importance of rental housing to kin networks.[16] It seems likely that Chicago families first rented separate flats to kin, and only then took kin into their own housing units, leading to the lower proportion of co-resident kin. Intriguingly, the proportion of co-resident non-kin in Chicago homes was very close to that in Kansas City and East St. Louis.

The many examples of sharing work and resources between units remind us that household boundaries among interwar working-class families were permeable, so that the quotidian differences between having renters in another unit and boarders in one's domicile may have been limited. There was almost certainly a gender difference, however; co-residence put heavy burdens on women to cook and clean, and the cleaning of halls, porches, and the like in multiple-family houses probably fell to them as well, but the maintenance of rental units most likely rested on men, like the Rhode Island carpenter who kept the flats in his house "all in good condition."[17] Whatever their housing type and conditions of housing tenure, working-class people diligently and creatively exploited their space.

Homeowning as a practice reveals much about the terrain of working-class reciprocity. Homeowning was not necessarily a nuclear-family matter, and often involved the collaboration of kin. Two-generation efforts were most common. A Polish couple with two school-age children was buying a two-family Chicago house jointly with the wife's mother.[18] Examples among Philadelphia immigrants include a Hungarian childless couple who jointly owned a house with the wife's parents; a Jewish mother and her daughter, a sweater finisher, who split the mortgage on the house in which they lived with the daughter's son, brother, and disabled husband; and a Polish mother who paid $20 monthly on the mortgage; she was living with a daughter who paid $12.[19] A few intriguing descriptions of home ownership hint at complicated understandings among kin. A Hungarian woman described her house as jointly owned by her and her father, even though her mother and husband also lived there.[20] Mary, a young Philadelphian whose life is discussed in greater detail below, spoke of her house as being owned by her mother, even though her mother was unemployed and her father was a steadily employed foundry laborer.[21]

Siblings also collaborated in home-buying, with unmarried or childless siblings often joining forces with those who had children. Three Philadelphia households are typical of sibling groupings. Nucha, a widow, and her unmarried brother teamed up with their married sister and her husband to buy the nine-room house in which they lived with their father and a total of four children.[22] A childless Italian couple was buying a six-room house equipped with a bath in partnership with the wife's sister, her husband, and their four children.[23] Three Scottish immigrants, two sisters and a brother ranging in age from twenty-six to thirty-seven and all employed, together bought a six-room house.[24] The W. sisters of Fort Smith, Arkansas, both divorced, not only shared the ownership of a cabin and enough land for gardening, chickens, and a cow, but also supported their mother, siblings, and children.[25]

The life of a twenty-one-year-old Italian immigrant shows the complexities involved in the ethics of mutuality among siblings. She was notably self-sacrificing and therefore passed up the chance to remain in Italy and contract an advantageous marriage with the financial help of her married sisters in the U.S. Instead, she migrated to Philadelphia so that she could add her earnings to what her sisters sent home to support their parents. The Women's Bureau agent who interviewed her remarked that she "displayed a very unselfish spirit and told her reasons modestly." This commitment to the family was, however, countered by a powerful desire to establish her own independence; her ambition, she stated, was "not to become dependent upon her family in Italy or her people here."[26] For her, house sharing was both a form of familial sacrifice and a path, however uncertain, to personal autonomy.

Ties That Bind: Female Kinship, Life Crises, and Co-Residence

The four bodies of raw data from Women's Bureau studies (Philadelphia immigrant women, meatpackers, Georgia, and Texas) allow us to probe the relationships behind house sharing and to examine in particular the bonds among women within and across families. Taken together, these studies found one in six expanded households, with about two thirds of those enlarged by the presence of kin. The proportion of expanded households with co-resident kin among Georgia women's households was highest, presumably because there were few immigrants in this group and they had tended to stick close to home and thus had many local kin. The lowest proportion—though still just over half—was among the meatpacking workers, probably because of Chicago families' far greater access to rental property.[27]

Connections with female kin far outstripped those among male kin.[28] Over half of the women in expanded households were living with female blood kin (some of those with male relatives as well), but only a handful (about one in a hundred) lived with male blood kin alone. Nearly a third of the women lived with their mothers (some of those with fathers as well), but only one in twenty lived with one or both of their husbands' parents. The connections among female kin were about twice as likely to be between those of different generations (mothers/grandmothers and daughters, aunts and nieces) as between those of the same generation (sisters, cousins).[29] This pattern probably reflects the tendencies of the older generation to help younger folk get a start and of younger people to care for sick or needy elders. Not surprisingly, native-born households were the most likely to include multiple generations of women. Bertha, an African American laundry worker in Oklahoma, was the sole support of a household of four generations of women: her mother, who kept house, a sixteen-year-old daughter, and an eight-year-old granddaughter, presumably the offspring of another of Bertha's children.[30] A Baltimore dwelling housed three generations of native-born white women, whose occupations recapitulated the changing opportunities for wage earning women: the oldest an industrial homeworker, the middle employed in an umbrella factory, and the youngest a stenographer.[31] An African American Kansas City meatpacker supported a co-resident aunt, daughter, sister, and sister-in-law.[32]

The female-centered pattern of co-residence can be partly attributed to women's closeness to their own kin, rooted in the household and family and in longstanding ties of interdependence and affection. Yet it also testifies to their conflicts with men. A Philadelphia woman's experience showed with brutal clarity the key role of female kin connections and the ways in which men might distance themselves from them. Mrs. King and her young daughter went to live with her parents after she was widowed. "All went well as long as her mother was living. Upon the death of the latter, however, the father made her feel that she was not welcome. She is now supporting a home of her own in complete independence of her father and brothers."[33] In a few cases we glimpse women sharing households in response to men's victimization of women. Desertion, as we saw earlier, not only left women without access to a male breadwinner's salary, but also tended to occur when women's responsibilities for infants and small children were heaviest. Two cases show, in different ways, how women picked up the burden left by deserting men. In the first, the deserter's family took up the responsibility he rejected. A Providence jewelry worker was deserted by her husband before her daughter was born, and when visited by the Women's Bureau agent eight years later was living with the husband's sister, his mother, and the mother's brother.[34] In the second, an Arkansas laundry worker asserted women's responsibility for their own kin. The eldest of seven children, she had supported her widowed mother and siblings until her mother remarried three years before the Women's Bureau agent visited. Now back in the labor force to support her deserted sister and niece, this "very attractive and efficient" woman told the agent that she "won't ask husband to support her family."[35]

Domestic violence, a problem less readily discussed, nevertheless made its appearance in an intriguing example that suggests networks of support for desperate women that went beyond kinship and neighborhood. Camilla, a young Italian immigrant living in an unnamed city, left her abusive husband to go to Philadelphia: "some one [had] told her of a good woman in Phila [sic] who would help her. She came to her present address [where] the woman (1st floor rear) took her in, fed her, cared for her child, practically supported them both for the two months she was hunting work." She found a job through a friend of her benefactress, who continued to care for her child, apparently without pay.[36] An impressive example of apparently disinterested benevolence, this was one of the rare instances when people extended themselves so generously to non-kin. Taken together, however, these three cases suggest an implicit consciousness of the ways in which the double oppressions of poverty and patriarchy placed special burdens on working-class women—burdens which, in the absence of a women's movement, individual women could lighten for others.

Co-residence was useful and readily available to cope with life-cycle changes such as marriage, childbirth, or aging or with disruptions caused by death, illness, or disability. Given that women tended to live longer and earn less than men, both widowhood and the infirmities of age weighed more heavily although not exclusively on them. A Rhode Island woman, for example, headed a household in which her blind mother and destitute elderly uncle lived.[37] Aged or aging parents and relatives often lived with children, but the benefits of such an arrangement could flow in both directions. An Italian widow of fifty-nine lived with her daughter, her unsteadily employed son-in-law, and her eight grandchildren, but evidently did so more for their sake than for hers. The $13 she earned at tobacco-stripping contributed to the household fund and was crucial to the younger generation's survival.[38] A widowed silk weaver from Germany lived with her three children, aged twelve to seventeen, and her seventy-eight-year-old aunt. The aunt provided child care, had probably done so for the five years since the weaver was widowed, and at the time of the interview did the laundry and cooking while the weaver cleaned, washed dishes, and made nearly all the clothing for the household. Presumably, the aunt was providing household services in the hope or perhaps with the understanding that her niece would take care of her if she became disabled.[39] Even when the benefits were less concrete, the satisfaction of doing a good job of family support could be sustaining. A thirty-five-year-old Italian widow who, along with her sixteen-year-old daughter, was supporting three other children and her dead husband's aging parents, gave the

Women's Bureau agent the impression that she enjoyed the challenge of keeping the household afloat.[40]

For the older generation, however, a one-sided relationship was hard to accept; the prospect of dependence could be disconcerting or even terrifying. A Welsh woman lived with her daughter, son-in-law, and grandchild and continued to work as a battery inspector even though, as she told the Women's Bureau agent, "The children want to keep me."[41] Nellie, a "frail little Polish woman" in Chicago, "live[d] in constant terror of not being able to pay for the equivalent of her board and lodging" to her son-in-law, saying that it was "hard to get along and not good to have an old lady who can't work."[42] Yet accumulated assets might also give women leverage as they aged. An Omaha woman shared her "cozy and warm" cottage with her divorced daughter and grandson; described as "feeble," she did little household work aside from some sewing, while her daughter held down a job making sausages and handled the housecleaning. The daughter felt the arrangement was "an even proposition. The home is her mother's and IP [Interviewed Person] pays all the bills."[43]

Widowhood presented economic problems of varying degree, in part dependent upon the widow's age, labor-force experience and job skills. At one end of the spectrum was a widowed Mexican immigrant in her mid-thirties who had never held a job until she was widowed and forced into the labor force to support her two children. She went to live with her mother and unmarried brother and, limited by her poor health, made small contributions to the family fund with fine appliqué work on children's dresses. She was acutely conscious of her dependent status and told the agent that she "could never live on this sewing—I just fool myself into thinking I'm working—helps my mind only."[44] The irony, of course, is that this woman was far from unskilled; the problem rather was that the labor market did not define and reward her work as skilled. Women more accustomed to wage-earning might be better prepared for widowhood, but even a less desperate widow might nonetheless enhance her life by sharing housing: a Providence factory worker lived in an airy flat with her two daughters, her brother and sister-in-law; without pooling resources, she told the visiting agent, "she could not afford so nice a place."[45] A grisly coincidence of widowhood led an Italian needle-trade worker to move in with her brother: their spouses both died. She took care of his preschool children as they settled into a day nursery and then returned to her job but continued to live rent-free at her brother's in exchange for taking full charge of the household work.[46]

Happier life-cycle circumstances, such as marriage and childbirth, also shuffled living situations and shaped housing choices. The burdens of household support shifted and in some cases the tables turned, with those earlier contributing to others' support ending up on the receiving end. Katherine, the daughter of German immigrants, had gone to work at sixteen to help support her widowed mother and brothers. When the Women's Bureau agent visited twelve years later, her mother had paid off the mortgage on the house and was working as a hosiery boarder while Katherine, now married with a child, was living with her (apparently without paying board) and doing all the household work.[47] What goes 'round had come 'round for Katherine and her mother. Childbirth was also the trigger for a change in the division of labor in the household of a Polish immigrant pork-trimmer in Omaha. She was part of a large household: two daughters who had left school, one of whom had a job; four more children in school; a child aged four; her car-mechanic husband; and her married daughter, son-in-law, and their year-old child. She had started work not long before the agent's visit, leaving the household work and care of the four-year-old to her married daughter just at the point when the latter would have recovered from childbirth. The married daughter told the agent, "We don't pay any board, we just live here." But the mother felt that "the help makes up for [the] expense."[48]

Co-residence might also be used as a kind of insurance against the uncertainty of marriage or the illness or death of a child. An English lace winder, the divorced mother of two teenagers and recently embarked on a second marriage, continued to board with her parents. Perhaps her parents needed her board money, although there is no evidence to suggest that that was the case; perhaps she was wary of the second marriage and hedging her bets by maintaining the living situation in which she had been for the last decade.[49] For Elvira, an Italian immigrant, the arrival of a newly married daughter and son-in-law allowed her to contribute to the family income. When her eighteen-year-old daughter married, the couple came to live with Elvira. Worried about the bills resulting from a child's protracted illness and death and about her husband's declining wages, Elvira turned over the care of her nine-year-old daughter and eleven-year-old son and most of the housework to her married daughter and took her first job just a month before the Women's Bureau agent's visit. The agent's note suggested that she did so with a certain glee: "Woman is enjoying the adventure of her first job. Seems glad of the chance to exchange places with daughter."[50]

In most cases, however, the dramatic dislocations in housing arrangements caused by illness or injury were less welcome. The most pointed evidence comes from a Women's Bureau study of women who had been involved in industrial accidents. The interviews, conducted in 1923–24 with 385 women in New Jersey, Ohio, and Wisconsin, reveal the importance of co-residence in coping with the loss of income and the effect of the injuries. Thirteen women moved in with relatives because of their accidents; typical were a white native-born woman whose aunt in the country took her in without charge,[51] an elderly woman who went to live with one married child while her husband went to live with another,[52] and an African American woman who first went back to the South to stay with kin and then returned to New Jersey to live with her daughter and son-in-law, where she assisted her laundress daughter.[53] Eight had relatives move in with them to assist in their care, among them a woman whose daughter and two grandchildren moved into the rooms which she usually rented out;[54] a widow whose niece came to care for her in exchange for occasional payments;[55] and a woman whose two sisters and married daughters all lived with and cared for her.[56] One moved in with friends who supported her[57] and another had a friend move in with her.[58] One lived first with friends and then with a brother, paying board in neither case.[59] Because the questionnaire for these interviews did not ask specifically about living arrangements and agents only rarely volunteered the information, these were surely not the only women who relied on some form of residential assistance in getting through their convalescence.

Illness unrelated to a job could be equally disruptive of working-class households. A Chicago candy-factory worker with an ailing husband moved in with her sister-in-law, though the record does not make it clear whether that woman was married to the brother of the worker or was her husband's sister.[60] A Georgia woman lived with her daughter and her married son; they had combined forces in order to care for a "very ill" cousin.[61] A German meatpacker and her husband in Omaha owned two cottages and had nearly paid off the mortgage on their house. They rented the cottages to their daughters who were "supposed to pay $15 [a below-market rate for that time and place] but you know how it is when your own girl is sick & gets behind."[62] A Lithuanian meatpacker and her husband lived with her father in a Chicago flat. When her father was ill a few years before the interview, she "helped pay [his] bills" and was currently giving money to a deaf brother still attending school.[63] Julia, a Yugoslavian dress-factory worker, and her husband lived with her brother, sister-in-law, and mother because the sister-in-law was partly disabled by rheumatism. The mother and sister-in-law tended to the children and helped with housework, but Julia had to handle the heavy housework and the laundry.[64] Some of these arrangements were explicitly temporary, while others had the air of permanence, but all allowed families to deal with the unpredictable loss of income and household labor brought by illness.

Economic Needs, Housing Assistance, and Market Values

House sharing could give a break to kin who were in economic straits or trying to get a start in life. Three cases from Philadelphia suggest some of the circumstances to which shared housing resources could respond: migration, immigration, and a complex of multigenerational needs. A month before the Women's Bureau agent called, a nineteen-year-old Polish woman had moved from her family's farm outside Philadelphia to her godmother's house in the city, where she was living rent free while she got settled.[65] A childless German couple took in her sister, brother-in-law, and niece when they arrived from Germany so that they could repay the cost of their passage and buy furniture before setting up independent housekeeping. Although the newcomers were contributing little if anything to the family fund during their period of adjustment, the recently arrived woman relieved her wage-earning sister (the steadiest earner in the house) of household work that she had formerly handled on her own.[66] Mary, the twenty-two-year-old Philadelphia woman introduced above, lived with her disabled husband who had been gassed in the World War, her two preschoolers, her parents, two brothers, and a sister-in-law in what must have been a very full six-room house.[67] The arrangement was viewed as a stopgap that allowed Mary and her husband to save money to buy a home of their own. In the meantime, she paid an unspecified "share" of the taxes, repairs, and similar expenses in lieu of rent. Such an arrangement served all concerned: the younger family members enjoyed below-market rent and could save for a home; the older generation was spared housing expenses and could save for old age.[68]

Not surprisingly, the most common economic trigger for doubling up was unemployment or underemployment. Thirty-four of the 150 families profiled in The National Federation of Settlements' study of unemployment before the 1929 crash turned to house-sharing as a direct result of unemployment. Seventeen took in unrelated boarders or began to board with unrelated people themselves; the other seventeen took in kin or went to live with kin. In two instances, the writer of the case studies suggested that the roomers provided unspecified benefits beyond the rent they paid: one woman "prove[d] an asset to [the family] in several ways"[69] and a sister of the woman householder in another family was deemed "a great help."[70] At best, though, co-residence in a situation of unequal power was bittersweet. A native-born Philadelphia couple had lived with the roofer husband's mother and stepfather during his seasonal unemployment and feared that they would have to do so again. Mrs. Jenkins told the settlement worker, "[His mother] was good to me all right and gave me everything for the children, and her husband, he gave us shoes for all the children, and him only a stepfather, too. But living with someone else ain't the same as having your own little home, even if they are good and kind to you. I hope I never have to give up my home again."[71]

Woman workers who experienced pay cuts or other financial reverses often received help from the family members in whose households they lived. An Axminster carpet weaver, who even after a 12.5 percent pay cut was still earning more than 19 out of 20 Philadelphia women interviewed, nonetheless received a break on board for herself and her three school-age children from her mother because of the pay cut.[72] An Italian widow's break came in the form of free room and board for her eight-year-old son, although she continued to pay her mother for her own room and board.[73] Two Kansas City meatpacking employees, both native-born of European descent, one described by the Women's Bureau agent as a "rouged type"[74] and the other a widow with a young child, relied on sisters to tide them over when unemployed.[75] The flexibility was not always, however, on the downward side; a Lithuanian meatpacker in Chicago chipped in more than her share of living expenses to her married daughter's household when "others [in the household were] not working." She did not do so because she was well off and easily able to bear extra burdens; already, at age forty, she had been fired once for being an "old woman," and summed up her situation to the Women's Bureau agent in gloomy terms: "Don't have so much to eat sometimes but get along."[76]

One housing pattern was born of sheer desperation: a married couple would split up, each of the partners going to live with a different family member, with the children sometimes similarly dispersed. A white District of Columbia family of eleven, for example, was limping through the worst months of the Depression on the wages of one daughter and the father's very sporadic earnings; when another daughter and her husband lost their housing, they took in the daughter and her two children while her husband went to live with his family.[77] A 1934 Philadelphia study of families experiencing unemployment found that five of twenty-five families headed by an unskilled worker had had to resort to this expedient.[78] Even this extreme step, though, could be part of a happier overall situation, as a Chicago study done at about the same time found: a newly married couple both lost their jobs and went back to live with their respective parents. When their child was born, the baby's father moved in with his wife's parents. The final resolution was achieved when he got sporadic work and the young family moved into a flat owned by his parents. The investigators reported that "there was no period when the parents did not stand ready to assist the young couple."[79] As with all the variations on living arrangements that people cobbled together, the critical thing was less the structural aspects of the situations than the relational. When good will and generosity obtained, the pinch of even the most difficult circumstances could be eased.[80]

Such were the economics of working-class households that even when co-residents paid below-market rent or room and board, it could still be a material benefit to the householders. Although money circulated freely in networks of reciprocity, cash payments were more likely to be reckoned according to a private calculus than market value. One of the many ways in which kin could help one another without the problematic direct offering of cash was to offer help at below-market rates. Flexible board or rent payments allowed struggling people to stay afloat and to enjoy a more comfortable standard of living. A Portuguese immigrant, her husband, and two teenaged children shared their "clean & neat" seven-room tenement with her sister and cousin. The lodgers paid $4 of the $9 rent and fifty cents toward the electric bill, receiving better housing than they could have found on their own and paying more than their proportional share of the expenses. They bought their own food, so that they added relatively little to the woman householder's domestic burden.[81]

Examples of housing costs below market levels abound in the documents.[82] A saleswoman in an Athens, Georgia, store had lived with the same friends for nine years, paying $20 per month instead of the market rate of $35;[83] a Joplin shirt stitcher and a St. Joseph candy maker told the agents interviewing Missouri women that they survived only because of the low rent they paid to, respectively, a sister and a daughter;[84] the grandmother of a Rhode Island man gave him an "allowance" on the rent.[85] The mother of a Cleveland factory worker and her unemployed husband charged them low rent and pitched in with "food at times when it was most needed."[86] Rents and boarding costs were not only low but also often flexible. Two Texas homeworkers benefited from such arrangements: the son-in-law of one was "indulgent" about collecting her rent,[87] and another paid her father-in-law $10 a month for the house she and her family lived in but, she told the Women's Bureau agent, "If we have it we pay it, if not he has to do without."[88] A Pawtucket, Rhode Island, woman commented that she didn't receive rent "half the time" from the flat in the house she owned.[89] Helen, a widowed Philadelphia shirtwaist maker with children aged six and seven, paid her parents half her earnings as board, a substantial benefit to her since her earnings ranged from $6 to $34.[90]

The ultimate rejection of the market was to provide free housing. An African American doffer in Georgia reported that she "just stay[ed]" with her married sister.[91] Even though a Rhode Island couple with eight children had subsisted for three years on pitiful earnings from industrial homework and the produce of their garden, they still allowed their married daughter to live in the second flat of their building rent-free. The agent noted no sign of discord over the arrangement, and the family may have felt that it was better to extend a helping hand to a family member than to try to extract rent from a stranger in a dismal economy.[92] An African American couple in Kansas City was allowed free rent for the winter by an unnamed relative.[93] Four Jewish sisters, all clothing workers, lived with another sister, their mother, and their uncle in an eight-room house that he owned. They were apparently enjoying this comfortable residence rent-free, for the uncle boasted to the Women's Bureau agent that "if they were paying rent it would be $45 a month."[94] A twenty-five-year-old Hungarian immigrant stenographer paid her mother only $5 out of her $18 salary, a sum the Women's Bureau agent noted would barely cover the cost of her food; she was in effect living rent free.[95]

When people offered housing to others at below-market rates, on a sliding scale, or for free, they were not simply acting on the basis of social and family connections and the personalism of daily life. They were also taking on the burden of the insecurities and dangers of working-class economic life and the irregular and insufficient wages that working-class people earned. If they were generous and flexible, it was not just because they valued those qualities but because generosity compensated for the stinginess of bosses and the perils of work, and flexibility at home offset arbitrary irregularities at work. Josefina S., a Mexican immigrant to San Antonio, lived with a sister who worried about the effects of fine needlework on Josefina's eyes; begging her to give up the work, the sister offered to pay for her training as a beautician or in any other field of her choice.[96] A Jewish clothing worker told the Women's Bureau agent that the aunt and uncle with whom she boarded were "good to her," by which she meant in part that they charged her no board when she was not working.[97] This woman apparently did not repay the overdue board when work resumed, nor did a young Italian woman[98] or a young Irish woman.[99] Just as workers lost irrevocably from sporadic or seasonal unemployment and from short hours, so too did those who provided them with housing. Others paid back board or rent when they could, among them a Jewish clothing worker living with a married sister in Philadelphia[100] and a young native-born married couple in Kansas City living with the husband's parents.[101] Shouldering this burden of debt, though, would have made recovery from slack times all the more difficult.

The finances involved in these housing arrangements were anything but standardized, even when situations seem to have been comparable. Two Providence jewelry workers boarded with their sisters: one paid a below-market rate of about $5 or $6 per week to live in her sister's "comfortable home" and her "sister often help[ed] her out" in addition, while the other paid $8 per week to board in her sister's "old tenement" and also helped with the housework.[102] Two white Georgia sisters, both employed, lived with a married brother; one paid "no set amount" and the other did housework in lieu of rent.[103] The Women's Bureau agents do not provide enough detail about these households to explain the discrepancy in payments, quality of accommodations, and work, but other cases offer a glimpse at the complex goals and calculations that could undergird such arrangements. They show us the ways in which selflessness could intersect with self-interest to produce a multi-leveled mutuality. An aunt's decision to "put up money" to help her divorced niece buy a house in Roanoke, Virginia, was certainly generous, but it might have served other family goals as well. Not only did the niece's young son and her ailing mother, probably the aunt's sister, live with her, but so too did two cousins, possibly the aunt's children, who paid board and thus "help[ed] finance the family." The aunt bailed her niece out of a bad situation, but she also might have been eager to assure that her sister and her own children had a secure place to live.[104] The whereabouts of the aunt are not specified; if she also lived in Roanoke, was she trading money for effort in setting her kin up in a house separate from hers? If she lived in the country, was she trying to cushion the lives of urban kin?

Four Philadelphia examples similarly reflect the complex family goals that led to particular economic and housing arrangements. A twenty-three-year-old single Jewish woman in Philadelphia was able to support herself thanks to her sister's charging her a below-market rate for board; the example becomes more complicated when we add in the fact that the boarder was also sending money to their sister in Rumania.[105] Why didn't the married sister send the money directly to the sister in Europe? We can guess that perhaps she could not get her hands on enough cash to do so, or that her husband would have objected to a direct remittance but tolerated the indirect subsidy to the resident sister. Another young woman paid board to her married sister and her husband when working, but when she experienced the seasonal employment endemic to her needle-trade job, they supported her so that she could continue to send money to family members in Russia.[106] Two milliners had similar situations: echoing the arrangement of the Rumanian sisters cited above, each lived with an aunt and uncle rent-free and sent money to family members in Russia.[107] This is one of the very few cases found when a pattern was group-specific: all four of these women were recent Jewish immigrants.

Co-Residence, Crowding, and Kin Relations

Co-residence had its ups and downs, captured in the comments of Teresa, a Scottish wool weaver who boarded with her married brother. We do not know if he had children. Although she was eager to assure the Women's Bureau agent that she was a self-supporting boarder, she also betrayed ways in which the boundaries blurred between her and her brother's family. She pitched in financially—"We might help each other."—as well as with housework—"Can't sit and see the others do it all." On the other hand, the hermetic aspects of co-residence grated on her nerves: "Gets discouraged sitting around the house in slack time. 'We get mad at each other sometimes, and say "You're a bum."' Feels the need also of some outside interest."[108] Teresa's ambivalence points to the seeds of discord in co-residence.

The crowding of too many people into too little space increased the chances that tempers would fray. Yet little evidence points to sustained conflicts. Mary's house, mentioned above, was not among the worst examples of overcrowding, with 1.5 people per room. The Women's Bureau recommended a standard of one person per room, but found that only about six out of ten households visited in Philadelphia and in the Midwestern meatpacking cities attained that. One in ten in Philadelphia, however, lived two or more people to a room.[109] But simple numbers—the incidence of overcrowding—do not suffice to explain the relatively low incidence of conflicts over shared space. This is another case where the interview schedules did not specifically ask about an item of interest, but it is one where I would use the iceberg metaphor with care. The Women's Bureau agents were finely attuned to the dynamics of the households they visited and commented freely on them. The depression-era investigators were biased toward the nuclear family and against co-residence arrangements, and they were dealing with families at their most stressed, but they rarely mentioned conflicts among co-residents. Unusual was a Philadelphia study conducted in early 1934; seven of the twenty-five families of unskilled workers had had to resort to doubling up with kin and the researchers argued that "[f]or six of these the change represented a very difficult experience, characterized by a sense of not being wanted, quarreling with relatives under these crowded conditions, or an acute sense of frustration due to the loss of independence as a family unit."[110] For at least some of these, it should be noted, the problems were psychological rather than interpersonal and may not have been expressed in outright conflict.

When conflict did break out, it was most often between generations rather than among siblings. As the older generation became less able to earn money and feebler in helping around the house, tensions mounted. A Scottish immigrant widow raised her only daughter through ten difficult years. She lived with her daughter briefly after the latter married, but soon departed because of her son-in-law's "ugly disposition."[111] When interviewed, she was sixty, living alone and in poor health, although still earning $18.90 a week as a silk winder, a wage that put her in the top third of the Philadelphia women interviewed. Whether mother, daughter, or son-in-law, or perhaps all three, were at fault in this breakdown of mutual assistance, we cannot know. Nor do we know what happened when, inevitably, the widow's health broke down. We can see one possible outcome in the life of a Jewish widow, also a Philadelphian, who had never earned wages until her son married a woman whose "attitude made it unpleasant to stay." The Women's Bureau agent found her living in a rented room and—without the Scotswoman's advantage of long and relatively lucrative labor-force experience—working as a cook in a small business dining room for the pitiful wage of $7 per week plus meals. When interviewed 14 years after she had taken this job, she had been away from work for some weeks because of illness. Her son supported her in her illness—whether willingly or grudgingly we cannot say.[112] The breakdown in house-sharing, however, surely meant increased cash outlay for the son and a grimly poor independence for the mother.

The older generation was more likely to hold the upper hand when a formerly independent child moved back into the family home, especially if a spouse and/or children also moved in. Wage-earning children could rapidly change from financial assets to liabilities, as New York newlyweds found. They were welcome in the husband's parents' home as long as they both worked and could contribute board that the parents were eager to put toward "a big marriage for their daughter Concetta." But when the young couple both lost their jobs, they were summarily thrown out. Living in three sparsely furnished rooms, they took their meals with the wife's parents until her "father lost his job and told them not to come there any more."[113] An unemployed Philadelphia cabinetmaker and his wife went to live with his parents, where they were made to feel distinctly unwelcome. The parents, worried about paying off their mortgage before infirmity overtook them, were clearly more interested in the young couple's rent than in mutuality and made "it most disagreeable for the young people when it is not paid." Desperate to earn something toward the rent, the wife began to take in industrial homework but her mother-in-law sabotaged her efforts by refusing to look after her five grandchildren.[114] In other cases, the older generation simply appears ungrateful. Grace, a divorced mother of two, moved from North Dakota to Iowa to take care of her ailing mother; after her recovery, the mother rewarded Grace by throwing out her and her children because she "wanted to live alone."[115]

The older generation was not always the source of difficulties, however. Some cases suggest an unwonted feeling of entitlement on the part of the younger generation. A widowed Arkansas laundry worker and her three children moved in with her parents, but after a year and a half, trouble seemed to be brewing. She, commented the Women's Bureau agent, "seem[ed] to accept dependency on parents [for room and board] as natural cause of events" and felt that her contribution of her husband's $1,000-life-insurance payment to the purchase of the house gave her "'a right' to the house."[116] A Georgia woman moved from entitlement into exploitation of her mother: when widowed, she and her two children had moved in with her ailing father, her cotton-spooler mother, and her seven siblings. When she remarried, she moved out and left her two children with her mother and only took them after her mother waged a long struggle to get her to do so.[117]

Finally, a Louisville, Kentucky, household shows how generational conflict could fan the flames of discord between spouses. A dress-factory worker and her unemployed husband, in an effort to keep the house they were buying, took in his father and sister: "We sort of thought that the money they paid would help to buy the food at least. But the whole arrangement is more bother than it's worth—they always complain that the suppers are not good. I know why this is,—'cause often I cook food to last several days since I have no time to cook every night. I come home too late and I've found that soups and some meats last a couple of days. Lately, I've found meats cost too much, so we have herring and potatoes and soups."[118] The bad situation was exacerbated by the husband's resolute unwillingness to help with the cooking; one senses an alliance between the husband and his kin against the woman.

Siblings, too, became entangled in conflict over housing arrangements, usually over aid given by the older generation to the younger. Two cases from the NFS study illustrate this pattern. The Dante family faced difficult circumstances indeed. Mr. Dante had worked his way into a clerical position and had moved his family from a cold-water tenement in New York City to a modern house in the suburbs complete with "a bathroom and a shower and a breakfast nook, which was the last word in elegance." Their situation rapidly deteriorated when he lost his job; and after a number of stopgap measures failed, Mrs. Dante took their two preschoolers to live with her parents. That household was in equally dire straits: their arrival brought the household population to seventeen, the crowding all the more unpleasant because they had recently had to move "from a comfortable apartment up town [sic] to a west side tenement of eight rooms." Her parents were both disabled, and the household was supported by her three sisters and her grandmother, who did day work as a domestic servant. Mrs. Dante more than pulled her own weight by caring for her many young siblings as well as her own children and her parents, but her sisters resented her presence and refused to have her husband in the house. "Much conflict and disharmony ensued," and Mr. Dante went to live with his married sister until he finally got a job and was able to re-establish an independent household. Other factors than those that the settlement worker pointed to may have made this situation especially difficult: Mrs. Dante's family was native-born of Irish descent, and some members may have resented her husband, who was an Italian immigrant. The resentment may have mounted when the Dantes initially fared so much better economically than her natal family. Something, certainly, must account for the sisters' rejection of help they obviously needed in order to care for the older and younger members of the household.[119]

A Pittsburgh family faced a similarly complex situation. Mr. Carbone, a carpenter, had enjoyed unusually steady employment until 1919; then followed nine years of increasingly sporadic work. Finally, four months before the settlement worker profiled the family, he, his wife, and their five children went to live with her mother and three brothers. Both generations took to the newcomers badly: the brothers "resent[ed] the additional expense [and] they constantly complain[ed], while Mrs. Tomalo, according to her daughter, "has the old country ways and doesn't want the children ever to go out anywhere or to dance or have a good time, and that causes all sorts of trouble." As with the Dantes and her parents, unmarried siblings supporting parents resented having to support siblings who were spared from the family economy to marry. In this case, the conflict between traditional and modern patterns of childrearing added extra bitterness.[120] The settlement worker was explicit about Mrs. Tomalo's attitude toward her grandchildren, but the Tomalo brothers may also have resented the Carbones' insistence on giving their children educational opportunities that they themselves had not had; one of their nephews was attending the Carnegie Art School on a scholarship.

In other situations, the very flexibility of household arrangements that was such an asset in coping with the vicissitudes of working-class life could lead to misunderstandings and sow the seeds of conflict. When arrangements were unclear or unequal, they might readily fertilize a seed of discord. A Yugoslavian immigrant shirt-maker and her five-year-old daughter had moved into the house owned by her brother and sister-in-law and paid "no regular board," did not assist in the general household work, and relied on the sister-in-law to cook and care for her child. While the sister-in-law may have been genuinely generous and eager to assist in an emergency, the "temporary arrangement" had already lasted 18 months when the Women's Bureau agent called.[121] Perhaps the shirt-maker had initially received extra consideration since her husband was barred from the United States by the new immigration-quota system, but as the arrangement became more permanent, life in the house might become more tense. A Jewish widow with an eight-year-old daughter lived with her mother, her junk-peddling father, and her eighteen-year-old brother, who "only work[ed] abt 1 wk a yr" [sic]. When interviewed, she was supporting herself by custom dressmaking, paying half the rent plus a handsome $10 per week in addition for board, probably about twice the actual cost of food for her and her daughter. She was clearly holding up the heavy end of the family budget, a situation with explosive potential given her casually employed brother, her father's declining earnings, and her daughter's increasing expenses.[122]

The many cases where financial responsibility was unclear seem similarly fraught with possibilities for bad feeling; consider, for example, the cases of a Georgia cotton spinner who paid to kin "what she could spare,"[123] and a German woolen-mill worker who gave her son "how much I can."[124] Who was the arbiter of what was owed in such situations? A Polish-born mother and her daughter, both sausage makers, lived with the mother's married daughter, buying their own food and only "pay[ing] what they can afford" for rent. Without knowing more about the total household income, we cannot gauge the degree to which the sausage makers were a burden to the household, but given the vagaries of the labor market, it seems likely that lean times would arrive and with them debate or even discord over just exactly how much they could afford for board.[125] Even when a child gave her entire paycheck to her mother, as we saw earlier, she might not defray all of her living costs; one mother was distinctly displeased with such a state of affairs. Her daughter, a timekeeper, earned only $13 and gave her entire paycheck to her mother, but the mother told the Women's Bureau agent that she had been unsuccessfully urging her daughter to get a "better paying job" since the $13 was not paying the cost of her keep.[126]

Yet another instability in some of these crowded households was their dependence on overwork by some of their members, typically women. Josephine K., a forty-five-year-old Polish immigrant, worked as a spooler in a woolen mill so that she and her ailing, sporadically employed husband could buy a house that their daughter, son-in-law, and two preschool grandchildren could share with them.[127] The daughter was too ill even to help with the washing and ironing, although she did look after her children, and the son-in-law earned little because of a war injury. The assistance of the older generation was vital to their survival, and it was most easily achieved in the context of providing shelter. Homeowning, in this case, amounted to a way for families to provide continuing care for their partially disabled members. From Josephine's perspective, however, this arrangement led to a grim load of overwork: fifty hours a week in the woolen mill piled on top of all the washing and ironing for a household of seven plus, in all likelihood, a substantial part of the rest of the household work. Perhaps she was headed in the same direction as Anna, a Providence woman who did wool-mending at home and was "kind to all relatives, take[s] them all in"; she had had several nervous breakdowns and might well have been headed for another.[128] At the time of the agent's visit, Anna's eight-room house sheltered her husband, their four children, her two sisters, one brother-in-law, a niece, a nephew, and her father-in-law.

From Mutuality to Collectivity

Despite the potential difficulties of sharing housing, the eruption of conflict was relatively rare. More typically, such mutuality opened the way to sharing other goods and services. Some households appear to have worked toward a long-term generalized collectivity. A twenty-year-old woman moved in with her widowed older sister, the mother of three young children. The arrangement was mutually advantageous: the younger woman was able to escape from an unpleasant stepmother and her room rent was a boon to her sickly and sporadically employed sister. They "help[ed] each other out, as can." Although the younger woman summed up their situation to Women's Bureau agent Caroline Manning as "sick, sick, sick. Work, work, work," Manning limned a picture of a well-organized, congenial household where the two sisters sat together doing needlework on an April evening.[129] Two Lithuanian immigrants in their mid-thirties made sausage in the same department at Armour's Chicago plant and shared the work in their flat. The Women's Bureau agent labeled their arrangement one of "partners"—we might speculate lesbian partners.[130] Close cooperation of another kind was the case in a Chicago African American household. The widowed mother worked in a meatpacking plant and her daughter was a cook in domestic service. They developed an elaborate division of labor that included sending out the laundry, the mother doing the ironing and the cooking, and the daughter the sewing and the cleaning. The mother described their arrangement to the Women's Bureau agent: "What daughter needs mamma needs. What mamma has daughter has." The daughter's husband, a laborer in a steel mill, figured in the description of the arrangement only in the agent's notation that his work had been irregular over the past year.[131]

Some families found that the sharing of living quarters opened the way to a more general pooling of resources and a broad sociability. Julia, the Yugoslavian dress-factory worker introduced earlier, and the others in her eight-person household cooked together and shared all their expenses.[132] An English aunt and niece, both in their sixties, were sharing both the work and expenses of a four-room flat, but their household was a shaky edifice indeed, with both in declining health and finding it hard to keep up their work in a lace factory.[133] A German immigrant and her daughter, wife of a sailor who was rarely home and mother of a baby and a toddler, lived companionably: "When one had money she buys grub, when the other has she buys it."[134] A married couple with three school-age children—she a tassel-maker and he a steelworker—rented part of their house to a childless couple with whom they shared meals. The female lodger made the weekday suppers and the tassel-maker cooked breakfasts and weekend meals.[135] A native-born couple, both working in meatpacking and parents of a toddler, invited a family of five recently arrived from the Kentucky mountains to share their tiny cottage until the husband secured a steady job. In the meantime, they pursued "joint housekeeping": three adults worked and the Kentucky migrant wife kept the house and cared for the children.[136] Nucha, introduced earlier, and her married sister pooled their efforts in shopping and cooking, but kept careful separate bills for milk and meat, even when cooked in the same pot, rather than buying them out of common funds.[137] These complex groupings were often described by the Women's Bureau agents—perhaps echoing their informants, perhaps supplying the phrase themselves—as living "as one family." Among those so labeled were two Italian-immigrant sisters and their husbands buying a house of six rooms and a bath;[138] a widowed Italian mother, her five unmarried children ranging in age from ten to twenty-one, and her married son, his wife, and their year-old twins;[139] and a Hungarian immigrant, her husband, and her mother.[140]

Other households established limits on mutuality, carving out separate turf within the shared space; perhaps these attempts to bring clarity to an inchoate situation were responses to past conflicts or the fear of future discord. In Josephine Z's house, where she lived with her married daughter and her married son, each of the three families bought and cooked their food separately.[141] Two Czech cousins, living with their husbands and children, also cooked separately.[142] A six-room Philadelphia house held two Jewish sisters, their husbands, the children of one, and their aged parents, who lived as two separate households. The Women's Bureau agent reported, "As 'it w[oul]d not look very nice to have bedrooms down stairs,' . . . all sleep up stairs & have other rooms down stairs. Yet families live absolutely independently." One household fraction included the childless couple and the old parents dependent upon them; the other included the second couple and their two preschoolers.[143] A divorced Virginia tobacco worker lived with her father and sisters rent free, but she bought and cooked food for herself and her children separate from the rest of the household.[144] Without knowing more about how these arrangements evolved, it is difficult to know whether they prevented friction by maintaining distance, whether they were instituted because of the friction generated by earlier more collective arrangements, or whether they simply grew out of different tastes in food and household habits. They, however, may have created as much discord as they prevented; cooking in the same kitchen could produce infinite occasions for misunderstanding and conflict.

Despite the tendency for most kin co-residence arrangements to be among women relatives, in-law relationships seem not to have been any more or less likely to produce conflict than blood relationships. One widow cheerfully supported her aged in-laws.[145] Another filled her nine-room house with her daughter, son-in-law, and grandchild, along with the daughter's brother-in-law and his wife.[146] The daughter did all the household work, but we know so little about this household that we can only guess whether this was in exchange for lower rent, for the mother's willingness to take in unrelated persons, a matter of mutual preference (perhaps the mother preferred her work in a bathing suit factory to housework), or for some other reason. An Italian immigrant hosiery topper married at seventeen, but within two months it became obvious that her husband would not support her. She swiftly divorced him and went to live in a house owned by her brother-in-law and filled with her parents, three sisters, a brother, and three nephews. Despite her interlude of independent living, she gave her mother her entire $20 paycheck, a sum that would have made her a major contributor to the household fund.[147]

Conclusion

Shared housing offered one means for working-class women and men to stretch limited resources. Whether assisting kin, friends or co-workers, household members negotiated complex arrangements of cash and labor as they worked to meet the material needs of adults and children. Women—including wives, widows, grandmothers, mothers, daughters, in-laws, aunts, nieces, and neighbors—were central to these arrangements. Providing domestic labor as well as wages, female kith and kin comprised an especially flexible resource in the context of shared housing. They also may have been better prepared, given gendered patterns of socialization, to handle the emotional and psychological pressures of close quarters. The mutuality of shared housing was not always an ideal solution to the problems of working families, but it was, in most cases, both available and manageable. Given the limited resources—both public and private—on which such families could draw, living together and pooling those resources provided the best chance for many working-class families to make ends meet.

4

What Goes 'Round, Comes 'Round
Working-Class Reciprocity

The contours of reciprocity, like mutuality, were shaped not just by tradition but by the personalities of those involved and the range of resources at their command; navigating among circumstances not of their own choosing, people met their own emergencies and those of kin and friends in ways ranging from grudging and humiliating to generous and self-sacrificing. Here, too, the possibilities for missteps and misunderstandings were infinite and the rules for appropriate behavior unclear and shifting. And as in the mutuality of shared housing, women played critical roles in the exchange of goods, services, and labor.

In its broad outlines, working-class reciprocity was largely female-administered; men figure primarily as wage-earners and only as shadowy figures in patterns of reciprocity. This is partly an artifact of the sources, which focused either on women's lives or on women as informants for relief and charity. Women's Bureau researchers in principle were concerned with the individual woman wage earner, but in fact they collected (systematically for some bulletins, anecdotally for others) information about the composition of women's households and, randomly, their connections with others outside the household. Still, social investigators of the 1920s and 1930s, especially in the latter decade, usually selected only nuclear families for their studies and took the nuclear family economy as their central project. As a result, they viewed obligations owed to those outside this unit as burdensome and viewed benefits received from those connections as helpful but temporary, peripheral to the goal of establishing the nuclear-family autonomy. Whatever their assumptions, the evidence they collected reflects women's real domination of this sphere, an echo of and an extension of their central role as household managers. Women pooled resources of paid and unpaid labor in a female economy bridging together the arenas of cash and barter, and thus the costs and benefits of reciprocity were inscribed in their lives.

Moreover, women often were more vulnerable to unemployment, felt more responsible for child care and household labor, and faced more difficult circumstances if divorced, abandoned, injured, or widowed. In their need to protect themselves against future crises, they might offer what they could when they had resources in hand in hopes of storing up good will for hard times. However limited their assets, they had to hope that in the long run what goes 'round, comes 'round.

Housekeeping

As noted in the previous chapter, a common feature of shared housing was the exchange of free or reduced rent for cleaning, cooking, child care, and other household services. Payment in kind offset unequal cash contributions to housing expenses. Such was the case in a very crowded four-room Philadelphia house. A widowed Polish immigrant sugar-refinery worker contributed $20 to the mortgage, while her married daughter paid only $12 on behalf of herself, her husband, and her five children, and the widow's adult son apparently made no contribution at all. The daughter took charge of the cooking and washing, relieving her mother of this onerous part of the household work.[1] Such arrangements were supported on both ends by women's waged and unpaid labor. In these exchanges, we see the valorization of household work; it might have little value in the labor market and be taken for granted by some, but the women in these interviews showed a deep conviction of its value.

Shared housing was, in fact, probably the only place that a woman could realize the value of her housework other than in marriage. Household work was a valuable cash-replacement activity: it could buy the housekeeper a home with minimal or no expenditure of scarce cash, and it could relieve a wage-earner of the burden of the double day and the temptation to spend money on services such as laundry. Acutely conscious of both the practical and the money value of domestic labor, working-class women rejected middle-class Americans' pastoralization of housework and instead recognized its labor value.[2] An African American meatpacker, separated, lived with her two daughters, one also separated, and a son. The separated daughter had exclusive responsibility for the housekeeping, and her mother stated succinctly the value of her labor as well as the difficulty of finding a clear language for it: "That's her job. I work."[3] An Irish widow paid the rent on the apartment where she lived with her daughter, son-in-law, and baby grandson. They in turn paid her $10 or $15 "if they have it," but she was conscious of the benefits she received from the arrangement: "I don't charge her nothing for she does the work."[4]

Not every woman found this sort of arrangement a good bargain, though; a German-born Chicago woman when first widowed lived with a daughter but found the housework she was expected to do "too heavy" and so moved to the home of a married son and happily went to work in a candy factory.[5] The labor involved in keeping a household going was still, in the interwar period, heavy work for most working-class families, and wage-earning might actually be easier. The arrangement could also turn problematic when the payment in kind was other than run-of-the-mill household work. A British hosiery worker made up for not being able to contribute to the family fund during slack periods by doing dressmaking and millinery for her mother and two sisters.[6] She enjoyed the chance to use her skills, especially since she was not confident enough in them to try them out in the labor market. By contrast, a Jewish clothing worker resented the demands her family made on her fine-tailoring skills. During her seasonal unemployment, her mother forgave her the usual $9 or $10 that she paid for board out of her $25 to $30 earnings, but when she was out of work her "married sisters all expect[ed] her to [make dresses] for them."[7] The difference between the two may have been in the quality of the dressmakers' relationships with their families, but it may also have been that the clothing worker resented having to offer for free the skills that she used to make her living. A Woonsocket, Rhode Island woman found the isolation of being the housekeeper weighed heavily on her when "so many members of the family died in quick succession, she became depressed and lonely, and she wanted to get some work that would bring her in contact with other people." Her job at a metal plating firm filled the bill; the Women's Bureau agent noted that "she is very enthusiastic about her work, thinks it very interesting and varied. 'I'm ambitious,' she said, 'and I have learned to do many things' about the shop just by watching."[8]

Households frequently recognized the importance of housework by designating one person as housekeeper; such was clearly the case in the households of 118 women visited by Women's Bureau agents, although this is yet another practice on which the schedules do not report systematically. One schedule, however, makes clear that this was a role that commanded respect, as an Iowa dry-goods store cashier told the agent in no uncertain terms: "'[My mother] is manager and everything and we could not do without her. She more than earns her way and should not be called a dependent', said Miss R."[9] In most cases—50—the designated housekeeper was of an older generation than the wage-earning woman, all but twelve (five mothers-in-law, five aunts, and two grandmothers) the mothers of the wage-earner. The other designated housekeepers were about evenly divided between women of the same generation (twenty-eight out of thirty-one being sisters or sisters-in-law) as the wage-earning woman and women of a younger generation (twenty-five out of thirty-three being daughters and another two daughters-in-law).[10] Not surprisingly, considering the close ties between female kinship and co-residence, women most frequently took charge of housework for women to whom they were related by blood.

The preponderance of women of an older generation as designated housekeepers speaks to the age discrimination that older women faced in a labor market that increasingly valued speed as well as to their diminished physical stamina and their difficulties in finding work if they had been long out of the workforce. Birdie, an African American meatpacker, told the Women's Bureau agent that her mother, in her sixties, did the housework because she was "unable to work out but able to keep house for IP [Interviewed Person] so latter thinks she should work."[11] Since the only other person in the household was Birdie's Pullman-porter husband, who would have been away a lot of the time, the work may well have been easy enough for the mother to handle. But many women with daughters old enough to be in the labor force kept them at home and took jobs themselves. In some cases, the major consideration seems to have been staying home with young children. Katherine, for example, had sent her sixteen-year-old daughter out to work when her husband had become disabled and had herself stayed home with her younger child; when the Women's Bureau visited twelve years later, Katherine was at work in a Philadelphia hosiery mill while the co-resident married daughter stayed at home with her two-year-old son.[12] Each had had her time at home with her child.

Among siblings, the choice of who would work and who would keep house seems to have been a matter of marital status or age. Typically, sisters who were or had been married kept house, even when they did not have young children. When all were single, it was often the eldest who acted as housekeeper. Isabella, a Scottish-born thirty-seven-year-old, both worked in a hosiery mill and kept house for her brother, a twenty-six-year-old printer, and her sister, a twenty-eight-year-old telephone operator. When a third sister who had been the housekeeper died, Isabella took on the housekeeping, staying at home for nine years to do so and then returning to the hosiery mill. This case makes it especially clear that age rather than income was the key, since Isabella's usual weekly earnings of $27 were almost certainly more than her sister made.[13]

Families deployed housekeepers to meet a broad variety of needs and developed various systems of exchange to do so. Probably the most common and pressing need was to relieve a wage-earning woman of the burden of the double day. Hughes found that fewer than 5 percent of the 728 women intensively interviewed faced the dual burdens of full-time work and no assistance with housework.[14] A Croatian meatpacker in Kansas City gave her sister-in-law free rent in exchange for housekeeping and child care. In this case, the arrangement seemed to grow out of the meatpacker's preference rather than financial pressure on either side; she told the Women's Bureau agent that "she likes to work would rather than keep house. [sic]"[15] A forty-nine-year-old native-born widow in the same city and occupation owned her house, in which she lived with (at least) a daughter, son, and daughter-in-law. The daughter, trained for but unable to find an office job, and daughter-in-law handled all the household work. The son and daughter-in-law paid their share of the expenses instead of a fixed amount, and the widow was careful to specify that her son was not contributing to her support.[16] Marital breakup might also necessitate creative arrangements, as was the case of an Italian couple who took in their daughter and year-old granddaughter when the daughter's marriage broke up. With no support from her estranged husband, the daughter could contribute only her labor as a housekeeper while her mother did hand-finishing in a shirtwaist factory.[17] A Polish-born worker in a lock factory and her brick-yard laborer husband bought and then added onto a small house. The addition, paid for out of the wife's wages, allowed them to rent two rooms to her sister, who then took care of their children aged four and seven.[18]

In the case of Mary, mentioned earlier, the arrangement involved a complicated mix of cash and non-cash exchange. Mary, her sister-in-law, and her mother "very systematically" shared the housework, but when it came to care for Mary's four-year-old daughter and one-year-old son, she paid her mother $5 a week.[19] An even more complicated intergenerational arrangement evolved in the household of two Kansas City women, the mother an office cleaner and the daughter a meatpacking worker. Three years before the Women's Bureau agent visited them, the daughter's husband had contracted tuberculosis and gone into a sanitarium, and she came with her baby to live with her mother. At first, she was the housekeeper, staying home with her baby and three younger sisters while her mother worked days. When the mother became pregnant again and could no longer work; she took over the housekeeping and the daughter took a job at the Cudahy plant. When the new baby was about eight months old, the mother took a job as a night cleaner in a courthouse and the two shared the housework and child care, much as married couples working different shifts might do. The father, an irregularly employed worker at a box factory, figured in the account only as an insufficient breadwinner.[20]

Virtually always, when a woman was living with kin, she mentioned that she helped with the housework, often "as she has time."[21] Because of the documents' focus on women, there is virtually no parallel evidence for male boarders. One intriguing case, however, suggests that men—at least young men—may also have offered labor in exchange for board. A Kansas City meatpacker struggled to support her completely disabled husband and her eleven-year-old son; she worked full-time and canned the produce of her sizable garden. Her employer was aware of the economic burden she carried and transferred her among departments in order to avoid laying her off. Still, she allowed her sixteen-year-old son and a nephew to live with her rent-free and charged them only the cost of their board because, she cryptically told the Women's Bureau agent, "they have other responsibilities." A dividend of having the boys live with her was that a neighbor did her laundry without charge in exchange for the boys' help with her small laundry business.[22] This example is one of but a handful of accounts of men's participation in household exchange. Such instances are far rarer than those of men assisting in housework, as chapter 1 argues. It appears that adult men performed housework only within their own households and that younger men might, if rarely, participate in the exchange of work between households.[23]

Even when there was no kin connection in co-residence arrangements and either the women interviewed or the Women's Bureau agents described the situation as boarding, the line between boarding and more reciprocal patterns of living was often blurry. A young Russian woman boarded with a friend and volunteered to help with the Saturday afternoon cleaning, although she was not expected to do any household work.[24] A young Irish woman similarly pitched in to help her aunt even though no help was expected.[25] The widowed Italian mother of five young children took in a married couple as boarders, asking a low rent in exchange for the wife's cooking and care of the children. They shared the expenses of food and utility bills.[26] A German immigrant couple both worked as sausage linkers on the night shift, and their boarder looked after their seven-year-old child while they worked, also occasionally pitching in with the housework. When the Women's Bureau agent visited this household, however, the mother had been out of work for three weeks because the boarder was in the hospital and unable to watch the child. It seems likely that the child-care services that the boarder had rendered were about to come back to her in the form of convalescent care by her landlady.[27] The Women's Bureau agent who visited the home of a Scottish immigrant sweater-maker was herself confused about the status of a lodger who did general housework, cooked, and cared for two preschool children, referring to her variously as housekeeper, lodger, and friend.[28] Boarding, as these examples make clear, was not a simple financial arrangement, but could include other obligations, including exchanges of labor on both sides.[29]

Child Care

Child care provides a convenient bridge linking reciprocity within and between households. The continuing cultural unease about the wage-earning mothers who were the focus of so many of my sources produced relatively plentiful information about how these women managed the care of their children. Given the worries about institutional child care that persist into the early twenty-first century, it is hardly surprising that day nurseries were not the preferred option in the interwar period. Just over 10 percent of the children in the households intensively studied by Gwendolyn Hughes were in day nurseries, and even this low proportion was probably inflated by the fact that Hughes had contacted about the same proportion of those households through these nurseries.[30] A similar proportion of mothers working in slaughtering and meatpacking had or had had one or more children in day nurseries, and about twice the proportion of Philadelphia immigrant women did so.[31] Day nurseries were an option that appealed to only a small minority of wage-earning mothers, but the reasoning behind their decisions can be glimpsed only rarely in the sources. One important factor was cost. Day nurseries, usually subsidized by some charitable institution, were typically the cheapest child-care option for those who could not rely on free care from kin or neighbors. A Nashville laundry worker, for example, kept her two children in a day nursery for ten cents a day, but when she worked Sundays she had to pay a woman a dollar to care for them for the day.[32] A few lucky women received day-nursery care for their children for free,[33] but most women paid about ten cents a day, or a dollar a week per child. Only three women paid so little to individuals for care. Two of those needed only after-school care, and one of them probably had a broader relationship of exchange with her neighbor: the evening that the Women's Bureau agent visited her, she was taking care of the neighbor's two babies.[34] The third may been given special consideration because of her abusive husband, who worked sporadically at best.[35]

Cheap rates were not the only consideration in the use of day nurseries; availability was also an issue. Numbers suggest part of the story, and here the revealing comparison is among the Philadelphia immigrant women, all of the meatpackers, and the Chicago meatpackers alone. About one in ten of all meatpackers turned to day nurseries, while one in five of the Philadelphia and Chicago mothers resorted to day nurseries, showing the relatively greater number of such institutions in big cities. But even in these urban areas the supply of nurseries did not meet the demand. Elizabeth Rose found a wide range of day care centers in Philadelphia during the 1920s and 1930s, primarily serving European immigrants and to a lesser degree African Americans, but the nurseries reserved their services for women in the most desperate straits, favoring "the struggling widow or deserted wife."[36] Even those who fit this description might find no place for their children and have to, like two Philadelphia immigrant women, leave their children with neighbors when the local day nursery was full.[37] Then as now, nurseries had inflexible hours: a third Philadelphian could not use the local nursery because it opened too late for her to get to work on time.[38] A number of women sent schoolchildren to nurseries for meals or after school, but not all institutions were so accommodating: a Polish immigrant, taking a job because her husband's work dried up, put her two-year-old and five-year-old daughters in the local nursery, but because it did not accept "children over six, Angeline [aged 7] had to shift for herself under such care as the neighbors could give her."[39]

Other women appreciated the reliability, quality, and flexibility of day nurseries. A Minneapolis woman worried about her six-year-old boy as he left the day nursery to start school. She fretted: "maybe I have [sic] to give up work unless I have some neighbor girl give him lunch, but you can't depend on neighbors. I can not take him to my sisters because one is a widow and works every day and the other is not very well."[40] Whatever their other limitations, day nurseries were at least more predictably available than individuals whose own complicated lives could compromise their reliability as child minders. Some women also believed that nurseries provided a better experience for their children than other options. A South Carolina woman hired "a girl" to look after her two preschoolers, but wished she had access to a day nursery so she could be confident that her children were getting "proper care."[41] Implicitly characterizing day nurseries as a desirable scarce resource, a Philadelphia hosiery worker, deserted by her husband, no longer took her school-age children to the local nursery, telling the Women's Bureau agent, "'Now they are big enough, leave someone else's children go. They can't take everybody.'"[42]

Even though Philadelphia nurseries, as Elizabeth Rose points out, had all the drawbacks of charity institutions and might offend parents with their condescension or relentless Americanizing, mothers found ways to incorporate them into the larger circles of assistance on which they drew.[43] Day nurseries shared with working-class practices of mutuality a willingness to adapt to women's situations, offering free or flexibly priced care. Mothers reported to Women's Bureau agents that they had earlier paid for care but were not presently doing so,[44] and they paid, as they fulfilled so many other obligations, only "as able."[45] Moreover, mothers might feel easier about bargaining over fees with an institution than with other women who were probably no better off than they themselves were. They used nurseries as stop-gap, short-term solutions to child-care problems and the harrowing circumstances of working-class life.[46] For example, in her utter desperation, a Philadelphia woman who had left her bigamous husband asked to bring her three-year-old to a settlement-house nursery even when she was not working, in order to keep the child warm because she could not afford a stove and coal.[47] In one respect, though, nurseries were completely inflexible: justifiably worried about contagion, they provided no care for children who were ill. The dreadful choice this occasioned was described by a Philadelphia woman whose drunken husband left family provision to her; when the children had sore throats and could not go to the nursery, she said, "'I give them their breakfast, put milk & lunch for them on the table, put matches, knives, anything that could hurt them, out of reach, locked the front door, & gate to back yard, and went to work and left them.'"[48]

The majority sought child-care solutions outside day nurseries, and their success depended on the kinds of reciprocal exchanges that characterized so many aspects of working-class life. A second look at the three groups discussed earlier—all meatpackers, Chicago meatpackers, and Philadelphia immigrant women—offers a perspective on the arrangements they made. Although women in these groups were supposed to be asked specifically about child-care arrangements, we should regard the information gained as a bare minimum. The question was frequently left unanswered even in cases where there were young children clearly in need of care, and responses giving details about arrangements tended to come in groups, as if the agents just happened to be more interested in child care that day or were stimulated by one interesting response to question the next few interviewees more closely. It is particularly difficult to know whether child-minders were paid or not; although in the absence of specific information, some judgments can be made based on all available information about household arrangements. That said, the overwhelming across-the-board preference was for care by an individual outside the mother's household: over half (from 52 percent to 57 percent) in each of the three groups relied on such care for their children. This is a far higher proportion than the approximately one in five of children aged five or under that Hughes found, a difference for which there is no ready explanation.[49]

Co-resident child-care providers were the second most popular child-care choice, used by one in five of both Philadelphians and all meatpackers and one in eight Chicagoans. The lower proportion in Chicago is clearly related to Chicagoans' lower incidence of co-resident kin, since all but a few co-residents providing child care were relatives. The meatpackers as a whole, having used day nurseries markedly less than the other groups, relied more heavily on fostering their children to others; about one in six did so, compared to one in thirteen Philadelphians and one in every ten Chicagoans.

Forty-seven of the Philadelphia immigrant woman workers were relying on someone in their households to care for their children. About half turned to women of an older generation: twenty-three to mothers, two to mothers-in-law, and one to a stepmother. Only one mother was directly paid, receiving from Mary, her cigar-worker daughter, an unusually generous $5 per week for looking after her year-old grandson and her four-year-old granddaughter. A look into the workings of this household, however, suggests that the payment was not part of a crassly instrumental arrangement but of a larger set of reciprocal practices. Eight people lived in the house: Mary, her mother, her father, two brothers, her husband, her two children, and her sister-in-law. Mary's mother, named as the owner of the house, charged her no rent but only a share of the taxes and general expenses; Mary and her sister-in-law "share[d] [house]work very systematically with Mother."[50] Eleven mothers and one mother-in-law appeared to be offering child care in exchange for some degree of support from the younger generation, and five mothers and one stepmother probably cared for grandchildren as a contribution to the younger woman's support. Here as in the case of other mutual assistance, the major axis of connection was between women of different generations; to these we can add two aunts, one being paid directly and the other receiving support from her niece. Four sisters-in-law cared for the children of wage-earning women, three probably for free and one who was paid, in the words of the child's mother, "not much,"[51] although one case of free child care involved a temporary emergency rather than a permanent arrangement. Two were in households where two married couples were sharing housekeeping on an apparently equal basis;[52] the third was helping the wage-earner during a temporary emergency;[53] and the fourth was partially disabled and being partly supported by the wage-earner.[54] A similar pattern emerged among the three sisters who provided apparently unpaid child care: one cared for her sister's children only while the sister was in the hospital;[55] a second was living with her parents in a temporary financial emergency and received child care from both her mother and her sister;[56] and the third was Nucha, introduced earlier as part of a complex joint household.[57] Finally, among non-kin, six boarders and two landladies looked after children living in the same house; one of each was paid a definite amount for doing so.

A similar picture emerges among women working in the meatpacking industry. Twenty relied on co-residents for child care, and again mothers were the most numerous; of nine, probably two were receiving partial support in exchange (in addition to one of the two mothers-in-law and the one aunt) and one was contributing her work to her daughter's support. The lone child-minding male was unemployed and probably receiving at least part of his support in exchange for looking after his two grandchildren, aged five and seven, after school.[58] One sister-in-law and one married daughter received cash payments for child care, and an unmarried daughter received her support in exchange for her work as housekeeper and child-minder. Two older boarders, one male and one female, received support in exchange for child care, and one woman received child care as part of a joint housekeeping arrangement between two couples with children.

Within the household, then, child care seems to have been provided as part of a complex household economy. Twenty-six cases of Philadelphia co-residents providing child-care support suggests at least an educated guess about who bore the burden of the arrangement: in twenty of those, the child's mother compensated the provider either in cash or in support and in six the mother appears to have received more than she gave in return; in the ten analogous cases among meatpackers, the child's mother compensated the provider in nine and received a net benefit in only one. The raw data for these two Bulletins records only five cases in which cash changed hands in exchange for child care by co-resident kin; the payments were made to a mother, an aunt, a daughter, and two sisters-in-law. Most payments were made in the form of what the Women's Bureau agents termed "support"—full or partial room and/or board. In the cases that appear to have been unpaid, we can only assume that child care was part of a complex mix of sharing and trading within the household. Some arrangements seemed convenient: an unemployed father of a meatpacker looked after his five- and seven-year grandchildren after they came home from school, and a married daughter cared for her own one-year-old along with her mother's four-year-old.[59] In other cases, there seems to be no particular reason why a given household member did child care.

The demands involved in child care also varied a great deal. The stepmother who oversaw her five grandchildren, aged six to twelve, after school, was more fully occupied than the woman who had only to keep her eye on her eleven-year-old granddaughter after school. Clearly the greatest effort was involved in caring for preschoolers. Tellingly, four of the six cases in which we know that money changed hands within the household involved the care of preschoolers, including Mary's mother, who was so well paid for caring for her two preschool grandchildren.[60] Conversely, only one of the seven cases where the provision of child care was not at the expense of the mother involved a preschool child, and this was the temporary emergency arrangement mentioned above where the care of the three-year-old was shared by his grandmother and aunt.[61] The greater effort required to care for young children received greater recognition within the household economy, and one form in which it came was cash.

More women turned to those outside their households for child care, but as might be predicted they did not go far, typically calling on a mother in the flat upstairs, a sister around the corner, or a neighbor.[62] Once again, information about payment for child care is very spotty, and when the care is offered by someone outside the household it is more difficult to guess at what if any exchange was involved. Among the women who worked in meatpacking, forty-seven are known to have relied on nonresident child-care providers. Most—some twenty eight—turned to neighbors, half of whom were paid, five of whom were probably unpaid, and about the others we have no way of knowing. Half of the ten maternal grandmothers who cared for their non-resident grandchildren were probably not paid, but we do not have enough information to speculate about the other five. Two sisters and a sister-in-law were paid. In one case this was a calculated plan to help out the sister: a white native-born St. Joseph woman took a job and turned the care of her five-year-old twin boys over to her widowed sister because she "thought it would help both if she worked and paid [her] sister."[63] We do not have enough information to support even a guess as to whether another sister, three mothers-in-law, and two aunts received payment for their help in child care. One of those mothers-in-law, we do know, not only cared for her three-year-old granddaughter but also made some of her daughter-in-law's clothing.[64]

Among Philadelphia immigrant woman workers, there was proportionally less reliance on neighbors and more on sisters: fourteen relied on neighbors and thirteen on sisters. The difference, presumably, is that fewer immigrant women had mothers in this country. One of those sisters had quit her job four months before the Women's Bureau agent visited, in order to care for her sister's children along with her own five- and seven-year-old girls while the sister was in the hospital. Clearly exhausted by the experience—"Too much work," she told the agent—she had begun to look for a new job.[65] Seven turned to mothers, two each to mothers-in-law and daughters, and one each to a sister-in-law and a cousin. We have even less information about payment arrangements among these Philadelphia women, but we do know that six of the neighbors received some kind of payment (two definitely did not), as did two mothers, a sister, a mother-in-law, and the sister-in-law. About the others, we cannot even speculate.

No single explanation for offering free child care to a neighbor emerges from the documents. Sometimes, minimal effort was involved: one woman left breakfast and a mid-day dinner for her children and without charge fed her neighbor's ten-year-old son as well, although only during the school year as his mother sent him to the country during the summer.[66] In other cases, it is more difficult to know what was involved. One neighbor provided after-school care for a thirteen-year-old boy free of charge;[67] a cooperative boy could be an asset around the house and even help to look after the neighbor's own children, but a rebellious youth could mean real trouble. But a third example suggests that calculations of effort were not the only element involved: Hughes quotes a woman who cared for her widowed neighbor's two children, providing them with all three meals. She was paid $3 per week, a sum that did not even cover the cost of the food she gave them; she was, in effect, contributing her labor without charge but, she told the interviewer, "we got to help each other."[68] Sensible of the fragility of their family economies, some women extended themselves to help others who were, for the moment, less well situated than they. A case from a Women's Bureau study of women on mother's pensions offers an example of volunteer assistance with child care; when the pensioners' relatives, who had cared for her child while she worked in a factory to supplement her pension, moved away, relatives on a farm took the children during the summer vacation and neighbors offered to look after them once school started.[69]

Women's Bureau agents reported on the amounts, ranging from one to eight dollars a week, that forty-two women paid neighbors for child care. The details are so murky that averages would not be meaningful: the numbers and ages of children cared for vary widely but not systematically, and it is not always specified whether meals or other services were provided.

Four women paid set weekly fees for their neighbors' child care: $1.50 each for a three-year-old boy[70] and a five-year-old boy,[71] $3 for a six-year-old boy not yet in school and his eight-year-old sister after school,[72] and $5 for a five-year-old boy.[73] The payment for child care was even less standardized than the payment that women received for work outside the home. Moreover, what a woman could earn for child care was far less than she might hope to earn outside the home; the child-care expenditures for these three mothers were, respectively, 11 percent, 20 percent, and 18 percent of their earnings. Such was the low rate at which child care was compensated that these wage-earning mothers realized a significant gain even after paying for child care. Two mothers paid no set amount for child care and benefited from the generosity of their neighbors. One neighbor looked after a three-year-old daughter and (after school) an eight-year-old boy out of friendship; the mother "gave them a gift at times."[74] Another neighbor asked no payment for caring for a five-year-old girl because, as the mother told the Women's Bureau agent, she was so poor; she gave the child-minder a dollar or two when she had it.[75]

Four women paid set amounts for child care to kin, either in or outside their homes, and all paid them more generously than women paid their neighbors. A cigar-maker paid her co-resident mother $5 a week to care for her four-year-old daughter and her year-old baby son; depending on her wage, this sum amounted to between 28 percent and 36 percent of her weekly earnings.[76] A silk winder paid fully 40 percent of her weekly wage of $15 to her sister, who took charge of her three sons aged two, seven, and nine.[77] A carpet-factory worker, working only three and a half days a week, paid her mother a dollar for each day she took care of her two-year-old grandson; with varying wages based on piecework, from 23 percent to 30 percent of her weekly pay envelope went to her mother.[78] A woolen-mill reeler paid her sister-in-law $4, one quarter of her weekly earnings, for the five days per week she cared for the woman's two-year-old daughter and five-year-old son.[79] The lamentably small number of cases clearly indicate that women paid a higher percentage of their earnings, and almost always a higher absolute amount, to kin than to non-kin for child care; this observation should, of course, be balanced by the fact that women directly paid non-kin more frequently than they paid kin. Nonetheless, the difference is worth pondering. Did women pay kin more generously as a way of subsidizing those who were poorer than they were? Did women pay kin more generously because they felt more compunction about exploiting their labor than that of non-kin? Was the ordinarily unpaid work of child care seen as more valuable when performed by kin than by non-kin? Did child-care providers feel able to drive a harder bargain with kin than non-kin? The possibilities are many, but the answers are unclear.

The interviews give us little more insight into the quality of child care or the difficulty of finding it, but we have a few telling glimpses. A Czech-born Omaha mother of a three-year-old son poured out her frustrations:

> Always a problem to get the child looked after. At one time an aunt stayed with them for $3 a week & living. One of the times when [the mother] was laid off, the Aunt went elsewhere for employment. Then [the mother] had gotten a young girl to stay thru the day for $3 a week. When this girl could get a better job, [the mother] felt it not fair to urge her to stay.

Finally, two months before the Women's Bureau agent's visit, the child had become ill and the mother had quit her job to care for him.[80] Intergenerational differences emerged in the accounts of a number of women who found problems with older relatives as caregivers. A widowed mother of three girls, seven-year-old twins and a ten-year-old, had taken in an aunt to care for her children while she worked in an Ottumwa, Iowa, slaughterhouse. The arrangement failed, however, because the elderly aunt "doesn't understand children" and she was forced to hire another woman to provide after-school care for her girls.[81] Others found that grandparents were often too ill physically or too "nervous" to care for their grandchildren, or that they were simply ineffective at the task.[82] In immigrant families, a language barrier could be added to these factors, as was the case in a Philadelphia family where the grandmother spoke "little English, [was] quite old, and not in very good health; the result was that the four-year-old was "being allowed to fall into irregular habits and she misse[d] her parents, results which the parents accepted for the moment because of their desperate need for the mother's income."[83]

On the positive side, three Omaha women were pleased with their child care. One woman's four-year-old daughter and six-year-old son were in the trustworthy hands of "a very reliable woman and old friend,"[84] another woman was confident that her mother-in-law was "just like a mother" to her five- and six-year-old children,[85] and the third assured the Women's Bureau agent that her neighbor, who cared for the children of two families, gave them "better care than [the mother herself] knows how to give them."[86] The fact that four of these five examples—by far the most revealing of mothers' attitudes toward child care—come from Omaha demonstrates eloquently the degree to which the historian is at the mercy of agents who decided for their own reasons what to focus on and what to take the time to record.

A final example shows both the hopes that might be embodied in the household economy and the distress that might result when carefully laid plans went awry. A Polish-born punch-press worker whom we shall call Irene, her machinist husband, and their five-year-old son set up housekeeping in a nine-room Philadelphia house with the woman's parents and her two brothers, seventeen and twenty. They had rented a large house planning to rent several rooms to lodgers, but the third floor was still empty after a month. Irene had agreed to pay half of the $50 rent, although presumably her smaller family did not take up as much space as her parents and young-adult brothers. When the lodging scheme did not get off the ground, she was forced to take a job to help pay her and her husband's share of the rent, and she was badly upset—her "eyes often filled," noted the Women's Bureau agent—because she had to leave her child with her mother "which is not right." Even worse, the family had so recently left their failed farm that they had not had time to establish relationships with neighborhood merchants and no coal dealer had been willing to sell to them. The agent called on a snowy, unseasonably cold late-October day when she was "cold in wraps for even the length of the visit." "Living in it," she lamented, "must be hard."[87]

In contrast to the isolated household above, Nellie, a Columbus, Georgia textile-mill spooler, shows the ways in which child care could be embedded in a larger working-class culture of caring. Nellie had six children, three still living with her, three living on their own. Her sixty-four-year-old mother lived with her and took care of the three youngest children and, presumably, pitched in on the work created by the two boarders who lived in the four-room house. Nellie's disabled husband lived with their married daughter in the country.[88] Yet this example also shows the fragility of such arrangements: when the elderly mother could no longer care for the children or help with the boarders, the precarious family economy might be fatally destabilized. Such was the case with Emily, an Oklahoma laundry worker whose sister split the rent and care of Emily's two children with her. When the sister became ill, Emily had to hire another woman to care for the young children at $3 per week; she told the Women's Bureau agent that "she is just managing to get along and doesn't know what she will do, if anything unexpected happens."[89]

The vicissitudes of health, especially of the elderly, played havoc with the best-calculated of domestic arrangements; a widowed South Carolina mill worker had counted on her mother, who lived upstairs, to look after her four small children, but the mother fell ill and the widow had to stay home sporadically to care for the children and, presumably, the mother as well.[90] Pearl, an Iowa divorced mother of two grammar-schoolers, had worked out an elaborate arrangement with her mother. She and her mother worked the day and evening shifts at a hotel in Des Moines. Pearl lived outside the city limits and paid tuition so that the children could attend city schools; during the day, they took their meals at their grandmother's, and the grandmother brought them to Pearl when the shifts changed at 3 p.m. The children clearly flourished under the arrangement; bursting in on the Women's Bureau's interview with Pearl to tell their mother "of [the] dollar [their] grandmother was going to give them next pay day to start a bank account, and of Hallowe'en party." Pearl, however, understood the perils of the arrangement: "if her mother got sick or could not work she would have to take care of her."[91]

Helping Neighbors and Friends

As imperfect as is the evidence on sharing and reciprocity within households, the record of such activities between households is even spottier. By far the least commonly mentioned of the three streams that might circulate among households—services, goods, and cash—was services. Some families mentioned that they had been "helped" by friends and family with whom they did not live, but whether this help was in services, goods, or cash it is impossible to tell.[92] An Augusta, Georgia, textile worker struggling desperately to support a disabled husband and three children, for example, told the Women's Bureau agent, "My friends help me."[93] Undoubtedly countless small acts of daily help and kindness slipped under the radar of those who studied working-class households. The occasional glimpse appears when a Women's Bureau agent happens to be in the right mood in the right place at the right time. Scattered evidence in other sources shows the types of assistance that passed between households. It might be as diffuse as looking out for a neighbor's interests. Two Washington, DC, families, for example, whose homes were advertised for sale for delinquent taxes in 1932, said that they learned of their plight only after neighbors alerted them to the notice in the newspaper.[94] This type of assistance is difficult to assess; it may have been offered either out of neighborliness or out of smug satisfaction at the homeowner's misfortune. The exchange of services between households is sometimes mentioned as an aside to another discussion. We learn, for example, of the way that obligations of mutuality might interfere with a family's economic fortunes in a settlement worker's profile of the Moran family. Mr. Moran, a sheet-metal worker, was unemployed because the family decided not to follow his factory when it moved to a neighboring town because Mrs. Moran, an Irish immigrant, was caring for her elderly aunt—her "only relative in this country"—who lived nearby. The other consideration in the Morans' decision was their reluctance to move their teenaged children to new schools; it is impossible to say if they would have moved had the aunt been the only consideration, but she certainly figured prominently into their calculations.[95] And we learn that a sixty-year-old Chicago candy worker was in the habit of helping a friend with housework only because the Women's Bureau agent offered that explanation for her inability to speak with the worker.[96] As we shall see below, settlement workers' and social scientists' narratives of family adaptations to dire economic straits provide some of our best evidence about inter-household assistance and reciprocity.

Rare anecdotes illuminate the ways in which women might use household exchange to allow for personal preferences, different skills, and different levels of resources. A Fall River weaver, out of work during the late 1920s because of illness, relied heavily on assistance from others but pulled her weight by trading her services for goods: "Then, the woman who runs a fruit store used to give me fruit which she could not sell, and I would put up half for her and half for us. Then she would get a piece of goods and say, 'Make a dress for your girl and one for mine.' This has all helped."[97] In Depression-era Chicago, a profile of the Allen family, in distress because of the ironworker husband's unemployment, revealed a similar pattern. Mrs. Allen and her sister developed a pattern of labor exchanges involving sewing ("Mrs. Allen mended for her sister, and the sister made clothes for her") and cooking ("the sister brought fruit, and Mrs. Allen canned all of it, retaining some for her work").[98] The Allens' extensive network of sociability and mutuality will bring them into the discussion again. Alice, a hard-pressed Oklahoma woman, separated from her husband and supporting five children between the ages of three and thirteen, could not afford to buy any services to lighten her household load but exchanged services with friends. Alice rented half of a "rough shell of a house" and the woman who rented the other half looked after her two preschoolers; the week before the agent's visit, Alice had devoted her only free day to helping another friend clean house. Since the interview took place in mid-May, the task was presumably spring cleaning and Alice might have expected similar assistance at a later date—and perhaps help with the unwashed laundry that had piled up while she aided the friend.[99] Men made only the rarest of appearances in such exchanges; one example is the Pittsburgh miner who made radios for his friends, but the source does not specify whether he sold them, traded them for other goods or services, or made gifts of them.[100] In another case, a New York glove homeworker told the Women's Bureau agent that she was able to do the work profitably only because her machinist father-in-law kept her machine in excellent working order.[101]

Two conspicuous exceptions to the lack of systematic information on the exchange of service were the Bureau's bulletin on women who had experienced industrial accidents[102] and Gwendolyn Hughes's "Mothers in Industry."[103] Hughes found that nearly six out of ten Philadelphia mothers who were working full-time had some assistance with household work from those outside the household, and that nearly half of those also had help from those within the household. Clearly the possibilities for exchange within the household did not preclude exchange between households.[104] Although the questionnaire did not ask specifically about household help, the Women's Bureau agents noted that twenty-three women relied on services provided by friends and family with whom they did not live, as opposed to the twenty-one to whom co-residents provided services. Tellingly, fifteen of the incidents of assistance were reported in Ohio, and only four in New Jersey and four in Wisconsin. There being no evidence that people in Ohio were on the whole more helpful than those in other states, we can assume that the larger number of instances recorded in Ohio had to do with the inclination of the agent to ask about or record such matters. One woman, divorced, had the help both of friends and of her landlady who cooked and cared for her without compensation beyond her regular rent.[105] The most common form of assistance was with housework, including personal care of the injured person and cooking. The

mother of a Wisconsin woman of Polish descent did her washing and ironing, a sister did her sewing, she herself did most of the light housework and
cared for her baby, and her husband helped with the heavier housework.[106]
An Ohio woman reported that "while she was laid up, her sister-in-law
attended to her & did her work for nothing."[107] A Wisconsin woman's
"neighbors came in and waited on her."[108] Most received this help gratis
from their mothers and/or sisters and daughters (ten women) or friends
and neighbors (nine women). Only two women paid a family member—
a mother-in-law and an aunt—for assistance.[109] Two more women, one
an Italian immigrant and one native-born of eastern European descent,
paid their mothers to take in their babies.[110] Three paid non-kin for specific services such as laundry.[111]

Child fostering was probably the most frequently recorded service exchanged between households. Among the fifty cases of child fostering reported in any detail in the Women's Bureau interviews, many ethnic
groups are represented: thirteen African Americans, seventeen women
who appeared to be white and USA-born, and twenty immigrants from all
parts of Europe, ranging from England and Scotland to Italy and Poland.
No single ethnic group had a monopoly on this practice, and the interviews
reveal a broad culture of caring for the children of others, principally but
not always kin. Fostering was about evenly divided between those of the
same generation as the child's mother—with twenty cases, all but one involving a child's aunt or an aunt and uncle combination—and those of an
older generation—with twenty-four cases. As in other matters, the connections between women and their kin, especially their mothers and sisters, were most powerful. Mothers were far more likely to turn to their own
relatives than to the child's father's kin when they could not care for their
children, and the nineteen maternal grandmothers or grandparents were
by far the single largest group offering foster care.

Fostering could be initiated by a child's parents, as in the case of a
Chicago African American meatpacker, who "gave" her daughter to her
mother,[112] by a larger family network, or even implemented against the
will of the parents or the foster parents. When the mother of two Iowa boys
died, their extended family patched together housing, child care, and financial contributions in order to keep the children out of an orphanage.[113]
A more ambiguous example is that of Elizabeth M. After her sister's death
she tried to adopt the sister's four children against the apparent wishes of
their father; finally she "found [a four-year-old niece] frightfully neglected
[and] bro[ugh]t her home." On the one hand, Elizabeth may have exag-
gerated her brother-in-law's parental shortcomings in order to fulfill her

longing for a child; she was childless after nine years of marriage, and both she and her husband had had extended illnesses which might have impaired their fertility. On the other hand, she and her husband had a very nice income; she earned about $23 a week and her husband was a steadily employed machinist. They supported a life described by the Women's Bureau agent as "contented, happy, care free. . . . have a good time. . . . go out a great deal."[114] Whether Elizabeth's desire for a child or concern for her niece was paramount, it is clear that she cared little for the rights of the girl's father. Mothers eager to be shut of the responsibilities of motherhood could be similarly inattentive to others and dump their children on unwilling kin. A St. Louis couple was left with their daughter's two children when the daughter remarried and moved across town, hence making the couple reluctant foster parents.[115]

Parents often fostered their children in emergencies or at moments of family transition. A Cleveland woman, deserted with an eighteen-month-old, was able to find only live-in domestic work and had boarded the child with her mother for four months when she was interviewed.[116] Illness and mounting debt had forced an Oklahoma widow to send her twelve-year-old son to an aunt in Texas and to board her younger son at a day nursery. A fourteen-year-old daughter, an older daughter separated from her husband, and a one-year-old granddaughter remained with the widow. The Women's Bureau agent noted, "When she can get caught up, the mother would like to find a house where she could have all the children at home together."[117] The vicissitudes of immigration separated parents and children; a Scottish couple had immigrated to Philadelphia, leaving their two preschoolers behind with kin while they earned the children's passage.[118] The state also intervened, however, and immigration laws played havoc with family immigration strategies. An English couple had brought their three-year-old with them when they immigrated, but their older children and the wife's mother had been kept in England for two years by the immigration rules.[119] A child barred from the United States because of whooping cough was adopted by her aunt back in Italy and subsequently fostered to the child's grandmother when the adoptive mother herself immigrated.[120] Fostering similarly served the interests of migrating African American women; three Chicago meatpackers reported having children aged from eight to fifteen living in the South.[121]

Fostering involved a stretching but not, in most cases, a breaking of the bonds between parents and children. Mollie, a Philadelphia cigar worker, illustrates this point in a number of ways.[122] Mollie's was the simplest and most typical type of fostering—one child in the care of its maternal grandmother. Like over two-thirds of the fostering parents, she contributed to the support of her child. Mollie paid the highest amount specified, $25 per month; the lowest sum mentioned was $4 per week.[123] At least five mothers, including Mollie, were paying enough to support the child and contribute to the support of the fostering maternal grandmother. Mollie, whose eight-year-old lived with her mother in Wilmington, Delaware, was also typical of the eleven mothers whose fostered children were near enough for daily or weekend visits. Some remained even closer to their children, such as the Philadelphia woman whose child had always lived with its grandparents but was cared for by the mother while the grandmother worked in a candy factory.[124] Mollie's fostered daughter was an only child, and eighteen other mothers similarly fostered all of their minor children. Seven, though, fostered some but not all of their children, showing no consistent age or gender preference about who was fostered and who was kept at home. Fostering, moreover, did not necessarily mean opting entirely out of child care, as the example of an African American meatpacker shows: her only child was with kin in the South, but she took responsibility for the evening and weekend care of her niece and nephew.[125]

As the case of child care demonstrates, the distinction among exchanges of goods, services, and money, although analytically useful, often disappears in the complex functioning of family economies. The Allen family mentioned above illustrates this point. As long as the ironworker father found work, the Allens developed a broad circle of friends to which they contributed both sociability and services: "[T]hey entertained their friends and went to many bunco parties. Mrs. Allen was a good cook and was in demand at the many birthday parties and weddings that they attended." When Mr. Allen lost his job, the family cut back their spending on housing, food, clothing, medical care, and insurance but still failed to make ends meet. Their friends and family intervened in many ways; Mrs. Allen's exchange of services with her sister was only one of the many resources that came their way. The Allens' experience can serve as a best-case example of mutual assistance, with generous and steadfast support from family and friends. "A friend who worked in the stock yards brought them bacon and inexpensive cuts of meat; another friend gave them a dozen cases of macaroni; someone else supplied ice. A friend gave Mrs. Allen a coat that had been left at her house and never called for."

Much lies behind these terse descriptions. The contributions of food and ice, for example, seem likely to have come their way as part of workers' assertions of "perks," or abilities and rights to appropriate the materials they made or used on the job.[126] The bacon may have been smuggled out of the packinghouse under an apron, the macaroni overlooked in checking a shipment, the ice delivery camouflaged in the driver's rounds. As an ironworker, Mr. Allen might well have asserted the same customary rights and would have been comfortable with sharing the bounty of his friends' perks, which represented a modest redistribution of wealth in hard times. Such gifts of commodities did not carry as clear and quantifiable an obligation to repay as a loan of money, as we shall see. Social skills also counted for something. Mr. Page, a truck driver, "was a good bridge player and was always in demand for a game in the neighborhood." When he lost his job, his wife "told their friends not to invite them to their homes because she could no longer return their invitations, but their friends come to visit them as often as before. They frequently bring their own refreshments with them. 'Take last night, for example,' said Mrs. Page. 'Some friends came over and played games, and had a very good time. Better, in fact, than they might have had if I had arranged a party, worked all day before and after the party, and spent a lot of money on it.'"[127] Mirra Komarovsky, who interviewed the Pages, contrasted them with the Scotts, whose social life entirely fell apart because of their poverty: "They have broken all relations with friends at the insistence of the husband, because they have no clothes to wear and no money to entertain with. The only visitor to the house is an old bachelor friend of the husband."[128]

Secondhand Goods

The gift of the "never called for" coat shows the importance of secondhand goods in the informal exchange networks among working-class people. The suspect explanation offered by the friend may have been true or may have covered up a more deliberate effort to find a way to give Mrs. Allen a much-needed coat. Working-class family economies were deeply dependent on the circulation of secondhand goods as one of the many expedients to stretch their insufficient resources. Mrs. Allen's coat sits in the deepest channel of the non-cash flow of secondhand goods. Secondhand clothing dominated the flow of secondhand goods, and it appears universally in the evidence, no matter the time, the place, or the source. One reason that the circulation of secondhand clothing was so brisk was that its value rested almost entirely in its use rather than as its potential to raise cash. A Utah family supported by a laborer father found when they desperately sold off clothing that "they have little of value";[129] clothing depreciated quickly and dramatically. At the same time, even the poorest, eager to help kin or friends, might be able to offer a bit of used clothing when they could afford no other assistance; one woman who was "poor and unable to do much to assist" her deserted daughter nonetheless gave her "considerable in the way of clothing."[130]

It is difficult to overestimate the importance of secondhand clothing in stretching already tight budgets a crucial bit farther; as a settlement worker said of a Buffalo mother of five children, "Clothes and shoes are the chief anxieties of [her] life."[131] The desperate family might simply stop spending anything at all on clothing, depending, as did a New York family, "on chance windfalls from anywhere."[132] A Little Rock, Arkansas, laundry worker told the Women's Bureau agent that "almost all her clothes [were] given [to] her."[133] Families in dire straits made used goods do very hard work indeed; one Rhode Island woman was still wearing secondhand shoes a year after they had been given to her.[134]

Secondhand clothing was more a woman's resource than a man's; one young man of twenty-two resented the shabbiness of his clothes, envying his eighteen- and nineteen-year-old sisters "because they can make their clothes over."[135] In another family, the mother and her daughter managed to "keep up [their] former standards in appearance" by wearing shoes and clothing given to them by friends, but such hand-me-downs apparently did not come the father's way and he felt "that his somewhat shabby appearance prevent[ed] him from getting work."[136] The pattern of adult women and children, but not the adult man, receiving secondhand clothes recurs over and over in the sources.[137] Many children may have had the same experience as those in a Philadelphia family of German immigrants; their mother told the Women's Bureau agent that she "always made the children's clothes out of old skirts which were big in those days and children were 12 years old before they ever had a dress made out of new material."[138] Only rarely were men the recipients of secondhand clothes, usually more formal attire rather than workaday garments. A typical example was the Minneapolis man to whom a social agency gave "fairly presentable suit of clothes" to wear as he hunted for a job; as the man told a settlement worker, "a guy hasta make a good impression nowadays."[139]

Secondhand clothing, moreover, usually needed the application of women's skills to make it useful. Thus it was both given and remade as part of the process by which it came to be the property of a new family. Mrs. Allen's coat may have been a perfect fit and the latest style, but more than likely it required some work before she wore it since she was "very much overweight."[140] The circulation of used clothing intersected with sewing, a persistently important aspect of domestic production. Secondhand clothing was rarely usable as it came to the recipient: it had to be altered to fit, updated in style, buttons and other fasteners replaced, worn spots mended. Clothing was often cut down for smaller wearers, allowing the use of the best of the fabric. Making over clothes was a skill of enormous value during hard times; those who didn't have it hastened to learn, as did Mrs. Allen's daughter Thelma, who became "very resourceful in making over hats and clothes."[141] It was no simple matter to make used clothing look new and fashionable; a settlement worker observed that the wife of an unemployed machinist was able to do a decent job of making over clothes for her children, but did less well for herself: "It was evident that she was wearing her unmarried sister's cast-off clothing, blouses that had been dyed."[142]]

Women responded differently to their place in the circulation of secondhand clothing. For some it was a way of life, such as the Fall River, Massachusetts, mother of seven children under the age of thirteen who boasted, "We have spent hardly a nickel for clothes ever since we were married [fifteen years ago]. Friends have given me things and in this way I have always kept the children clothed."[143] Others saw it as a sign of their disadvantaged class position. A New Orleans woman, for example, told a settlement worker that "she has never had to do this before but now 'she must forget her pride' in order to manage."[144] And for some it was ultimately a labor of futility; as a Czechoslovak immigrant mother of nine opined, "I cannot patch the clothes any more,—they are all patches." When a local settlement house gathered some used clothes for her, she went "over late in the evening to carry the things to her home. The neighbors did not see her, and the children did not know how the things all got there."[145] But some rose proudly and energetically to the challenge, as this account of another New Orleans woman shows: "When one of the workers at the settlement took over some things where the material was good and suggested that Mrs. Broussard make them over for the children, she was overjoyed. 'Now,' she said, 'that will give me a little more money to spend for food. I won't have to buy the dress for sister that she needs so badly and I can make a coat out of this skirt for Susanne. I will dye some of these things and you must come and see what I make of them.'"[146] In some instances gifts from kin seemed preferable to those from charitable institutions. E. Wight Bakke, investigating the lives of unemployed families in New Haven, Connecticut, during the Great Depression, learned from an indignant mother about the social costs of accepting clothes from charitable organizations: "Secondhand clothes from the rest of family are all right. But the other day a neighbor's child had it flung into her face by a schoolmate, 'That looks like the coat I gave to the Red Cross.' I'll not let that happen to [my daughter]."[147]

Secondhand clothing probably dominated the goods that flowed between working-class families, but new clothes and food made prominent appearances as well. Children and their clothing came in for particular attention. The wife of a Georgia cabinetmaker not only looked to her own children but "would often have children who were less well cared for than hers into her home, and would dress and feed them."[148] An Iowa cigar worker first took in her nephews when they were orphaned but continued to buy their clothes even after they went to live with other family members.[149] The four daughters, aged from six to eleven, of an Italian immigrant couple in Pittsburgh were dressed in clothes given by their maternal grandmother and aunt and made over to fit them and shod in overshoes and stockings given by a teacher at their school.[150] A determinedly self-sufficient family, in which the father and children scavenged enough wood to fill the family's fuel needs, accepted no aid "except a few clothes for the children from interested friends."[151] Someone might take a special interest in one child's welfare. An Arkansas saleswoman bought shoes and clothing for a neighbor's child so that she might go to school; the saleswoman did so at some pains since she was widowed and partly dependent on cash contributions from a single brother.[152] Other cases in point are the maternal aunt who bought clothing and eyeglasses for her fifteen-year-old niece[153] and the neighbor who bought a young man an overcoat.[154]

That neighbor's gift of the coat had grown out of "feeling indebted for past kindnesses"[155] and thus introduces us to the calculations of reciprocity among working-class families. Perhaps the neighbor had benefited from the efforts of the boy's mother, who was a "dependable, hard worker" in church and neighborhood organizations.[156] Engagement with the community clearly brought rewards to an Italian family, for some years a member of a cooperative that bought oil and cheese at cost. When the family fell on hard times, "these neighbors insisted that the family continue to avail themselves of this service and pay for the things as they could."[157] A sociable couple in New Orleans—"Visiting from the front steps with their neighbors was a regular social function on Sunday winter afternoons."—reaped the benefits of friendship when the husband's diligent efforts to find work failed. They received both regular assistance in the form of a neighbor's daily gift of a pint of milk for the children and special treats when "The neighbors run in with a special dish or a bowl of soup, 'to help

Mary out.'"[158] Clearly concern for the children was important here, but the extra effort with special treats suggests real affection and esteem for the parents as well.

The example of the Taber family shows that people might feel an immediate need to reciprocate for some things but not for others. When the letter-carrier father lost his job, according to Mrs. Taber, "Often on Saturday night at eleven o'clock there was no Sunday dinner, and would have been none but for my mother. I well earned what she gave us, though, by cleaning house for her." On the other hand, the family seemed to feel no pressing need to reciprocate for aid to the children; as the settlement worker put it, "The normal wants of childhood have been satisfied in a good measure for these children by their numerous aunts and uncles."[159] In another family, supported by daughters aged eighteen and twenty-one, an elder daughter whose husband was institutionalized was welcome to bring "her four children every night to share the evening meal" because, as Tessie, the eighteen-year-old, put it, "Rose helped fine when she was home." By contrast, Tessie had nothing but contempt for her brother who lost his job because he was "too proud" and had "been loafing around for a year and a half. I guess he knows us girls is easy marks."[160] These examples suggest, though not conclusively, that continuing reliance for food led to a more direct calculus of obligations owed than did occasional aid for clothing and the like, especially when provision of food was directed to the needs of children.[161]

Food, Furniture, and Funds

Food seems not to have incurred the immediate obligation to repay when the giver had special access to food or when it was intended for children. The family of a Buffalo laborer found that "their food isn't as much of a problem as it would be if [the wife's] parents did not keep a grocery store."[162] A Washington, DC, African American couple benefited from a connection to rural roots. Deeply in debt for their house mortgage, taxes, medical care, and furniture, they told a Woman's Bureau agent that "[t]he only way they can meet all these payments and 'not starve' is by depending on the food that relatives (on a farm in Maryland) send them every week."[163] A Mexican couple in San Antonio eked out a very lean existence for themselves and their two young children with beans brought by the husband's father from the warehouse where he worked.[164] An Anglo couple in the same city was typical of the families who received occasional aid, often directed at the children, from neighbors and kin. The Women's Bureau agent noted that a "neighbor bro[ugh]t in some beans for the children's dinner while agent was there"; the household was in some disarray—the agent described it as "Bare—cluttered—disorderly," and noted that "Neighbors help her more than she realizes." This seems to be a case where the parents were not coping and the neighbors chipped in.[165]

Other dependents might also spark the sympathy of neighbors. A Chicago candy worker supporting her eighty-nine-year-old mother was grateful that a friend gave the mother "coffee and sometimes milk."[166] Other assistance seems to have been more occasional and ad hoc: a neighbor brought some groceries to a Virginia tobacco worker whose husband was in prison for bigamy.[167] Special occasions often provoked outpourings of generosity. One woman returned home in despair from a fruitless trip to the market because she "couldn't get anything that seemed really like Christmas"; however, she found that her husband's old boss (who had had to lay him off because of a slump in the building trades) had "brought a beautiful turkey" and that a neighbor had left "a dish of macaroni, some green peas, even some celery and a *beautiful cake*."[168] The generosity might be combined with an expression of community standards: a childless Omaha couple, both meatpackers, "prepared a thanksgiving basket—chickens—vegetables—bread—apples—for one family with husband laid off because they felt bad for wife and children but said husband was n.g. [no good]"[169]

We find occasional evidence of more handsome assistance given by kin and friends. The Philadelphia woman whom we met earlier when she asked that her child be taken into the day nursery to keep warm received a gift of a stove from a neighbor; that, along with coal supplied from the House of Industry settlement house, allowed her and the child a measure of comfort at home.[170] A Mexican family moved from California to San Antonio and received a houseful of furniture (except for beds) from friends.[171] In Depression-era Connecticut, investigators found that more families sold their furniture than added to their stock, but those who did add mostly did so through gifts from friends or kin.[172] These examples of the circulation of furniture outside the cash market are fairly rare; most families, as we shall see in the next chapter, used furniture as investment capital. An Omaha couple with two young children had their own cottage thanks to their fathers: the husband's father gave them a house lot, and the wife's father built the house for them.[173] Unmarried relatives sometimes extended themselves with special generosity, as did the Arkansas saleswomen's brother, but usually it was a mother's sister who offered help. The sister of a Boston Yankee woman "stepped into the breach in every emergency," but also gave the family the handsome gift of a piano.[174] The sister of another Boston woman, this one an Italian immigrant, drew down her own savings to keep the sister's family out of debt.[175]

Of course, wealthier relatives both helped and shunned kin in need. The woman who was surprised by the Christmas food was fortunate in having a sister who had married well and occasionally bought the children clothes and once paid the rent.[176] By contrast, a family that moved from a small town to Indianapolis, where the father's career in clerical work foundered, experienced "some break in relations with relatives as relatives all appear to be more successful than this family." The settlement worker's account of the family's declining fortunes, however, attributes them also to the fact that "ties and associations have been broken" by their move; if community connections helped some families, their lack could lead to a spiraling decline for others.[177]

Mutuality and reciprocity might extend to the world of paid work, with family and kin sharing resources that maximized earnings or helping young people to acquire training that would increase their earning potential. Upstate New York glove makers clubbed together to buy machine oil by the gallon because "it was cheaper that way."[178] Josefina, a young Mexican homeworker in San Antonio, lived with her sister and brother-in-law, who were prospering. Appalled at the toll that fine needlework was taking on Josefina's eyes, her sister offered "to pay for beauty culture courses or anything if she will stop working at home."[179] Another San Antonio homeworker shared her sewing machine and her industrial homework with a friend "who has no machine and the dresses are partly machine made."[180] In the upstate New York glove-making district, sewing equipment circulated briskly, another aspect of the importance of secondhand goods to working-class families. Sewing machines, sewing machine motors, and tables for sewing machines were sold, given, and borrowed; about four in ten of those who referred to secondhand equipment (the questionnaire did not specifically target the type of equipment) had obtained it outside the cash market. These non-cash transactions were largely among kin (eleven of the sixteen exchanges involved family members, three were among friends, and two were unspecified), among women (nine of the donors or loaners were women, and sex was unspecified in five cases), and intergenerational. The nine female kin donors or loaners included four mothers-in-law, three mothers, and an aunt, but only one sister.[181]

Working-class people also shared automobiles and telephones, especially in situations where these were not conveniences but necessities for wage-earning. This type of sharing is also one of the few situations where men make an appearance. Women who did industrial homework often relied on others to provide transportation to collect and deliver the work. An elderly Anglo widow in San Antonio existed on only two meals a day, and was able to do that well only because a neighbor gave rides to and from the factory and saved her carfare.[182] Another San Antonio Anglo woman was in the habit of taking several neighbors with her when she drove to the factory.[183] A study of Houston workers during the Depression pointed out that "like the automobile, the telephone is a business asset" for workers such as electricians and longshoremen who work at different locations, need to be in contact with hiring halls, and have tools to transport.[184] Of 40 electricians' families queried, only half still had telephones. The researchers guessed that "doubtless they find the borrowing of a neighbor's telephone less difficult than borrowing his automobile."[185] Longshoremen, whose Houston-area work was spread thirty miles along the Gulf of Mexico, shared rides and the cost of gas.[186] The Depression produced an extended slack time in the Cleveland construction industries, and one man "used his ford [sic] to look for work and the gas was paid for by other men also job hunting, who went with him."[187]

As the previous example suggests, cash was a significant medium of circulation in working-class reciprocity. People loaned or gave others money for every conceivable purpose. A woman borrowed money from her sister first to help pay the house mortgage and then to go to the dentist, but "had to use it for food instead."[188] A cousin redeemed a man's suits and a woman's fur coat from pawn, although the family's ring and watches were left at the pawnshop, not having the use value that the clothing had.[189] Four Washington, DC, families, two African American and two Euro-American, took loans from friends to pay the taxes on their houses. One had done so for six or seven years out of the previous ten, and another had been lucky enough to get an interest-free loan that she repaid promptly.[190] A man's brother and sister loaned him enough to pay his union dues and to give the grocer a payment on the family's "book" so that more credit would be forthcoming.[191] A father assumed the payments on the used car that his son needed for his frequent work out of town; this family conscientiously repaid loans from family, either directly "or by giving its value in service,—perhaps making clothes for the children."[192] Not all were so punctilious. A Nebraska family of seven spent a summer toiling in beet fields, netting $500, "the only money Mr. Aller had ever had ahead"; he loaned $200 to a brother-in-law who never repaid him.[193] Most common of all, however, were contributions to the support of relatives who had fallen on hard times. A study of 107 Washington, DC, families whose homes were in danger of being sold because of unpaid taxes found that over a quarter of them were making cash contributions to friends or kin who did not live with them; four were recipients of such contributions.[194]

Given the mobility of working-class people, there was a high incidence of contributions by kin who had immigrated or migrated from the family home. Of the thirty-two Philadelphia immigrant families where cash circulated, twenty-two sent remittances to family members still in Europe, ranging from England and Ireland to Poland and Russia to Italy.[195] Of those twenty-two, eighteen were sent by single women. Only one woman had received a remittance from abroad—her brother in South Africa had bankrolled her move to the United States[196]—but four women in Texas received remittances from male relatives in Mexico, and none sent money back to Mexico.[197] A Chicago meatpacker, though, sent money to a sister in Mexico who had been left with four children by her deserting husband.[198] An intriguing case is that of the Chicago meatpacker whose husband in Lithuania "broke his leg ten years ago and never has worked since"; she sent him about $5 per month and a Christmas package of $80 worth of clothing.[199]

Migrants around the United States did not forget their kin at home. Two sisters in San Antonio who had lost their jobs and fallen back on industrial homework in a desperate attempt to hold onto to their comfortable bungalow received "a dollar or so" from their brother in New York.[200] A brother in West Virginia sent "a little money as able and clothes for the children to be made over" to his mother and five siblings in Omaha.[201] A Missouri woman went back to her hometown to visit her mother every week and give her the little money she had left after paying her living expenses.[202] African Americans sent money to kin still in the South; a Chicago meatpacker, for instance, sent money to Arkansas to an ailing sister with six children,[203] and a childless Kansas City couple were sending money to both their mothers.[204] Many of these cash remittances were to contribute to the support of fostered children or those who cared for them.

Borrowing money in an economy where the rules were fluid and often ambiguous allowed people a certain flexibility, but it also produced anxiety and potential conflict. Friends and family were often in no better shape than the person seeking a loan. When hard times hit broadly, friends and family, however willing, might no longer be able to extend credit.[205] Even those most hard pressed, though, might go to great lengths to assist kin in need. An upstate New York Italian immigrant woman bought a sewing machine for $147.50 so that she could do industrial homework on gloves; hard pressed because her husband was unemployed, she still shared her meager earnings, ranging from $6.90 to $10.35, with her widowed sister.[206]

A reputation for prompt repayment was a valuable asset in this fluid economy, but even then it had limitations. A New York woman explained the rules to a Henry Street Settlement worker: "Fortunately she has relatives who can lend to her, but 'if you don't pay them back, the door is closed.' She is still owing them, which may be one reason why now, as she says, 'I do my own remedy to save money. What you going to do?'"[207] Building up a record for reliability served a Wisconsin Railroad laborer well: "He knows that he can borrow enough money for necessities from his friends who trust that he will repay them." This happy situation, however, was not simply a matter of dollars and cents but of culture as well; he told the settlement worker that "he is willing to borrow from other Italians, for they are his friends, but he will not ask other people. These others, he says, are always sending notices asking one to pay while an Italian trusts and waits until one is able to pay."[208] Another Italian immigrant, a New York building-trade laborer, found that his countrymen could be importunate indeed: "Neighbors lent them money, always counting on a building's being 'caught.' When pay day came during the three weeks in which Mr. Zappula had work, his neighbors hastened to call in the evening, and he was distracted, wondering whom to pay first."[209] One woman "in a burst of confidence in her ability to earn," took out a Morris Plan loan to repay her debt to her neighbor, only to lose her job.[210] Working-class families often incurred many different types of debt and faced hard choices in repayment. A family plagued by illness and the father's unemployment went into debt for rent, food, hospital care, and to a friend. When the father, a carpenter, secured six months' work, however, he paid off some of the debt to his landlord and his grocer, even though the debt to the friend was the largest one. It was an unhappy choice—to protect his family's food and shelter at the cost of irritating a generous friend.[211]

The extremes of generosity and predation appear in the circulation of cash among working-class people. An uncle bought a two-story cottage for his niece, her husband, and seven children—a highly generous act, though the uncle may have been eager to find a home for his aging brother, the niece's father, who then made his home with her.[212] The sister of a Washington, DC, woman whose house was in danger of being sold for unpaid taxes paid some of the taxes and promised to buy the house for them if the sale could not be forestalled.[213] On the other hand, a Philadelphia family, forced by the father's unemployment to give up a comfortable house with all the modern conveniences and move to a tiny place without a bath or an inside toilet, endured the further indignity of putting up its expensive radio set for a loan from a friend of less than a fifth of its value.[214]

Collective efforts and pooling resources could be gratifying, as they were for the Iowa woman who had combined with other kin to keep orphaned boys out of an institution. Looking back on the effort with satisfaction, one family member commented that "the family is getting along fine."[215] But many, especially when they felt that they could not hold up their end of the bargain or when others seemed to fail them, found the world of working-class reciprocity a cold one. An English immigrant to Philadelphia, plagued by a drinking husband, supported her mother for the last ten years of her life on meager rag-sorter's wages. The Women's Bureau agent painted a picture of a miserable and bitter woman: "Interviewed in her door way. Seemed ashamed to have agent go inside. Shutters were closed & room gloomy. Dressed in shabby old worsted skirt evidently very old & Black cotton waist. Waist gapped open showing that IP wore no underwear. The outfit might have come from a rag bag. She said 'I can just pay the rent & get food. I have to eat don't I? I can't buy any clothes.' Her hair was thin & dirty. Upper teeth out & lower in very bad condition. The struggle for existence seemed almost too much." The siblings, who had been happy to leave their mother's care and support to her, shunned her: "'My brother & sisters never come near me. Perhaps if they saw crepe on the door they'd come.'"[216] Even under the best of circumstances, the tangled connections of working-class reciprocity bumped closely up against the specter of dependency; an upstate New York glove maker summed up the dilemma: she "said when she first came to Gloversville 20 yrs. [sic] ago, she thought it would be nice to work on gloves & have her own money so she wouldn't need to depend on anyone else. Said now she sometimes wonder if it was a good idea as now others have gotten to depend on her."[217]

As we saw above, engagement with the community was an important factor in making available assistance from others; the cruel irony is that those who were down on their luck often felt compelled to withdraw from social contacts in an attempt to conceal their material neediness or because they could no longer provide the reciprocity and the niceties of sociability. Two young women had cut back their social life because "in their five small rooms [shared with their mother and six other siblings] they have no place to entertain their friends and . . . feel they cannot visit their friends because they cannot entertain in return."[218] Mirra Komarovsky's study of unemployed men and their families in the mid-1930s offers broad evidence of the pains suffered by those whose budgets limited their social lives: an out-of-work carpenter said: "'As soon as you are out of the dough, your friends don't want to know you any more. They are afraid you will ask them for something. People on relief are black sheep. I used to make wine, and friends would drop around several times a week. It was nothing for me to give them a gallon to take away. I don't see anyone coming around now.'"[219] A former electrician opined, "'You don't have any friends unless you have got the dollar.'"[220] The wife of a former glassworker said "'Our friends certainly did turn out to be fair-weather friends. Once they know you're down and out, they act as if you had a disease.'"[221] The burden of maintaining social contacts often fell disproportionately on women, who provided the food and drink that lubricated sociability; one woman noted, "'The least you can offer is a cup of coffee and a piece of cake, and even that costs money.'"[222] Clothing, too, was a special issue for women, many of whom told Komarovsky that the want of decent clothing kept them from more formal social contacts such as church services and organizations.[223] Komarovsky allows that the picture she draws may have been unduly bleak because those whom she interviewed were all "native-born Protestant skilled laborers" and part of "an urban and a mobile group" with "relatively weak kinship ties." She speculated that "it is probable that an Italian or perhaps a Jewish group would have a more closely knit family unit."[224]

When the balance of rough equality and good feeling was disturbed, bitterness could result; such was the reaction of a Boston woman "who has become rather hardened in her attitude toward friends who started out as she did, but who have been more fortunate about getting ahead."[225] The resentment could turn even uglier when it happened within families, and it would be hard to find a case more disastrous than that of the Dantes, a New York couple with two young children. When the clerical-worker father lost his job, the family lost its modern suburban home and the mother and children moved in with her parents. The household was a crowded one, with seventeen in eight rooms. The parents both fell "seriously ill" and the support of the household weighed heavily on Mrs. Dante's three wage-earning sisters. They became deeply resentful: "because his wife's sisters would not have [Mr. Dante] in the home where they were the only breadwinners and he was earning nothing, he went to live with his married sister. Mrs. Dante grew more and more discouraged and although she was much needed to care for . . . [her ill parents and her younger siblings] in her mother's home, her sisters made her feel that the presence of herself and two children was an added burden." The result was "much conflict and disharmony." [226]

Conclusion

The many and varied cases of reciprocity outlined here, including the exchange of goods, services, labor, and cash, suggest the necessity and the hazards for working-class families of relying on the kindness of relatives, friends, and neighbors. Although patterns varied across time, place, and circumstance, some key factors shaped such exchanges. Those with rich networks of sociability and strong reputations for integrity and helpfulness were the most likely to have help extended to them when in need. Whether assistance required repayment, how soon, and in what form depended in part on earlier traditions of reciprocity, the person being helped, and the ability of the individual giving assistance to provide the resources. Someone who was repaying an earlier debt, who had the means to do so at the time help was needed, and who was providing resources specifically for children, had less expectation of a return than persons who had not been recipients of earlier largesse, were needy themselves, and were supplying goods or services for adults. Injury, illness, or short-term unemployment might also inspire more liberal forms of aid than situations that demanded long-term support. Moreover, in general, family members were expected to offer help whenever possible, whereas friends, neighbors, and co-workers felt less pressure to assist, especially if they were in dire straits themselves.

Yet there was no clear set of rules and obligations that regulated exchanges of goods, services, or labor. Some friends and neighbors were more generous than family members, and some family members were more willing to help than others. Women, who were central to the webs of reciprocity, were not thereby automatically rendered more caring or generous. Indeed, disagreements over who should help, what form the help should take, and how such assistance should be repaid inspired disappointment, resentment, and even estrangement among relatives as well as friends and neighbors. And those with wide-ranging social networks when times were flush might find themselves isolated or ostracized in hard times.

Still, despite the uncertainties and miscommunications that marked exchanges among working-class families, traditions of reciprocity were deeply engrained. In part, this was because there were few alternatives in the early twentieth century United States to collective responsibility in working-class families and neighborhoods. In addition, some immigrant groups carried traditions of mutual aid with them to their new homeland and nurtured new forms of reciprocity in the communities they created. Native-born American workers could also draw on customary patterns of exchange built in union halls, socialist political movements, or churches over the previous century. Inventive in the face of necessity, working-class families, and especially working-class women, relied on the old adage "what goes 'round, comes 'round" to buttress themselves against economic crises and social upheavals over which they otherwise had little control.

5

The Family Economy in the Marketplace

Studies of working class family budgets and standards of living often neglected the collection of information on the central subjects of this final chapter, failing in particular to enumerate household appliances and to investigate the purchases of household services. In completing her useful 1927 study *The Income and Standard of Living of Unskilled Laborers in Chicago*, for example, Leila Houghteling included in her interview schedule a question about "indications of comfort," specifying automobiles, piano, victrolas, radios, and telephones. But she omitted those items which would contribute to the convenience if not comfort of the women in the household: sewing machines, washing machines, electric irons, and the like. Even the instructions about filling in the "other" category direct Houghteling's investigators away from such items and toward "unusually good furniture, expensive rugs or lamps, etc."[1] And yet perhaps the most fruitful ways to connect the family economy and the market lie precisely in these relatively uninvestigated areas. If we imagine, for example, the decision of families contemplating the purchase of a washing machine in the 1920s or 1930s, we find them facing choices which imply whether they would enter into installment buying plans, calculating whether to a buy a new or used machine. The choice could involve balancing both the savings to be realized by not having to buy the commoditized services of laundries and the possibility of "freeing" women in the family not for leisure but for increased participation in waged labor.

If an important part of the working-class family economy was forged in the crucible of relationships among families, individuals, and households, another part took place in the marketplace, where working-class families made choices about how to spend their money, about how to use credit, and about how to retrench in hard times and enhance their material lives in good times. Like the practices of assistance among working-class people, relationships to the market were less than rationalized; much took place below the radar of formal institutions and legal arrangements and was deeply personalized. Precisely because the working-class purse was so shallow, families and individuals had to make many hard choices. They might buy some things with an eye to imitating other people or keeping up with peers, but emulation and conformity figured far less into their consumption than it did for families who commanded larger discretionary incomes. As a result, we find not a dominant pattern of working-class consumption, but a tangle of dynamic and idiosyncratic relationships to the marketplace. Central among the tangle of life decisions connecting the family to the market were those that structure this chapter: whether to buy goods and services that could replace the household labor of women, whether and when to engage, as sellers and buyers, the market in second-hand goods, and how and when to negotiate credit.

Replacing Women's Household Labor

Because the Women's Bureau data focused on wage-earning women, they shed special light on the purchase of services to replace the household labor of women. From their point of view, the line between the purchase of goods and services often blurred. For a woman, to purchase a dress was not just to buy the thing, but to buy the labor that went into it instead of supplying it herself; buying a loaf of bread bought her way out of the long and delicate process of producing it herself. The three most frequent services purchased were baking, sewing, and laundry, in that order. Once again, we turn to the Women's Bureau studies that tell us the most about housework and expenditures, those on Philadelphia immigrant women and on women working in meatpacking and slaughtering. The former asked about what work was done outside the home, with the agents' instructions suggesting that they inquire about the purchase of clothing, baked goods, and laundry services.[2] The latter provided a check-off grid on which agents were to indicate whether interviewees received assistance with cooking, laundry, cleaning, child care, sewing, and doing dishes. The information in both cases is more imperfect than the normal run in the schedules because it came toward the end of the schedule and often shows signs of being hastily or carelessly provided. Perhaps in recognition of this, the published bulletins gave short shrift to this matter, barely considering it at all in the Philadelphia report and dealing with it briefly in the meat-packing report in a largely anecdotal section of less than two pages and an appendix table.[3]

These imperfect data show most definitively that women rarely baked bread. About half (477) of the Philadelphia immigrant women were specif-ically noted as buying bread. One can well imagine why so many women headed toward the bakery or grocery store. Bread baking requires time, equipment, and space that were lacking in the lives of wage-earning women.[4] The long process of rising and kneading required continuing at-tention over an extended period of time, a routine incompatible with the women's job schedules. The ability to control both the ambient tempera-ture of rising bread and the oven temperature of baking bread exceeded the heating and cooking facilities of most working-class homes; bread baking would have been a chancy enterprise. Storing both the raw materials and the baked bread would have strained the resources of cramped households, and bread baked on weekends would at the very least have been stale and possibly moldy within a few days. Store-bought bread was readily and widely available and relatively cheap, its purchase requiring relatively little effort and money from busy woman householders. Women's Bureau agents noted only two Philadelphia women who baked most of their bread and four who baked some of it; they were all non-Jewish immigrants from east-ern Europe, married and in their thirties, and in no way distinct from oth-ers of the same age, marital status, and ethnicity.[5] The study of women in meatpacking and slaughtering said virtually nothing about bread baking, and we meet only one woman who baked, a South St. Paul pork trimmer in her 40s. When the agent visited her on a Sunday, she was both baking bread and trying out lard. (Her comment—"Then I know it's good."—reflected critical distance on the processes at the Armour plant where she worked.)[6] Store-bought bread, clearly, was one of the most universal expenditures of working-class households in the interwar United States.

Sewing, usually in the form of ready-made clothing, was the next most popular service sought in the marketplace. A bit over half (55 percent) of the Philadelphia immigrant women and just under a third (31 percent) of the meatpackers bought at least some of their clothing. Behind these proportions, however, lurks a much more complicated picture than the relatively simple one of bread-buying. Sewing, like bread baking, required skill, but of a more complex nature. Some knowledge of sewing was nearly universal. As a young Italian immigrant to Philadelphia put it, "anyone with a big family knows how to sew." Nonetheless, taking dressmaking lessons in night school, she was acting out her understanding that there was a big gap between being able to do what informants referred to as "plain sewing" and the kind of skilled work that would produce a stylish and well-fitted wardrobe.[7] An artisanal pride in fine sewing coexisted with an appreciation for stylish ready-made clothing. At least a dozen other Philadelphia women either expressed a similar desire for training in dressmaking or spoke proudly of their dressmaking skills.[8] One Philadelphia woman earned her living making machine-made "better dresses" in a factory and bought fine fabric remnants from her boss to use at home to make all her own clothing ("even hats coats suits") and to make Easter dresses for her nieces.[9] More commonly, informants told Women's Bureau agents that they did only plain sewing or made "plain dresses,"[10] "everyday dresses,"[11] "house dresses,"[12] or "work dresses,"[13] and purchased "holiday" clothes,[14] "best" dresses,[15] "fancy" clothes,[16] or "Sunday clothes" (a phrase most commonly used by African American women).[17] Another common strategy was for a mother to make her children's clothing and to buy her own ready-made.[18]

Virtually no one made clothing for adult men; one of the few exceptions was an unusually energetic Philadelphia meatpacker, mother of seven, who did all the family's washing, ironing, and cooking and baked some of its bread in addition to making all of her sons' and husband's shirts and her own and her daughters' dresses. The quirkiness of decisions about what to buy and what to make is underlined by her decision to purchase the family's underwear.[19] Some had turned almost entirely to the market for sewn items, such as the numerous women who told the Women's Bureau agents that they did only mending.[20] It should be noted, however, that mending garments skillfully and durably was a skill in itself and an important way to extend the life of clothing. One Philadelphia woman showed the agent "old worsted skirts patched in many places," presumably still useful as work clothes.[21] Sewing could be a means of remaining independent from the cash market, although that too could have its price. An Iowa meatpacker boasted that she "'never had anything made in [her] life' or bought ready made," but the result was that she did not have the wardrobe necessary to move into the sales job to which she aspired.[22]

Skill was not the only determinant of whether or not to make or buy clothing; time and money were obvious factors. Many gave up sewing while working and went back to it only when they were laid off or on short hours.[23] Seven Philadelphia immigrant women pursued this tactic but, interestingly, always did their own laundry. An Italian immigrant mother of six, a clothing-factory worker, knew precisely what the lack of time was costing her: she would, she told the agent, "pay a dollar for a dress for one of little girls and could make two better dresses for a dollar's worth of material."[24] Other women made dresses only when they were too short of money to buy them. A young Jewish knit-goods worker told the agent, "When I get the money, I buy dresses."[25] Sewing machines sat squarely at the intersection of time and money. A machine obviously increased productivity. A Philadelphia woman cited the lack of a machine as the reason she didn't sew; she did, however, she told the Women's Bureau agent, bake cakes.[26] One woman with a "good Singer machine" made all of her own and her grandchildren's clothing,[27] but a deserted mother of four eked out a miserable living as a rag picker and had to do all her family's sewing by hand.[28] There were limits to what a machine could do to ease a busy woman's life. An exasperated cigar maker bemoaned the fact that she had no time to use her sewing machine.[29] The family's capital investment in the machine was worthless without the time to use it. Women's Bureau agents kept an eye out for household appliances, but since the schedules did not ask specifically about them there is no way to know how consistently they reported them. Still, it is noteworthy that in the 1887 households visited for the studies of Philadelphia immigrant women and women in meatpacking and slaughtering, investigators noted only six sewing machines.[30] Two women did all of their own sewing—one of them "a great deal" of it—by hand.[31]

The many women who bought clothing, particularly that which was more difficult to sew satisfactorily, still spent parsimoniously. A single Philadelphia clothing worker in her late 20s was working hard to support her frail parents and shopped carefully for her dresses. The Women's Bureau agent noted that she "had on a good one from Gimbels—on sale $8."[32] A young divorced Philadelphia woman, back in her parents' home, worriedly rehearsed her budget to the agent; after she paid her $4.50 board to her parents, $9.50 remained to her, "very little . . . to buy clothes with. Can't get shoes for less than $6 or a coat for less than $5 and wanted to buy a new coat this winter but hasn't been able to get enough money together."[33] A study of the families of unionized Houston workers during the Depression argued that economic hardship had "cut most deeply into the expenditure for clothing."[34]

The Philadelphia women who continued to do their own washing even when too pressed to sew reflect women's less frequent recourse to paid laundry services than to store-bought clothes and bread. Relatively few studies offer a systematic view of sewing and laundry practices. During the 1920s, one in five or fewer working-class women appear to have used commercial laundries: only 15 percent of the Philadelphia immigrant women, 20 percent of the meatpackers, and 17 percent of wage-earning mothers in Philadelphia in Gwendolyn Hughes's study.[35] By contrast, a 1930 study of San Diego Mexican families found that despite "their relatively low incomes and native customs" three times as large a proportion used commercial laundries, about four in ten regularly and another two in ten occasionally.[36] The readier recourse to laundries among the Mexican families probably grew out of a complex convergence of factors. Wage-earning probably did not make the difference: 44 of the San Diego Mexican women were in the labor force, albeit on an "irregular, part-time" basis,"[37] but wage-earning was universal among the women surveyed by the Women's Bureau and by Gwendolyn Hughes. Neither the lack of household infrastructure nor the weather provides an explanation, as all the Mexican homes had running water, compared to about seven eighths of the households in the Hughes study,[38] and the San Diego climate was far milder than in other areas surveyed and would have made washing and hanging clothes outside relatively pleasant.

Four more likely explanations help to account for the difference. Between the 1919 Hughes study and the 1930 Heller Committee interviews, laundries expanded their more affordable services such as "wet wash,"[39] giving women an alternative to the high prices of fully finished laundry. Second, the San Diego women appear to have chosen to sew rather than to wash: eight of ten families (79) had sewing machines, five of them electric, a far higher proportion than in the two Women's Bureau studies.[40] Third, it may have been those so-called "native customs" that predisposed Mexican women to use laundries: the authors of the Heller/Panunzio report argued that women were unfamiliar with laundries because they were not common in Mexico, but it could have been precisely the novelty of them that made them more attractive. Finally, the San Diego families studied spent relatively little on fuel. Wood stoves were fixtures of their households, even when they had access to piped gas and electricity, and nearly half the families got free wood, either by "gathering it along the tracks or the beach or . . . from yards and shops where they worked."[41] In addition, the families were, according to the authors of the study, "exceedingly careful in not wasting gas" and "not infrequently baking is done on a communal basis by groups of families."[42] Money not spent on utilities may have gone for laundry services. The example of the San Diego Mexican families offers a glimpse into the complexity of the family economy and the wide range of factors that helped to shape market choices.

The Women's Bureau investigators who visited Oklahoma wage-earning women in 1924 for some reason paid particular attention to laundry, and their comments on five white women reveal the range of women's laundry practices and the mixed economy of home and commercial laundry. The hardest-pressed was shut out of the commercial market entirely: a single mother with five children devoted her Sundays to her washing because she could not "afford to hire any done, or to lay off any time during [the] week."[43] Two others paid to have their laundry done, one in an apparent trade-off for the effort it took to keep a boarder and the other because she was simply overwhelmed. The first, a widow with a high-school age son and a boarder, did all her own housework except for the laundry.[44] The second, a deserted woman with two teenagers, did a great deal of her housework in the evenings after work but took her laundry to a washerwoman—not to the laundry where she worked—because she "just [couldn't] manage that."[45] In between these were two women who paid for some but not all laundry services, washing the more delicate items at home and leaving the heavier work to the laundry. A single mother of three daughters had "most of the washing done but was washing some dresses for the little girls Sun[day] morning, as the laundry is so hard on them. Washes some of her own dresses too."[46] A widow with two woman boarders took off Monday mornings from work to do the smaller pieces of her laundry, but had the large pieces washed at a discount at the commercial laundry where she worked, using the company's pressing machines to iron them "before or after hours or at lunch time."[47] Among them, these five women ran the gamut of laundry decisions, from relying entirely on the marketplace, to picking and choosing among services, to rejecting paid laundry services for one reason or another. When times were hard, giving up paid laundry services was one of the first ways to economize. The wife of a Philadelphia roofer told a settlement worker, "When [my husband is] working steady, I can just manage, but when he's out, things go back. First I stop on the damp wash, then on the food and then the rent goes behind."[48] In a family economy with uncertain income and unpredictable demands, the ability of households to substitute family labor for market transactions in clothing and laundry was an important source of flexibility.

The more systematic information in the Women's Bureau studies of Philadelphia immigrant women and Midwestern meatpackers offers a more detailed view of the use of commercial laundry services. Only 3.5 percent of the total paid to have all their washing and ironing done by others;[49] these women numbered about a quarter of those who spent any money at all on laundry services. Most relied on commercial laundries but some of them hired washwomen, lodgers, or their landladies to do the work. Nearly half of those who spent to have any laundry done had it partially done on a "wet wash" or "rough dry" basis, utilizing the partial services offered by commercial laundries, beginning in 1910 and becoming widespread during the 1920s. The great irony is that these services, which so relieved the home-front burden on working-class women, were laundry entrepreneurs' efforts to cut costs by "eliminat[ing] marking, sorting, and ironing—labor-intensive processes carried out by relatively well-paid workers."[50] While as consumers they might benefit from cheap "wet wash" services, as workers they faced the same relentless cost-cutting pressures on their own wages. About one in six of the laundry spenders sent only part of their wash out—flat pieces, heavy pieces, or large pieces—and the remaining one in eight used laundry services sporadically, usually according to the weather (doing the laundry in winter without adequate facilities was especially grueling),[51] shifts in their economic fortunes,[52] and their health.[53] Fully three-quarters of those who devoted some of the family fund to buying laundry services still did some of the laundry, at least some of the time, and did the bulk of the ironing themselves. That commercial laundries could conflict with women's sense of the proper and appropriate is shown by the occasional remarks about the toll that laundries took on clothing.[54] A Philadelphian did all her own washing "because I've worked in a laundry and have seen what's done there!"[55] Other women expressed an artisanal consciousness about housework that conflicted with the industrial quality of commercial laundries; one Philadelphian did her own wash because "no one does wash to suit me so I do it myself."[56]

Another way to explore the use of cash to replace household work is to look at those women in these two studies who routinely bought both clothes and laundry services. Forty-nine fell into this category, three of whom received laundry services as part of their boarding arrangements.[57] The other forty-six might be generally described as among the more economically successful and, more important, economically self-confident. The median earnings of the women who paid for laundry services exceeded the median of those visited by $1.40 per week, or nearly 10 percent, and they were more than half again as likely to earn over $20 per week as all the women visited; by contrast, their husbands' earnings (less frequently reported) were just at the men's median earnings. Members of this group owned or were buying their homes at a higher rate: four in ten as compared to about one in four for all Philadelphia women visited. But a less readily quantifiable characteristic also seems to have motivated these women and their families to spend scarce cash to ease women's burdens: the women were in families that seemed to be particularly enterprising and inclined to take charge of a situation rather than let it take charge of them. Elizabeth, a Polish immigrant Philadelphia hosiery topper, earned the remarkable wage of $35.00 per week, 80 percent higher than the median for her occupation; her husband, as an upholstery weaver, almost certainly earned more than the median Philadelphia male textile worker's wage of $27.00. Their income was handsome indeed in comparison to other families visited, but they had five sons to support and a mother-in-law to whom they probably had some obligations. Elizabeth had consciously sought out a high-paying occupation and was working to pay for and improve the family's six-room house. Her husband was also a paperhanger and used his skills both to decorate the house and to earn extra money by moonlighting. Tellingly, the sons told the agent that they wanted to follow their mother into the hosiery industry.[58] Mercie and her husband, African American meatpacking workers in Chicago, together earned between $38 and $50 per week, depending on his seasonal wages;[59] Mercie also provided for the needs of two lodgers. They and their two schoolboy sons, like the majority of the Chicago families visited, lived in a rented apartment; theirs, a five-room "good apartment & modern" with central heating and a bathroom,[60] was both larger and less crowded than the majority of the Chicago families' residences. Mercie told the agent that she wanted to "live well" and was willing to pay an astounding $80 monthly rent, a figure that was probably inflated both by the amenities of the apartment and the "race tax" paid by African American families in the rental market. Despite the heavy burden of rent and worries about her husband's irregular wages, Mercie still did no sewing except mending and sent her laundry out for "rough dry," a step beyond wet wash in that it ironed flatwork and dried and starched clothing.[61] Anna, a Polish widow also working in a Chicago meatpacking plant, had managed to keep her three teenagers in school at an age when many were already in the workforce or staying home to take charge of housework; she had kept the family's head above water on a wage of about $22 a week. Her seventeen-year-old son proudly reported to the agent: "Everything paid for on time. Never late." Anna did little sewing and paid for wet wash services at the laundry.[62] Small signs, these, but they offer a glimpse of women and families who exerted a control, however tenuous, over their economic lives, one aspect of which was to ease the woman householder's load with purchased services, a sign of respect and acknowledgment of her work.

Families also purchased washing machines and irons to ease the burdens of laundry. Machines did some of the heavier work of washing clothing, but left much to be done by hand. Machines of the 1920s and 1930s required continual attention for filling, emptying, and the wringing of clothing, work that women were spared by commercial laundries. Machines may have raised the standards of cleanliness for clothing and actually have increased women's work, as Ruth Schwartz Cowan has argued, but there is no evidence that the women in these studies perceived them that way; this effect may have been felt more by the middle class during the interwar period.[63] An electric washing machine was a substantial investment, with the least expensive, those requiring more attention and labor from the user, running around $60 during the 1920s and about $30 by the mid-1930s.[64] Few working-class families could buy washing machines for cash, given a price that was more than most working couples earned in a week, and most probably turned to installment purchase. Despite the cost and the limitations of the affordable technology, a washing machine might supplement or replace the labor of an ill or disabled woman householder, as appeared to be the case in an Omaha family headed by an ailing widow who had two wage-earning daughters and three more children under the age of eight.[65] Even in families with straitened circumstances, a washing machine might rank as a necessity. An Italian immigrant laborer in Wisconsin insisted on keeping up the payments on the family's washing machine despite his unemployment, a house described as "bare," mounting debts, and pressing needs for clothing and health care. As he told a settlement worker, "with four children there are a lot of clothes to wash and the work is too hard for my wife."[66] Husbands with mechanical skills could limit the cash outlay for a machine by improvising one, as did a Philadelphia man who made a water-powered machine that could be attached to the hydrant in the yard. This husband was a poor earner, often ill and seasonally out of work, but he earned the label of "helpful" with housework.[67] Some families, like that of the Wisconsin laborer, appear to have purchased washing machines because of the workload involved with a family of young children; the family with the water-powered machine had children aged two and six. The investment in a washing machine paid off in the short run if it enabled a mother of young children to earn wages. A Philadelphia family had three primary school children but also an ambitious pair of parents willing to take some risks for the future: they had undertaken to buy a house even though the husband was still a pipefitting and plumbing trainee. The wife, eager to have a more comfortable material life and to educate the children, went to work in a hosiery factory and was earning the handsome wage of $33. "Head over heels in debt," they had nonetheless purchased an electric washing machine.[68] Although the Women's Bureau agent did not comment on the quality of this family's house and furnishings, agents often commented favorably on the homes of those who had washing machines, nine out of twelve of whom were buying their homes or owned them outright: one had a "very good house" that the family had built itself;[69] another a "very well furnished" house with central heating and modern plumbing;[70] another had a "very good cottage—well furnished and in A-1 repair," including a bathroom and a furnace.[71] The exception to this picture of washing machines churning away in relatively comfortable homes was that of a three-room "bare" cottage in "poor repair" that sheltered two married couples and a total of four children; in this case, the washing machine had been brought from Kentucky by one of the couples, apparently their only possession of any value.[72] They were not the only ones to see a washing machine as a capital investment, and families were aware that they could raise cash by selling a machine in the secondhand market.

At Second Hand: Clothing, Furniture and Tools

Working-class family economies in the United States of the interwar period depended heavily on secondhand goods as one of many expedients to stretch insufficient resources. Used items could offer an indirect entry to consumer culture, stretch a tight budget to supply comforts not otherwise available, provide both investment and use value, and enhance wage-earning possibilities. Three main streams of circulation of secondhand goods deserve attention: clothing, primarily for direct use; household goods, such as furniture, which served as investment goods; and tools that helped in making a living.

By far the broadest and deepest of the circulating streams of used items was that of clothing, which appeared universally in all times, places, and sources, and was segmented by gender and generation. Secondhand clothing was both a finished product and a raw material, with women diligently repairing and refashioning used clothing into garments that fit the wearer and the current fashion. Used clothing came from myriad sources: secondhand clothing dealers, family, friends, employers, teachers, and non-profit organizations' rummage sales.[73] Even the poorest, eager to help kin or friends, might be able to offer a bit of used clothing when they could afford no other assistance.[74] My sources privilege transactions outside the commercial market; dealers in used clothing make no more than a cameo appearance. Therefore much of the discussion of such clothing belongs to chapter 4 in which the focus is on mutual support and reciprocity among working-class families. However, the ways that secondhand clothing influenced the consumption choices of families left it enmeshed in market choices and central also to this chapter's dramas.[75]

Secondhand clothing stretched tight budgets a crucial bit further. A study of electricians and longshoremen in Houston revealed that "the depression-era economy seems to have cut most deeply into the expenditure for clothing." Among their replies to questions about clothing expenditure were: "Damn little this year" and "Furnished by someone else."[76] As we've seen, the value of clothing rested almost entirely in its use rather than in its potential to raise cash. The desperate Utah family disappointed in their attempts to raise cash by selling their used clothing—they learned that "they have little of value"[77]—nonetheless benefited greatly from the used clothes that they received as gifts and bought at rummage sales. Such were the economies of buying secondhand garments that this family of eight, including six children aged two through seventeen, spent a total of $10 per year on clothing and relied on the mother of the family to make over what little they bought. But even for those doing relatively well, secondhand clothing freed up scarce cash for things that mattered most; one African American family bought most of its clothes at Goodwill (a nonprofit outlet similar to the Salvation Army) except for "Sunday best" and shoes.[78] In a study of San Diego Mexicans, two of the three families who spent the most (between two and three times the median expenditure) on clothing also received gifts of used clothing. Since these families ranked in the top income quintile of those interviewed, the example defies easy assumptions that used clothing always flowed to the poorest.[79]

Clothes donated by employers, which might be seen as badges of humiliation and were entirely unacceptable as a substitute for wages, might be eagerly received when they were of high quality and in near-new condition.[80] One young woman wrote about her happy relationship with an employer's wife: "His wife became interested in me and gave me her daughter's cast-off clothes which, made over, made me some of the prettiest clothes that I have ever had."[81] A complicated path of circulation is suggested by the comment of a Connecticut woman frantic to outfit her daughter for school:

> "Finally in desperation I wrote to a friend who used to work for a 'rich lady.' This friend used to send pretty things to Virginia but has not done so recently. I don't know whether she is still working for that lady, but if she is, I guess she won't mind my writing."[82]

This incident is one of the few in which we know who initiated the exchange, the giver or the recipient.

The vast majority of secondhand garments, as we have seen, were women's and children's; adult men's clothing appears infrequently.[83] This was partly for material reasons: men's work clothing and suits were likely to be worn until threadbare, with the best clothing moving into everyday use as it wore out. Cultural factors probably figured in as well. Men's fashions changed little during these decades, and so men had little incentive to replace serviceable clothing with new versions of the same styles. Husbands' clothing didn't catch the attention of most women interviewed; women typically mention that they purchased their own and their children's clothing, omitting mention of men's, or that men purchased their own clothing out of spending money they withheld from the family fund.[84] As a result, women apparently had limited opportunities to contribute their husbands' clothing to the secondhand stream and they and their children reaped most of the benefits from used clothing.

A generational dimension was involved as well. In most cases, siblings or parents gave the clothing to the woman householder, who distributed it within the family and remodeled and repaired it as her skills, time, resources, and inclination allowed. A few intriguing cases, however, show how secondhand clothing could become implicated in intergenerational conflict. A young woman whom we know only as Mary struggled with her very traditional Polish-immigrant parents over her use of makeup, her interest in clothing (her mother felt that "clothes [. . .] was a sin."), and her disobedience. She finally quit school and took a job as a domestic servant. As a YWCA worker reported, "The woman who employs her gave her some of her pretty dresses and this convinced Mrs. M. [her mother] that Mary was working for a person who was leading her astray."[85] In this case, the parents' fears about their daughter were justified: she became an occasional prostitute. In many families, young women could look only to hand-me-downs for the clothing they craved; the ways in which these goods could become entangled in complicated family dynamics are shown by the tale of a fourteen-year-old Chicagoan, the daughter of Polish immigrants who were tolerant of her aspirations even though they could not afford them.

> Friction between the mother and child has arisen because the mother is unable to give the girl money for the little things she wants and should have. Many irritating and distressing incidents have occurred because of the shortage of money. For instance, the child's shoes were worn out and beyond repair. For several weeks she wore galoshes until they too gave out. Desperate, Mrs. Topolski walked several miles to the home of a relative for aid and this sister gathered up all the shoes of her sixteen-year-old daughter that she could spare. The visitor found Mrs. Topolski at home, surrounded by twenty-five worn-out, high-heeled slippers, figuring on how to get one pair of shoes out of the mess for Angeline. The girl came running in full of hope, and burst into tears at the sight.[86]

A mother's frustrations and hopes, a daughter's resentments and desires, all come into sharp focus around that pile of secondhand shoes. The peer cultures of the high schools that more and more working-class children were attending during the interwar years placed a high value on fashionable clothing, and young women felt this pressure especially keenly. In one touching case, the peer group helped out one of its own to meet group standards: when a Minneapolis high-school girl wanted "to dress up better her friends give her clothes; one girl gives her a coat and another a dress and so on."[87]

Gender and generation figured less prominently in the circulation of secondhand furniture. As might be imagined, adults made the decisions about the disposition of household goods, and husbands and wives seem to have done so together as part of joint economic strategizing. Although working-class families gained almost entirely as the recipients of secondhand clothing, they benefited from being on both the demand and the supply sides of the circulation of secondhand furniture. Consider the case of the Faileys, a Louisville, Kentucky, family with five school-age children and a father skilled both in carpentry and plumbing who had been fortunate enough to secure year-round employment. At their most prosperous, they had a home "better furnished even than one would expect in the circumstances," but during Mr. Failey's second winter of unemployment they finally had to sell the furniture "bit by bit to purchase food." After a series of crises, Mrs. Failey began to refurbish the smaller quarters to which they had moved with secondhand furniture from Goodwill Industries.[88] As the Faileys' fortunes plummeted, they first contributed to and then purchased from the stream of secondhand furniture, in both cases doing better than they would otherwise have done.

Unlike clothing, which kin and friends exchanged without the mediation of cash, most furniture circulated in the cash market. Household goods figured but rarely in exchanges among friends and kin. Among the few examples was a Mexican family previously mentioned who moved from California to San Antonio and received a houseful of furniture (beds excepted) from friends.[89] In Depression-era Connecticut, investigators found that more families sold furniture than added to their stock, but those who did the latter mostly did so through gifts from friends or kin.[90] In most cases, however, furniture was bought and sold for cash, as families rarely had enough extra furniture to share or the financial security to forego the money they could gain from its sale. My sources are mute about whether furniture was being sold to dealers or to other families, but they do show that the purchase of secondhand furniture, especially on installment payments, was an important money-saving strategy. One Kansas City meatpacker, for example, paid off her used furniture at the rate of two or three dollars a month, whereas those who bought new furniture usually paid more than that every week.[91] Buying secondhand furniture did not necessarily mean buying second-rate furniture, for furniture loomed large in a family's investments and was often well cared for, moving into the used-furniture market in good condition.

As an investment, furniture was likely to be sold when times were hard or when the capital tied up in it could be better used elsewhere. The use of household goods in this fashion suggests the tenuousness of ownership of valuable goods such as furniture, jewelry, and automobiles. The working-class acquisition of such items was not a steady process of accretion but a cyclical one in which goods acquired during good times had to be sold or pawned in bad times. In some cases, the secondhand market offered the primary entry into higher-end consumption. The emergence of a market in used automobiles during the 1920s, for example, gave many working-class families their only access to this icon of mass consumption; twenty-four of twenty-six San Diego Mexican families owning cars, for example, had bought them second hand.[92]

Selling household goods met many different types of family emergencies. Proceeds from the sale of $500 worth of furniture, for example, cushioned the slide of a Mexican immigrant from skilled auto painting to chronic unemployment, providing cash to feed his family as debt mounted for rent, medicine, and utilities.[93] Thrown out of work by technology, a Pittsburgh pipe-cutter and his family struck out in a new direction by opening a grocery business financed in part by the sale of their living-room furniture. The business failed, and they lost their remaining furniture; the bare necessities of furniture that they then bought on the installment plan were later repossessed, "leaving only mattresses, broken chairs, and a hot plate."[94] Three times this family entered the trade in secondhand furniture, but only once from a position of comparative power. A Wisconsin Quebecois family sold its $1,100 (about half a year's pay for the carpenter father) worth of furniture to finance its move to Minneapolis for a new start.[95] When another family's only wage earner was injured on a foot press, the family sold its furniture to get along until she had recovered.[96] A Massachusetts family was able to keep its house only because the bank that held its mortgage allowed them to suspend payments in exchange for a lien on their furniture.[97] Even when a family moved before destitution set in, they might have had to contribute their furniture to the secondhand market if they were buying it on installments, as dealers often refused to allow debtors to move their purchases any distance.[98]

The sale of furniture certainly involved heavy economic costs, since families sold as used what they had bought as new, but it also involved psychic costs. When pushed, families tended to sell the more luxurious—and often most expensive—pieces first; pianos and Victrolas were often the first household items to go, followed by parlor furniture.[99] Far from a simple matter of selling off non-essentials, the sale of these items often cut deeply into the family's sense of itself. One New Haven, Connecticut, man ruefully told an interviewer: "You didn't buy a piano and victrola just to have them, you know. Now us—we bought them to keep the children happy and at home. When you sell—you sell those things that are a part of you."[100] Selling furniture as part of breaking up housekeeping was an unsettling ordeal. A Kentucky woman confided to a settlement-house worker: "I hated to part with my furniture; I didn't know when I'd ever get as nice again, but we had to sell it all, even my folding bed." She and her family first lived with her parents but soon "wore out [their] welcome" and ended up in furnished rooms, a sorry comedown from the snug little cottage they had once owned.[101] Adding to the distress was the fact that families, once having made the painful decision to sell, sometimes had difficulty in finding a buyer at a reasonable price; the Vanzettis, a Philadelphia family, had given up their flat and gone to live with Mrs. Vanzetti's mother, but failed to sell their dining room furniture.[102]

Furniture bridged the gap between those secondhand items which had use and investment value and those that might be used in wage earning. An Oklahoma widow filled a rented house with furniture and built up a thriving business taking in boarders, but when the house was sold she had to sell her sizable stock of furniture "at a loss."[103] On other side of the fence was a Rochester, New York, woman whose husband was chronically unemployed. They had had to sell their furniture but were saving to buy more, presumably secondhand, so that the woman could "take roomers."[104] Evidence about the role of furniture in wage earning is anecdotal, but one source offers remarkable detail about the use of used sewing machines, a common household item that could easily do double duty in making over secondhand clothing and earning cash. In 1933, Women's Bureau agents visited 305 upstate New York women doing industrial homework on leather gloves.[105] Their interview notes tell us that forty-one women, or nearly one in eight, used secondhand tools in their work; an additional woman had sold her old machine to another homeworker. The interview schedule did not specifically ask about secondhand equipment, and so these machines were probably only the tip of the iceberg of a flourishing market in used capital equipment. About six in ten of the women had purchased their used machines, although it is impossible to know if they did so from other workers, from manufacturers selling off old-model machines, or from commercial dealers. The other four in ten reported that they had received their equipment as gifts or had borrowed it. The cash market in used equipment, then, accounted for only 60 percent of the transactions; as with hand-me-down clothing, although to a less dramatic degree, a substantial stream of secondhand items circulated outside the cash market.

In all, fifty used items were mentioned: thirty-three machines, fifteen motors, and two tables. The predominance of machines over motors can probably be attributed to the durability of the basic sewing machine; carefully maintained, as these interviews testify that they were, a machine could last many decades. Motors, on the other hand, were less readily tinkered with by the homeworkers and more prone to burning out. Tables probably figured relatively little in the secondhand trade because they could be re-used with new machines or turned to entirely different purposes if the owner ceased to work at sewing. These items figured differently into the different sectors of the market—cash purchases, gifts, and loans. Machines were most likely to be conveyed definitively: all but four were bought or received as gifts. About half (seven) of the motors and both of the tables, on the other hand, were borrowed, presumably with the idea that they would someday be returned to the lender. Presumably, motors were regarded as too valuable and tables as too enduringly useful to be given as readily as machines. The non-cash transactions in used sewing equipment were largely among kin (eleven of the sixteen exchanges involved family members, three were among friends, and two were unspecified), among women (nine of the donors or loaners were women, and the sex of five was unspecified), and intergenerational (the nine female kin donors or loaners included four mothers-in-law, three mothers, and an aunt, but only one sister).

These transactions were embedded in larger networks of reciprocity and exchange, another aspect of the pattern of mutual assistance among women that we observed in the case of hand-me-down clothing and that has been more broadly found in a wide variety of times and places. The intergenerational aspect is especially intriguing, suggesting a familial culture of industrial homework in which older women either gave their used equipment to younger kin when they bought new machinery or passed along their equipment when they retired from the trade. One mother, for example, was buying herself a new machine on installments for $158.50 and turned her old one over to her eighteen-year-old daughter, not only passing along the machine but also training her in the skills of glove making.[106]

Although the Women's Bureau agents did not record homeworkers' comments on the meaning of this secondhand equipment to them, their dire circumstances suggest that it was crucially important. One woman who worked with a secondhand machine and motor supported herself and her two children entirely on industrial homework after her husband died; the availability of used equipment surely eased her transition to a very different life.[107] Another woman working with a secondhand machine and a borrowed motor had a similarly difficult situation: her husband had been unemployed for nine months, her two working children were unable to support the family, and she had to turn to glove making even though she was "sick and [it was] hard for her to work."[108] Even for those in less desperate straits, used equipment served a variety of pressing needs. The mother of an eighteen-month-old daughter was working on a machine and motor loaned by her mother-in-law until her child was old enough for her to return to the factory.[109] The daughter of a blind woman who could not be left alone worked at home on a secondhand machine and motor.[110] Unlike many varieties of women's wage-earning, industrial homework on gloves required a capital investment, and secondhand equipment dramatically lowered the cost of entry.

Men, too, took advantage of secondhand tools in their wage-earning efforts, but because my sources privilege the female perspective, I can offer only a few tantalizing examples of men both drawing on and contributing to the circulation of used goods. In Depression-era New Haven, Connecticut, a man laid off from a lucrative job as a munitions worker bought a used truck for $15.00, overhauled it, and replaced its body and cab, and set out on a successful new career as a hauler.[111] A Philadelphia man who used his truck to moonlight on hauling jobs had to sell it, adding to the secondhand stream, when he lost his principal job and could no longer afford the $10 monthly garage rent.[112] Other sources might well illuminate men's participation in the circulation of capital goods: we can imagine some men purchasing the tools of their trade from those leaving the field or from elderly retiring workers, and other men inheriting both tools and skills from their fathers.

The importance of secondhand goods in all three streams of circulation—clothing, furniture, and tools—suggests that we cannot fully understand working-class family economies without taking such practices into account. Nor, for that matter, can we understand the culture of consumption and its continuing connections to home production. The dense circulation of secondhand clothing allowed women to use their domestic skills to fashion clothing that they could never have afforded new and to outfit themselves and their children in current styles. Clothing had long been a badge of status, but became even more so in the interwar period when the mass production of fashionable goods raised the bar for public appearance; access to secondhand clothing made it possible for those who could not buy directly into this world to participate in it nonetheless. The flourishing market in used furniture allowed working-class families to play both sides of the street as sellers and buyers. Furniture provided an investment that paid dividends in its use and in the enjoyment of it, and it could also be sold to realize needed cash. Families could enjoy, even if only briefly, the pleasures of an overstuffed parlor set or a piano or a Victrola and hope, once they had to be sold, to acquire similar items again when things looked up. Their contributions to the market in used household goods provided opportunities for other families to buy needed and desired items at less than full retail prices. The third stream of circulation, that of goods that could be used in wage-earning, was a key element in helping working-class families to expand their slender budgets by allowing them to acquire low-cost capital goods to enter a variety of pursuits either as wage earners, in the case of the industrial homeworkers, or as independent entrepreneurs, like the women who took in boarders and the men who engaged in hauling. And finally, the circulation of used clothing and of used capital goods shows the continued importance of ties of mutuality outside the cash market and of the ways in which those ties could be used to open small doors into the world of mass consumption for working-class families in the interwar period.

Installment Credit and Negotiating the Market Place

The rationalized budgeted family economy, mediated by installment debt and vividly evoked from different points of view by Lee Rainwater and Lendol Calder,[113] penetrated only shallowly into the world of the working class as it is revealed in my sources. Two factors account for this. First, the labor market in which wage-earners toiled remained highly unrationalized in the interwar period and failed to provide the kind of dependable steady income that would enable families to systematize their expenditures. Second, the more regularized granters of credit such as personal finance companies and the larger installment sellers preferred to extend their services to those who were, by and large, wealthier than those whose lives are documented in my sources. Instead, families devised market relationships that met their particular and changing needs: sending laundry out when women were employed and doing it at home when they were laid off; buying furniture at prosperous moments from small local merchants who were flexible about payment schedules and reselling it in leaner times. Book credit for food was common, as was relying on the good will of landlords when the rent was late. But what emerges in the lives of these families is not the embrace of credit but the rejection of it, a rejection rooted not in moralism but in savvy understanding of their world. Credit was dangerous rather than evil and by and large worked against the interests of the debtor. Resorting to it was not a choice so much as a necessity, a way of maintaining the usual activities of life in the face of what was typically a roller-coaster of good and bad times or, even worse, a steady slide downward. A Rumanian immigrant captured the uncertainties of working-class market life when she told a Women's Bureau agent of her hopes to soon pay off the mortgage on the family house if she could get work.[114]

Chapter 3 looked at homeowning as a key piece of a larger pattern of sharing resources among working-class families, but homeowning had other powerful appeals. A well-located home could ease wage earners' daily lives and save the time, the cost, and the wear and tear of a long journey to work; the family of a Philadelphia machine knitter was saving to buy a home near his factory in Germantown.[115] Aesthetic considerations motivated others. A Polish immigrant working in food processing saw homeowning as a way to have more pleasant and comfortable surroundings; the

Women's Bureau agent quoted her as saying, "Want my home, not stay in hole like here."[116] A German immigrant expressed a wish "to have schoene haus"[117] and an Italian immigrant dreamed of "a bungalow in [the] suburbs."[118] Buying a house could offer some stability and security in an uncertain economy. Homeowning had an enduring appeal as old-age security; a Philadelphia clothing worker in her late teens disclaimed any ambitions for herself but wanted "to buy a home for my parents—they're getting old now. It looks far off on my salary."[119] But the goal of homeowning could have a powerful generational element as well. As mentioned above, after an Ohio woman lost her finger in a work accident, her mother, taking advantage of the daughter's minority and minimizing the seriousness of her loss, paid about half of her compensation on the house the family was buying, telling an investigator, "She would only spend it on clothes."[120] A paid-off mortgage lifted the pressing obligation of monthly rent and provided an element of predictability in tight and unstable budgets; the mother of an African American widow supporting a household of six said to the Women's Bureau agent, "if we had to pay rent, I don't know how we'd live."[121] Such security did not necessarily bring comfort with it: the woman's house, though large, was described as being "in poor repair" and had an outside privy. Owning a house meant a certain geographic stability, savored by the South St. Paul woman who told the agent "we don't have to keep moving."[122] Residential continuity wasn't the only way in which this woman tried to bring order to her life; we encountered her earlier as the woman who baked her own bread and tried out her own lard. Paying off a mortgage, however, could be a will-o'-the-wisp. Such was the experience of a New Jersey woman who was injured in an industrial accident just as she and her husband were on the verge of paying off their mortgage; medical bills and the loss of income precipitated them back into deep debt.[123] An Omaha family, aware of the possibility of losing their house, refrained from improving or painting it until it was paid for.[124]

The racial politics of American real estate practices, as refracted in one Omaha neighborhood, point up the mixed results of strategies for homeowning security. Kate, an Omaha sausage-maker, was bursting with pride over her house but feared for her family's substantial investment in it. They had bought it as "not much more than a shack" and spent over half again as much "repairing it, putting in furnace, bath, electricity and raising it on to a new foundation"; but by the time the Women's Bureau agent visited, they were worried that the move of African Americans into the neighborhood was undermining the house's value.[125] A Croatian immigrant, Kate, was in peril of having to pay the price of what David Roediger and James

Barrett have referred to as the "in-between" racial status of southern and eastern European immigrants.[126] Real-estate entrepreneurs inflamed whites' racial fears and induced them to sell property at rock-bottom prices, reselling it at inflated prices to African Americans. The investment of Kate's family was indeed at risk from such tactics, but her Black neighbors were not to blame. The tale of Virgie, a nearby African American neighbor, shows that African American migrants and eastern European immigrants shared both aspirations and material status. Virgie and her family were buying a house barely a block away from Kate's—a five-room cottage described as being in good condition.[127] With six children to Kate's four, and living on less money (Kate and Virgie probably earned about the same wages,[128] but Virgie's husband probably earned only about two-thirds what Kate's did), Virgie and her family had not been able to improve the cottage and still used an outside privy, as did about two-thirds of the families visited in their six-by-seven-block neighborhood. Virgie was the only African American visited who was buying her house in the neighborhood, and her experience resonates with Kate's in ways that might have transcended race. As relative newcomers to Omaha, both families had gone into debt for furniture as well as for their houses—Kate's family owed $150 for a parlor set and a radio, and Virgie's $200 for unspecified furniture. Both were committed to the neighborhood. Kate's family had signified its desire to put down roots by its investment in the house. Virgie's family had come from Oklahoma three years before the agent's visit and "felt that they had done pretty well—better off than they would be there" and Virgie's husband was "anxious to get [the] house paid for." Their neighborhood was an area in transition, physically as well as racially: the houses of families visited ranged from small, dilapidated places without plumbing (though the agents labeled only African American-occupied dwellings as "shacks") to Kate's spiffy modernized home. In another world, Kate and Virgie could have made common cause in building a solid improving neighborhood instead of being pitted against each other in the struggle for security in a racialized economy.

The economics of class weighed as heavily on working-class families as did those of race. The anchor of property could restrict as well as stabilize. A Chicago woman was disillusioned with her family's two-unit dwelling: the apartment was often vacant and the taxes and special assessments were a heavy burden. She hoped, she told the agent, to sell the house, having decided "it doesn't pay to own."[129] A Kansas City woman, plagued by family health problems and embittered by a daughter's ingratitude, numbered her house among her many trials: "bought this house, roof leak, then floor rotten, fix me floor, then other bad, all the time some thing."[130] Not surprisingly given their limited financial resources, working-class families often, like this woman, had no choice but to purchase houses that demanded continuing effort and investment. A Chicago family was paying $79 per month on their home's mortgage and new roof, taking the lion's share of the husband's wage of $22 per week;[131] a Philadelphia clothing worker, whose parents were paying a mortgage on a six-room house, complained that "It's a house that takes every cent."[132] Unexpected expenses repeatedly competed with the mortgage payment for a share of the family fund: illness and accidents[133] could put homeowning in peril. Buying a house was a long-term project in family economies that existed very much in the short term because of the unsteadiness of employment and the variability of income. An African American hotel maid in Oklahoma learned this when her husband lost his job just after they bought a house.[134] A widowed Czech immigrant in Omaha, struggling to support five children and an aged mother, opined that she thought "it better to rent" because the upkeep on her house was a continuing burden.[135] Home ownership was within the grasp of women on their own. A Georgia textile worker, widowed nineteen years, "has brought up 2 daughters, bought a lot and built a house with savings."[136]

Taxes burdened home buyers and owners heavily. Two elderly Chicago couples had managed to pay off their mortgages but their wage-earning children were so hard pressed to support the families that they had to borrow to pay the taxes.[137] In December 1932 and January 1933 Women's Bureau agents interviewed 107 District of Columbia families, 44 of them African American, whose tax delinquency had been published.[138] Twenty-four of the families displayed some degree of indifference to paying their taxes and to the potential loss of their houses, and the agents judged that in fifteen other cases "other desires [took] precedence." Those other desires might include Christmas presents[139] or "unnecessary expensive improvements" to a home where "The *entire* first floor is beautifully panelled, with just the correct kind of electric fixtures"[140] but more often they involved heavy sacrifices, for example, to send a young woman to college,[141] to support destitute boarders who could no longer afford to pay their rent[142] or even buy their food,[143] to provide medical care,[144] or to support kin and friends. A family headed by a white policeman found that it could live better—with all the modern conveniences including an electric refrigerator—by giving up its house and renting an apartment;[145] they were many years away from the post–World War II era when federal mortgage guarantees made it cheaper to own than to rent for many working-class families.[146] Many had made the investment in a house at an untimely moment:

the male insurance agent who bought an old dilapidated house at age fifty-five,[147] or the street-paving foreman's family who bought a house three years before his pay was slashed by half,[148] or the African American couple who were both government workers devastated by pay cuts—as the wife told the agent, they "had a place for each dollar."[149] Many had supported their home-buying efforts by taking in roomers and found that they were unable either to rent the rooms or collect the rent from their roomers once hard times hit. One woman who had pursued this strategy also pointed to the lack of fit between the yearly demand for taxes and the uncertain and irregular income of working-class families: her income from roomers was falling—"all I can get from them is by the dribble"—and she pointed out that "You can't pay taxes when your money comes in that way and your taxes are in the hundreds."[150]

The marketplace was a place of misery and defeat for many. An Atlanta factory worker sagged under the weight of medical bills and winter layoffs, telling the agent that "she has got so far behind financially, that she doesn't know how she will ever catch up."[151] A native-born Kansas City meatpacking worker paid regularly on her food bills but could not get caught up and had to go further into debt to outfit her children for school.[152] The Eastern-European parents of a young Omaha meatpacker were in the same pickle: they described their situation as "almost never caught up—coal—groceries—payment on house—catch up with one, get behind on another."[153] A United States-born Sioux City, Iowa, woman presented a pitiful picture indeed, as the agent's account showed: "Husband left her 'when baby was born.' A very miserable little house, no furniture, small window with glass broken out and rags stuffed in to keep out the cold. Wants to go back to a house she used to live in, but people will not rent to her, she left owing the rent for several months back. Also had so many creditors coming to collect bills that the people don't want her in the house."[154]

Women wore the badges of their defeat on their bodies. A Women's Bureau agent commented about a Georgia textile worker, "She seemed to have been a woman of some education but the hard work and the worry of always being in debt is taking the life and strength out of her. She was wrinkled and bent beyond her years."[155] A St. Louis candy-factory worker catalogued her defeats: a failed teenage marriage, a return to her parents' household and a long struggle to support her mother after her father died, expensive problems with her eyes, saying that "she has nothing to look forward to but 'a struggle to get along the best she can.'"[156] An Atlanta laundry worker resorted to credit not for luxuries but because "she can't make

The Family Economy in the Marketplace **163**

a living and has gone into debt for things she has needed."[157] Women's Bureau agents heard many a tale of the self-denial that debt and low wages could exact. A Georgia woman, for example, moved to Atlanta after her husband's death, taking a room in a women's residence, paying off heavy medical and funeral expenses for her husband and sending money to an invalid aunt. After two weeks in the city, she told the agent, she had "not spent one cent on herself except the $4 a week for room and board," devoting the other $6.30 she earned to paying her debts and supporting her aunt.[158] Perversely, misfortune could produce a windfall. A factory worker sustained a back injury for which she was paid less than $200 in workers' compensation, but that amount enabled her to pay some debts and bring payments on furniture up to date.[159]

Consumer goods that might seem to be evidences of a connection to a consumer culture of pleasure were not always what they seemed to be. An Atlanta widow bought her son a bicycle on the installment plan—not because he wanted to ride for sport but because he needed it for his work with the post office. The story ended badly when the bicycle was stolen, the son lost his job and could not find another, and the mother was saddled with payments on the stolen bike.[160] A Missouri needle-trade worker told a Women's Bureau agent that she worked to make "it possible 'to live,'" by which she meant that she had "clothed family, given some educational advantages to children, paid insurance, [and] kept up home furnishings," while her husband paid for rent and food. Her efforts "to live," however, were undercut by low wages, the high cost of living, and her inability to save.[161]

Clothing, probably for many the most readily available consumer treat, did not always bring consumer pleasure with it. An Atlanta saleswoman, required to dress nicely in the silk department where she worked, ran into debt to her firm and owed $50 when the Women's Bureau agent interviewed her.[162] One can well imagine that she took limited pleasure in the clothing that saddled her with debt. Installment purchases of course entailed higher costs but in combination with other factors they could put consumers in a highly disadvantageous position. Most clerks at an Oklahoma City store bought their work dresses on installments, but the required dark colors were available on installments only in taffeta, a fabric that wore very poorly. One woman complained, "I thought I would never get [the taffeta dress] paid for and now it is splitting so I can't wear it any more"[163]

Good credit and neighborhood connections could be a substantial asset in the working-class family economy. A New Jersey woman who was injured on the job at the same time as her husband was out of work testified that they "had lived in [the] neighborhood some time and [their] credit was good. Otherwise would have had [a] hard time."[164] Nonetheless, most women interviewed saw credit as a trap; we see in these sources only passing glimpses of credit as a road happily taken. One exception would be the 305 glove homeworkers interviewed in upstate New York in the summer of 1933. Many, probably most, of them, had bought their sewing machines on credit, making regular payments on their machines, although one woman had "paid it off in work."[165] For these women, debt was an investment that paid obvious returns in the money they earned with the machines. Even so, the disadvantages of an unregulated credit system appeared in these small towns. One woman, for example, had been buying an electric machine when she became too ill to operate it and "had to trade in p[ay]m[en]ts on it" for a foot-treadle machine "at a big sacrifice."[166]

The Women's Bureau report on slaughtering and meatpacking from 1932 tells us the most about how working-class families viewed credit. The overwhelming impression that we gain from women's responses is one of fear and mistrust. The agents asked "To what extent family has resorted to extended credit for rent, food, clothing, etc.?" Women's Bureau agents recorded comments about debt and credit by about one in ten of the women interviewed. Only one woman said anything at all favorable, a Chicago African American woman who kept two boarders, did all her own laundry, and worked an especially grueling job in a slaughterhouse. She talked happily about the furniture and piano she was buying on installments: "always want to buy a new piece, easy way to buy."[167] This woman probably spoke for many others who were hesitant to admit their material cravings to the agents, possibly because she and her husband, a post office worker, had steady and relatively well-paid jobs and could engage in long-term planning more confidently than most. A Polish immigrant working in the same plant explained what might be called serial installment buying, a conservative engagement with credit that was typical for the women interviewed: she was about to make the final weekly payment on her radio and was looking forward to buying a new stove, also on installments.[168] Another Chicago meatpacker, an African American woman, made explicit the logic behind this strategy: "You have to buy things by the piece cause if you can't pay regular they take your things away."[169] Cementing ownership of one item before taking on indebtedness for another made excellent sense in the unpredictable economy of the working-class family; it was bad enough to have to pay a premium for goods bought on credit, but it would have been even more galling to lose all one had paid if an item were repossessed.

Even so, many felt the temptation of credit, especially when underlined by real need. Many families resorted reluctantly to credit when they had made a move, either to the United States or within the country. Two years after leaving their Chicago farm, a Chicago couple had paid for the stove and other items they'd bought to set up housekeeping and were struggling to remain current with all their bills; the husband told the agent, "It takes will power not to" go into debt.[170] A Lithuanian meatpacker with a disabled husband, a ne'er-do-well son, and two other children was acutely conscious that to go into debt was to step onto a slippery slope, and framed her economic strategy accordingly. The agent recorded her sentiments thus: "Safest to pay cash. Have a book—first thing one knows there is a bill so big it can't be paid. Can only buy coal 1/2 ton or 1 ton at a time now."[171] Anna, a United States–born Kansas City woman, felt somewhat the same, saying that the "grocer would give credit 'but we might run a bill and then not have the money to pay it.'"[172] Resist though she might, another Kansas City woman with a disabled husband and two school-age children had gone into debt "beyond her courage" and owed $400 on shoes, clothing, and medical bills.[173] Another Kansas City woman took her chronic indebtedness for food in stride; the agent commented that she owed money at a number of stores to the tune of $50 or $60 and that she "did not regard this as a burden but just a normal state of affairs."[174] A revealing comment made by the neighbor acting as a translator for a Lithuanian-speaking woman suggests that others had abandoned themselves to the inevitability of going into debt for the necessities of life, at least in their corner of Chicago: "She ain't got no money. Sure she buys on credit, clothes for the children and everything."[175] Credit may have been the accepted thing in that Chicago immigrant community, but Anna, quoted above, suggested that such was not universally the case. She told the agent, "My mother doesn't want to owe anybody and have people talking about her."[176] Anna's point was underlined by a Washington, DC, government clerk who owed "a few small bills" and found that after her tax delinquency was advertised "these people have been very disagreeable to her over the bills."[177] The Women's Bureau agent judged that one family was so "destitute [that they were] more worried about food than taxes."[178]

Some stretched their money farther by avoiding credit, as did a young Chicago woman who usually patronized a "cash place" where things were cheaper but sometimes ran "a book at another place if short of money."[179]

A strain of self-denial ran through comments made by women of all racial and ethnic groups. A United States-born single woman, boarding in Kansas City, said in response to the Women's Bureau question, "I don't believe in [credit]. What I can't pay for I don't get."[180] The agent rendered the comment of a Chicago Polish immigrant as: "Not got money not buy."[181] And a divorced African American mother left no doubt about her stance: "No mam [sic] no credit no where what we can't pay for we don't get."[182] A Chicago Polish immigrant, a widow raising three grandchildren, told the agent that she "often goes without things she needs"[183] in order to avoid debt; for a Lithuanian widow in the same city, this meant that she, her daughter, and her son-in-law "Don't have so much to eat sometimes but get along."[184] An Irish immigrant keeping house with her brother told the agent that "[we] do without what we haven't money for"[185] and an African American meatpacker in Kansas City said that she paid "cash for what little I get."[186] An African American in East St. Louis learned her lesson the hard way, and doubtless to the sorrow of the grocer with whom she had run a book: she said that her bill "got so bad I changed store—now if I haven't money we go without."[187]

Many suggested that paying their bills was a source of satisfaction and a sign of success. A childless Kansas City couple, Polish immigrants, told the agent that they "don't like to have bills. . . . Like to be on our feet."[188] Some avoided credit by saving for what they wanted; such was the case of a young South St. Paul couple, both meatpackers; the wife told the agent that she was saving her wages and "when we have a house and furniture, I'll stay at home."[189] But for most families, financial solidity was precarious. An Omaha couple had been making payments on and improving a house for eleven years; the wife, plagued by repeated layoffs from her meatpacking job, memorably summed up their shaky position by telling that agent that they hoped to pay off the mortgage soon, "if I can [go] back to work and anything won't happen."[190] For most, though, "if . . . anything won't happen" was a forlorn hope indeed.

But for many families, survival was a matter of fancy economic footwork. One Chicago family managed to "keep [the] balance every month" —that is, avoid running into debt for food, rent, and fuel, by paying irregularly on the furniture they had bought on installments and buying the minimum of clothing.[191] One Chicago African American woman told the agent that staying out of debt "takes up to the last notch,"[192] another that "[I] just have to manage close" in order to do so,[193] and a third said that she "just makes it" without resorting to credit.[194] A Polish widow with seven children kept the bills from piling up "but it takes every cent,"[195] and a married Polish mother of two said that she could "just about make it" without debt.[196] An East St. Louis meatpacking worker professed her amazement at her ability to avoid debt: "don't hardly see myself how I make out."[197] Seasonal shifts in income could wreak havoc with the most carefully calculated budget. One African American meatpacker found things "pretty tight" in the spring and summer, but managed to pay off her bills within two weeks and resorted to sales to buy her son his school clothes.[198] Winter, with its demands for more heat and light and slack work for men in the outdoor trades, was harder for others, such as the Lithuanian immigrant meatpacker, plagued by layoffs and short hours, who fell behind on both food and coal during the winter.[199]

Families developed a variety of strategies to rationalize their economies in the face of the unpredictability of the larger working-class economy in which they lived. Families had a clear sense of their limits in the marketplace and tried to contain their indebtedness within them, an effort that could be all too easily undone. An Ohio woman, injured in a workplace accident, reported that her "family had to economize and go into debt to grocer beyond [their] usual habits."[200] A Chicago African American widowed mother of three had developed her own system of installment payments: "Pays grocer every 2 weeks. Takes two weeks to pay rent then 2 weeks to catch up on groceries."[201] One can only imagine the sleepless nights that must have accompanied such a juggling act. Another Chicago African American woman paid her rent in small weekly installments to avoid falling behind,[202] as did a United States–born South St. Paul woman.[203] An East St. Louis woman paid clothing and food bills in alternate weeks.[204] Lest the historian make too much of the fact that the only such payment schemes recorded by the Women's Bureau agent were devised by native-born women, whether of African or European descent, it is worth noting the appeal of small but regular payments to a Czech-immigrant widowed meatpacker. She told the agent, "it would be easier if we could pay taxes a little at a time—the way we buy clothes. Can never get $50 ahead for taxes."[205]

Even in families about whom we know less, we can discern the outlines of economic strategies framed to fit their needs. Food, not surprisingly, was the most vexed issue for most families. Six of the women visited for the Women's Bureau report on meatpacking and slaughterhouses said that they gave top priority to paying the food bill, among them the African American in Chicago who said that "The grocery bill has got to come right along,"[206] and the Croatian immigrant in Kansas City who said, "You got to make it on the groceries."[207] Only three, among them a Lithuanian immigrant living in Chicago who said "Got to pay rent [when due] no question,"[208] named the rent as their first concern. As we saw in the previous chapter, many lived with, or in housing owned by, relatives who were lenient about rent payments, but even non-family landlords were often tolerant of rent in arrears. Unusually helpful was a Chicago woman who not only trusted her tenants to pay the rent when they could, but also looked after their four-year-old while they were at work.[209] In the personalistic world of working-class housing, it made sense to cultivate continuing ties of good faith in the hopes of eventually collecting back rent.

The two items on which families were most likely to fall behind were food and medical care. Seventeen had difficulty paying their food bills, some of them chronically, like the Chicago family whose food bill never went below $15[210] and others because of specific circumstances. In the latter group were another Chicago family who "had it in the book" to the tune of $150 when one of the breadwinners was ill and had whittled the debt back to $90 when a Women's Bureau agent called a few months later[211] and the St. Joseph, Missouri, family who had trouble paying the food bill off and on during the winter.[212] Twenty-three families let their medical bills mount up and paid other bills instead. The burden of such expenses was great. A homeworker on gloves in upstate New York "looked exhausted and ill" to the agent. She did prioritize paying what was owed for medical care but reported, "I work so hard it all goes to doctors' bills."[213] Many women, such as a Kansas City sausage linker with three sickly children,[214] took jobs mainly to pay for health care. Such bills seem almost universally to have taken last priority and accounted for the only debt, aside from house mortgages, of twenty-four families.[215]

Conclusion

If working women and their families joined a consumer society during the interwar period, they did so amidst cries of deprivation more often than amidst cries of exultation. Calculations regarding what services to buy hinged on how labor, especially women's labor, could be saved in order to be redeployed, not centrally on how leisure could be created. Vistas of new possibilities to consume commodities were most likely to emerge in the secondhand market. These possibilities were apt to be associated with refashioning used items for household use, as in the case of clothing, or with getting a living, as in the case of secondhand machines. Far from being caught up in a burst of credit buying designed to produce immediate gratification, those interviewed by the Women's Bureau were seldom beckoned by lenders and often wary of debt. Credit followed on the need for families to survive far more than it did on desires for personal fulfillment. For these working people, the Age of Consumption was also about production, and the threat of want, at every turn.

Class, Gender, and Reciprocity
An Afterword

by David Montgomery

Susan Porter Benson has left a distinctive imprint on the writing of American social history primarily because of her independence of mind. Although she was very much aware of and made use of the newest styles of historical interpretation, she consistently refused to adhere uncritically to intellectual fashions. She contributed significantly to the history of twentieth-century consumerism, but she never enthroned consumption as the driving force of modern society. Note, for example, that her influential first book, *Counter Cultures: Saleswomen, Managers, and Customers in American Department Stores, 1890–1940*, subjected human interaction in the urban "palace of consumption" to thorough and persuasive analysis by focusing on the tasks, earnings, prospects, and behavior of the women who worked in those stores.[1] She drew heavily on studies of scientific management, which were then influential, but insisted that turn-of-the-century managerial innovations had a meaning for saleswomen that differed significantly from the experience of skilled craftsmen, who were the favorite subjects of those studies. Her analysis of family relationships in *Household Accounts* shows the influence of the linguistic turn, but the book investigates women's values and social relations by scrutinizing what the women actually did. For Benson class was more than one of many identities: it was rooted in relations of production, but it was also re-created in all manner of everyday human interactions. She also insisted that all these interactions were shaped by gender (as were the relations of production), yet gender roles themselves were malleable and often a contested terrain.

Counter Cultures examined the hundreds of thousands of women who earned wages in the new urban bastions of both bargain hunting and conspicuous consumption. The saleswomen's relationships to their jobs, their co-workers, their managers, and their customers revealed the importance of class. Her analysis brings vividly to the reader's mind E. P. Thompson's famous formulation that "class happens" when people encounter and differentiate themselves from others with conflicting interests.[2] Benson insisted, however, that women's upbringing and the social roles assigned to them decisively shaped the ways class happened in department stores. In doing so, she opened a window on an important domain of women's wage earning in industrial society. She also reminded us here and elsewhere that the category "service sector," to which commentators now consign so much employment, encompasses a wide variety of work settings, relations to employers and to other workers, and prospects for advancement. Within the department store itself, the position of the youthful clerk in the bargain basement was vastly different from that of the older, often married, and career-oriented woman selling high fashion clothing.[3]

Benson drew heavily on the voluminous published literature dealing with store management for insights into the work practices and experiences of saleswomen, and into their relations with predominantly male managers and with customers—women "on the other side of the counter." She was a consistent critic of historians who viewed scientific management solely from the perspective of its assault on the skills and power of craftsmen.[4] Moreover, the term "resistance," which appears so often in writings about subordinate groups, is too limited to encompass the range of collective behavior that is described in the stores' managerial literature. The personal bonds and animosities saleswomen experienced on the job, the various ways they conducted themselves in others' presence, and the ways in which they took advantage of some managerial practices while frustrating others revealed the women's own sense of self and of solidarity. The department store was a hotbed of modern managerial methods and experiments, and although saleswomen benefited from some new personnel practices, they often showed scorn for store rules designed to increase productivity, made their own use of payment plans, and turned the very rhetoric of professional personnel management against arbitrary and degrading regulations that managers imposed.

Household Accounts follows the trail of class and gender out of the workplace and into working people's homes during the decades between the two world wars. In this new work Benson directs her attention to consumption, while rejecting the notion that social life was then shaped by "consumerism." It is commonplace today to celebrate the pursuit of individual self-interest in "the market" as the key both to understanding modern economic life and to promoting social welfare. Benson challenged both the explanatory capacity and the morality of acquisitive individualism. *Household Accounts* argues persuasively that "people do not function in the marketplace as autonomous individuals solely in response to marketing and desire but as part of families in which consumption is an object both of struggle and of shared aspiration."[5]

Her evidence is drawn from numerous surveys of household management conducted by investigators from the federal Women's Bureau, social workers, and scholars. As Benson had noted elsewhere, in the aftermath of the achievement of women's suffrage, the role of the state itself became "a terrain of more intense struggle" among women. The issue in those struggles was: "Should [the state] enforce equality between the sexes, or should it expand the mechanisms of special protection to the women worker?"[6] In this book she has carried the implications of that observation further, examining both the increasing governmental attention to women who were not (or were only episodically) wage earners and whose husbands were often unemployed or incapacitated, or who had simply absconded. The high levels of consumption and the "rugged individualism" acclaimed by President Herbert Hoover in no way corresponded to the experience of these women. Benson's use of evidence gathered by the investigators alerts the reader to two rather conflicting considerations. First, it reveals how the many women in those situations managed heavy responsibilities when they had little control over the material conditions in which they did so. Second, it warns users of such evidence that the stock phrases employed by investigators to describe working-class women fit the reality those women experienced poorly and are often hard for the historian to interpret.

Benson's findings bring to mind Dot Jones's study of women in Welsh coal-mining areas, where their opportunities for earning wages were few but their arduous work held the key to family survival. Early marriage, frequent childbearing, squalid surroundings, and endless rounds of household toil made the young wives of Rhondda Valley miners die at a younger age than their husbands, who spent their days among noxious gases, roof-falls, and maverick explosions.[7]

Moreover, it is clear from this evidence that the "family wage" often attributed to working-class husbands was more a wish than a functioning instrument of patriarchy. Earnings drawn from mining, meatpacking, construction, and textiles, which loom large in the studies used here, reveal that even those men who aspired to be model breadwinners could seldom do so. Lawrence Glickman has shown that the very term "family wage" was not used by workers before the Progressive Era. It was introduced by academic economists and social gospel advocates, while the goal then espoused by trade unionists was a "living wage."[8]

Ever since state bureaus of labor statistics and tariff commissions had begun to study workers' incomes in the nineteenth century those agencies had usually compared the earnings of adult males to some index of the cost of food, housing, and other necessities. Taken literally they suggested the conclusion that everybody starved. A major contribution of Peter Shergold in *Working-Class Life: The "American Standard" in Comparative Perspective, 1899–1913* was to reckon with the market for secondhand goods and seasonal food bargains, in which wives of industrial workers routinely shopped.[9] In the 1920s as in the depression years, the earnings of children, especially daughters, were still critically important to household accounts.[10] Benson has insisted that homemakers were also sellers as well as buyers in the market for clothing, furniture, and utensils. In contrast to the middle-class women who are featured in most studies of twentieth-century consumerism, however, the women she studied found the market a place of perils and uncertainty, and avoided resort to credit wherever possible.

Most important of all, Benson has rejected the notion that all levels of American society found individual fulfillment as consumers between the two world wars. Her findings underscore the crucial role of mutual support and reciprocity in working-class households and neighborhoods. She argues that such reciprocity existed mostly among women, while men figured primarily as contributors of greater or lesser portions of their wages. Women shared or exchanged tasks, goods, child care, and sometimes food, not only within families but also between households. By no means was the sharing always harmonious. Although it could be a source of friendship and generosity, sometimes it was marked by bitter conflict. But there is no escaping its importance. Women's mutuality, especially through religious and ethnic organizations, could far outweigh the husband's work role in determining a family's social status, as Ewa Morawska has shown.[11]

Clearly this reciprocity—"what goes 'round comes 'round"—lies at the heart of both Benson's analysis of working-class households and her own lifelong dedication to assisting and sharing with others. Her life and her scholarship both remind us of the meaning of mutuality in everyday life.

Notes

Introduction

1. Robert Anthony Orsi, *The Madonna of 115th Street: Faith and Community in Italian Harlem, 1880–1950* (New Haven: Yale University Press, 1985), xix. Orsi is quoting LeRoy Ladurie.

2. Orsi, 78, 80, quotation on latter page.

3. Ibid., 82–83.

4. Ibid., 92–93.

5. Orsi himself suggests the same fit between Jewish and Italian family cultures, see 95.

6. See my essays, "Living on the Margin: Working-Class Marriages and Family Survival Strategies in the United States, 1919–1941," in *The Sex of Things: Gender and Consumption in Historical Perspective,* ed. Victoria de Grazia with Ellen Furlough (Berkeley: University of California Press, 1996), 212–43, and "Gender, Generation, and Consumption in the United States: Working-Class Families in the Interwar Period," in *Getting and Spending: European and Consumer Societies in the Twentieth Century,* ed. Susan Strasser, Charles McGovern, and Matthias Judt (Cambridge: Cambridge University Press, 1998), 223–40.

7. Judith M. Bennett, *Ale, Beer, and Brewsters in England: Women's Work in a Changing World, 1300–1600* (New York: Oxford University Press, 1996); Steve J. Stern, *The Secret History of Gender: Women, Men, and Power in Late Colonial Mex-*

ico (Chapel Hill, NC: University of North Carolina Press, 1995); and Gracia Clark, *Onions Are My Husband: Survival and Accumulation by West African Market Women* (Chicago: University of Chicago Press, 1994).

8. On the maternalist reformers who were most likely to advocate policy changes for working-class families between 1870 and 1940, see Linda Gordon, "Putting Children First: Women, Maternalism, and Welfare in the Early Twentieth Century," in *U.S. History as Women's History: New Feminist Essays*, ed. Linda K. Kerber, Alice Kessler-Harris, and Kathryn Kish Sklar (Chapel Hill: University of North Carolina Press, 1995), 63–86. Also see Robyn Muncy, *Creating a Female Dominion in American Reform, 1890–1935* (New York: Oxford University Press, 1991), William H. Chafe, "Women's History and Political History: Some Thoughts on Progressivism and the New Deal," in *Visible Women: New Essays on American Activism*, ed. Nancy A. Hewitt and Suzanne Lebsock (Urbana: University of Illinois Press, 1993), 101–39, and Linda Gordon, *Heroes of Their Own Lives: The Politics and History of Family Violence* (New York: Viking, 1988).

9. On the importance of shared stories, see *Interpreting Women's Lives: Feminist Theory and Personal Narratives*, ed. The Personal Narratives Group (Bloomington: University of Indiana Press, 1989), especially 261–264, and Susan Porter Benson, "Gender, Generation, and Consumption in the United States: Working-Class Families in the Interwar Period," in *Getting and Spending*, ed. Strasser, McGovern, and Judt, 223–40.

10. A good introduction to this literature is part 2, "Intrahousehold Distribution and Control," in *Persistent Inequalities: Women and World Development*, ed. Irene Tinker (New York: Oxford University Press, 1990). The three articles in this section—Amartya K. Sen, "Gender and Cooperative Conflicts," Benjamin Senauer, "The Impact of the Value of Women's Time on Food and Nutrition," and Hanna Papanek, "To Each Less Than She Needs, From Each More Than She Can Do: Allocations, Entitlements, and Value"—discuss the four themes I have isolated here and offer excellent bibliographical surveys of the relevant literature.

11. Judith E. Smith, *Family Connections: A History of Italian and Jewish Immigrant Lives in Providence, Rhode Island, 1900–1940* (Albany: State University of New York Press, 1985), *All Our Kin: Strategies for Survival in a Black Community* (New York: Harper and Row, 1974), and Margaret Byington, *Homestead: The Households of a Mill Town*, Russell Sage Foundation (1910; Pittsburgh: University Center for International Studies, 1974).

12. For example, see Loren Baritz, *The Good Life: The Meaning of Success for the American Middle Class* (New York: Harper and Row, 1982), Susan Strasser, *Satisfaction Guaranteed: The Making of the American Mass Market* (New York: Pantheon Books, 1989), and Lizabeth Cohen, *A Consumers' Republic: The Politics of Mass Consumption in Postwar America* (New York: Random House, 2004).

13. Ruth Schwartz Cowan notes that during the 1920s "more than half of the households were still living below—and, in some cases, far below—what was then

defined as the minimum standard of 'health and decency'" (*More Work for Mother: The Ironies of Household Technology from the Open Hearth to the Microwave* [New York: Basic Books, 1983], 181). See also Lizabeth Cohen, *Making a New Deal: Industrial Workers in Chicago, 1919–1939* (Cambridge: Cambridge University Press, 1990), 102–4. The situation of course worsened during the 1930s.

14. The consumption of African Americans is conditioned at least as much by race as by class. Both historically and currently, racism has hampered African Americans in achieving a style of life commensurate with their incomes. Earl Lewis, to offer a historical example, notes that middle-class Norfolk blacks during the 1910s and 1920s had to pay higher insurance rates—and, we might add, devoted more income to home maintenance—because the city provided only substandard services to their neighborhoods. See Lewis, *In Their Own Interests: Race, Class, and Power in Twentieth-Century Norfolk, Virginia* (Berkeley: University of California Press, 1991), 80. Attorney Patricia Williams is but one of legions of African Americans who tell vivid anecdotes of the ways in which their race still offsets their class position in the marketplace; during the height of a recent Christmas shopping season, she was denied entry to a Benetton store guarded by a buzzer-operated locked door. Patricia J. Williams, *The Alchemy of Race and Rights* (Cambridge: Harvard University Press, 1991), 44–51.

15. Burton J. Bledstein, *The Culture of Professionalsm* (New York: W. W. Norton, 1978); Paul E. Johnson, *A Nation of Shopkeepers: Society and Revivals in Rochester, New York* (New York: Hill and Wang, 1978).

16. There is, of course, a problem in seeing a plant manager and a stenographer in his office as members of the same class, although they are both members of the white-collar group of which C. Wright Mills wrote so perceptively; see his *White Collar: The American Middle Classes* (New York: Oxford University Press, 1951). Also see Ileen DeVault, *Sons and Daughters of Labor: Class and Clerical Work in Turn-of-the Century Pittsburgh* (Ithaca: Cornell University Press, 1990), Sharon Hartman Strom, *Beyond the Typewriter: Gender, Class, and the Origins of Modern American Office Work, 1900–1930* (Urbana: University of Illinois Press, 1992), 273–313, and Jerome P. Bjelopera, *City of Clerks: Office and Sales Workers in Philadelphia, 1870–1920* (Urbana: University of Illinois Press, 2005), 9–31.

17. I use the term *consumption* in preference to *consumerism*. By the former I mean cash-mediated market behavior; I use the latter in a narrower sense, to refer to the self-conscious advocacy of the consumer's interest.

18. See, for example, Jessica B. Peixotto, *How Workers Spend a Living Wage: A Study of the Incomes and Expenditures of Eighty-Two Typographers' Families in San Francisco*, Cost of Living Studies 2 (Berkeley: Heller Committee for Research in Social Economics of the University of California, 1929), 173, 219, 221, 224. I developed this point at greater length in a paper delivered at the Annual Meeting of the Organization of American Historians in 1991, and Ruth Schwartz Cowan makes a similar point in somewhat different terms in *More Work for Mother,* 189–90.

19. Susan Porter Benson, *Counter Cultures: Saleswomen, Managers, and Customers in American Department Stores, 1890–1940* (Urbana: University of Illinois Press, 1986), 75–78, 89–91.

20. Roland Marchand, *Advertising the American Dream: Making Way for Modernity, 1920–1940* (Berkeley: University of California Press, 1985), 64.

21. Cohen, *Making a New Deal*, 103–4; Benson, *Counter Cultures*, 90. Martha Olney, *Buy Now, Pay Later: Advertising, Credit, and Consumer Durables in the 1920s* (Chapel Hill: University of North Carolina Press, 1991) notes a dramatic expansion of credit but does not investigate who incurred that debt.

22. E. P. Thompson, *The Making of the English Working Class* (New York: Vintage Books, 1966), 9.

23. Kenneth L. Ames, "Trade Catalogues and the Study of History," in *Accumulation & Display: Mass Marketing Household Goods in America, 1880–1920*, ed. Deborah Anne Federhen et al. (Winterthur: The Henry Francis du Pont Winterthur Museum, 1986), 10.

1. "Living on the Margin"

1. Benda family case study, folder 2, box 43, Helen Hall Papers, Social Welfare History Archives, University of Minnesota, Minneapolis. The National Federation of Settlements asked member settlement houses to provide case studies of families experiencing unemployment during the winter of 1928–1929. Some 300 cases were submitted, of which 150 are published in *Case Studies of Unemployment*, ed. Marion Elderton (Philadelphia: University of Pennsylvania Press, 1931). Seventy-six of the original cases are in the Helen Hall Papers, and of the 76, 29 have not been published. Because the published versions differ minimally from the manuscript versions, I will refer to published cases in the more readily accessible Elderton collection and to the Helen Hall Papers only for the unpublished ones.

2. Susan Levine, "Workers' Wives: Gender, Class, and Consumerism in the 1920s," *Gender and History* 3 (Spring 1991): 45–64; Elizabeth Ewen, *Immigrant Women in the Land of Dollars: Life and Culture on the Lower East Side, 1890–1925* (New York: Monthly Review Press, 1985), 96–109; Kathy Peiss, *Cheap Amusements: Working Women and Leisure in Turn-of-the-Century New York* (Philadelphia: Temple University Press, 1986), 21–26; Judith Smith, *Family Connections: A History of Italian and Jewish Immigrant Lives in Providence, Rhode Island, 1900–1940* (Albany: State University of New York Press, 1985), 60–61, 74–76.

3. Christina Simmons, "Companionate Marriage and the Lesbian Threat," *Frontiers* 4 (Fall 1979): 54–59.

4. A good survey of European peasant marriages is Barbara A. Hanawalt, *The Ties That Bound: Peasant Families in Medieval England* (New York: Oxford University Press, 1986).

5. Jeanne Boydston, *Home and Work: Housework, Wages, and the Ideology of Labor in the Early Republic* (New York: Oxford University Press, 1990), 88–92.

6. Herbert G. Gutman with Ira Berlin, "Class Composition and the Development of the American Working Class," in *Power and Culture: Essays on the American Working Class,* ed. Ira Berlin (New York: Pantheon Books, 1987), 385–92.

7. See, for example Elderton, *Case Studies of Unemployment,* 187, 333; and Mirra Komarovsky, *The Unemployed Man and His Family—The Effect of Unemployment upon the Status of the Man in Fifty-Nine Families* (New York: Dryden Press, 1940), 9, 26.

8. Schedule 7-9-739, box 101, Raw Data for Published Bulletins, *The Immigrant Woman and Her Job,* Bulletin No. 74 (1930), Records of the Women's Bureau, RG 86 (National Archives, College Park). For this and most other bulletins, the schedules cited are in the home-visit folder unless otherwise noted. Schedules for bulletin numbers 60 and 88 are particularly easy to locate by schedule number; the folder name is not required. On some schedules, the number is absent or illegible, and the citations will use the informant's last name. Schedules for bulletin number 88 were assigned a two-part number sequence that identified the city and then the informant. The citations will provide city names when this portion of the assigned number does not appear on the schedule. I will include a folder name only in the few cases where it is necessary to easily locate the cited schedule.

9. Schedule 7-8-687, box 101, Raw Data for Published Bulletins, Bulletin No. 74, Records of the Women's Bureau.

10. Schedule 21-43, box 123, Raw Data for Published Bulletins, *The Employment of Women in Slaughtering and Meat Packing,* Bulletin No. 88 (1932), Records of the Women's Bureau.

11. Elderton, *Case Studies of Unemployment,* 102.

12. Schedule 59, folder "Housing Survey 1933 District of Columbia—Schedules," box 14, Division of Research, Unpublished Studies and Materials, Records of the Women's Bureau.

13. Caroline Manning, *The Immigrant Woman and Her Job,* Bulletin of the Women's Bureau, No. 74 (Washington, DC: Government Printing Office, 1930). I tabulated the women's responses in three categories:

Unemployed—with no regular trade or job mentioned—36.7 percent.
Slack work—with regular trade or job mentioned, or reference to short hours, irregular schedules, or seasonal work—41.7 percent.
Low wages—28.0 percent.

Percentages add up to more than 100 percent because 14 women mentioned more than one factor.

14. Elderton, *Case Studies of Unemployment,* 26.

15. Baldwin, box 31, Raw Data for Published Bulletins, *Women in Tennessee Industries: A Study of Hours, Wages, and Working Conditions,* Bulletin No. 56 (1927), Records of the Women's Bureau.

16. Elderton, *Case Studies of Unemployment,* 347.

17. Enochs, Raw Data for Published Bulletins, *Women in Oklahoma Industries:*

A Study of Hours, Wages, and Working Conditions, Bulletin No. 48 (1926), Records of the Women's Bureau.

18. The irony is that many working-class men pursued union militancy for the express purpose of asserting their status as breadwinners. The IWW "homeguard" provides one clear example: see David Roediger, *Towards the Abolition of Whiteness* (New York: Verso, 1994), 133, 158–59. The CIO was the best bet for the family economy during this period, but none of my documents deal with the families of men involved in CIO organizing. For a discussion of the impact of the CIO on the family economy, see Lizabeth Cohen, *Making a New Deal: Industrial Workers in Chicago, 1919–1939* (New York: Cambridge University Press, 1990), 346–48, 358–59.

19. Schedule 24-22, box 123, Raw Data for Published Bulletins, Bulletin No. 88, Records of the Women's Bureau.

20. Ibid. Schedule 37-20, box 122.

21. Lombardi, box 8, Raw Data for Published Bulletins, *Women in Rhode Island Industries: A Study of Hours, Wages, and Working Conditions,* Bulletin No. 21 (1922), Records of the Women's Bureau.

22. George Chauncey, *Gay New York: Gender, Urban Culture, and the Making of the Gay Male World, 1890–1940* (New York: Basic Books, 1994), 79.

23. Jacquelyn Dowd Hall et al., *Like a Family: The Making of a Southern Cotton Mill World* (Chapel Hill: University of North Carolina Press, 1987), 165–66.

24. Elderton, *Case Studies of Unemployment,* 160.

25. Schedule 26-12, box 123, Raw Data for Published Bulletins, Bulletin No. 88, Records of the Women's Bureau.

26. Ibid. Schedule 56-34.

27. Schedule 17-92, box 121, Raw Data for Published Bulletins, Bulletin No. 88, Records of the Women's Bureau.

28. 9th case, "Case Records from United Charities, St. Paul," folder "#88 Correspondence," box 117, Raw Data for Published Bulletins, Bulletin No. 88, Records of the Women's Bureau.

29. Elderton, *Case Studies of Unemployment,* 126.

30. Schedule 7-8-701, box 101, Raw Data for Published Bulletins, Bulletin No. 74, Records of the Women's Bureau.

31. Ibid. Schedule 7-9-722.

32. Ibid. Schedule 7-8-566, box 100.

33. Ibid. Schedule 7-12-925, box 102.

34. Schedules 11-40, box 120, and 17-108, box 121, Raw Data for Published Bulletins, Bulletin No. 88, Records of the Women's Bureau.

35. Ibid. Schedule 36-23, box 122.

36. Ibid. Schedule 32-39, box 122.

37. Manning, *The Immigrant Woman and Her Job.* Perhaps the most obvious sign of a husband's insufficiency was desertion. Of the Philadelphia women interviewed for Women's Bureau Bulletin 74, 68.4 percent had ever been married. Of that total, 5.4 percent had been deserted either permanently or temporarily.

38. This practice was especially common in England, even more so that it appears to have been in the United States. See, for example, Ellen Ross, *Love and Toil: Mothers in Outcast London, 1870–1918* (New York: Oxford University Press, 1993), 56–90; and Jan Pahl, *Money and Marriage* (New York: Palgrave MacMillan, 1989), 40–42.

39. Elderton, *Case Studies of Unemployment,* 42.

40. Osborn family case study, folder 5, box 48, Helen Hall Papers.

41. Schedule 36-35, box 122, Raw Data for Published Bulletins, Bulletin No. 88, Records of the Women's Bureau.

42. Ibid. Schedule 11-16, box 120. See also schedule 11-46, box 120, and schedule 36-22, box 122.

43. Ibid. Schedule 32-33, box 122.

44. Schedule 2-3-3, Raw Data for Published Bulletins, *Industrial Homework in Rhode Island with Special Reference to the Lace Industry,* Bulletin No. 131 (1935), Records of the Women's Bureau.

45. Schedule 7-1-35, box 97, Raw Data for Published Bulletins, Bulletin No. 74, Records of the Women's Bureau.

46. Schedule 5-3-18, Raw Data for Published Bulletins, Bulletin No. 131, Records of the Women's Bureau.

47. Rowe, box 25, Raw Data for Published Bulletins, Bulletin No. 48, Records of the Women's Bureau.

48. Schedule 32-48 (African American woman) and schedule 36-40 (Polish immigrant woman), box 122, Raw Data for Published Bulletins, Bulletin No. 88, Records of the Women's Bureau. It is significant that these women, both meatpackers, worked in different industries than their husbands did; the former was married to a tire builder, the latter to a foundry worker. Women who worked in the same industry as their husbands were much more likely to know how much their husbands' wages were. For a father who hid the amount of his wages from his daughters, see Schedule 1085, box 33, Raw Data for Published Bulletins, *Industrial Accidents to Women in New Jersey, Ohio, and Wisconsin,* Bulletin No. 60 (1927), Records of the Women's Bureau.

49. Schedule 7-9-722, box 101, Raw Data for Published Bulletins, Bulletin No. 74, Records of the Women's Bureau.

50. Bennett family case study, folder 9, box 105, Helen Hall Papers.

51. Komarovsky, *The Unemployed Man and His Family,* 16.

52. Benda family case study, file 2, box 43; see also O'Dowd family case study, file 7, box 43, both in Helen Hall Papers. Husbands who turned over all their income to the family income are mentioned in Elderton, *Case Studies of Unemployment,* 187, 332.

53. Komarovsky, *The Unemployed Man and His Family,* 31.

54. Ibid., 27.

55. Ibid., 76.

56. Caruso family case study, file 5, box 48, Helen Hall Papers.

57. Sciarro family case study, file 14, box 43, Helen Hall Papers.

58. Komarovsky, *The Unemployed Man and His Family,* 32.

59. Schedule 7-3-297, box 98, Raw Data for Published Bulletins, Bulletin No. 74, Records of the Women's Bureau.

60. Komarovsky, *The Unemployed Man and His Family,* 77.

61. Schedule 24-42 box 123, Raw Data for Published Bulletins, Bulletin No. 88, Records of the Women's Bureau.

62. Ibid. Schedules 42-36 and 56-67, box 123.

63. Ibid. Schedule 41-1.

64. Skipper, box 3, Raw Data for Published Bulletins, *Hours and Conditions of Work for Women in Industry in Virginia, Bulletin No. 10* (1920), Records of the Women's Bureau.

65. Schedule 7-7-455, box 99; schedule 7-2-52, box 97; schedule 7-2-245, box 98; and schedule 7-12-939, box 102; all in Raw Data for Published Bulletins, Bulletin No. 74, Records of the Women's Bureau.

66. Barbara Ehrenreich, *Hearts of Men: American Dreams and the Flight from Commitment* (Garden City, NY: Anchor Press, 1983), 42–51. Kenon Breazeale pushes the emergence of a male consumer back to the 1930s, linking it to *Esquire* magazine, but does not make the same links as Ehrenreich does between male consumption and dereliction in the breadwinner role. See "In Spite of Women: *Esquire* Magazine and the Construction of the Male Consumer," *Signs* 20 (Autumn 1994): 1–22.

67. Mary Simkhovitch, *The City Worker's World in America* (New York: Macmillan, 1917), 101.

68. Ibid., 95.

69. Case 9, folder "Mothers' Pensions 1925–26," box 3, Division of Research, Unpublished Studies and Materials, Records of the Women's Bureau; see also case 73.

70. Elderton, *Case Studies of Unemployment,* 36. For other examples of good managers, see 207, 215, 270, 296, 300, 321–22, 323–24.

71. Schedule 32-16, box 122, Raw Data for Published Bulletins, Bulletin No. 88, Records of the Women's Bureau.

72. Elderton, *Case Studies of Unemployment,* 85.

73. Ibid., 27.

74. Ibid., 299.

75. Ibid., 38.

76. Ibid.

77. Schedule 7-7-485, box 99, Raw Data for Published Bulletins, Bulletin No. 74, Records of the Women's Bureau.

78. Elliot family case study, folder 10, box 43, Helen Hall Papers.

79. Elderton, *Case Studies of Unemployment,* 187.

80. O'Dowd family case study, folder 7, box 43, Helen Hall Papers.

81. Schedule 41-19, box 123, Raw Data for Published Bulletins, Bulletin No. 88, Records of the Women's Bureau.

82. Ibid. Schedule 56-16.

83. Cortino, folder #25 Survey Materials Home Visits [*sic*] Schedules (Chicago), box 12, Raw Data for Published Bulletins, *Women in the Candy Industry in Chicago and St. Louis: A Study of Hours, Wages, and Working conditions in 1920–1921,* Bulletin No. 25 (1923), Records of the Women's Bureau.

84. Case 21993/21996, folder 1553, box 99, Mary Van Kleeck Papers, Sophia Smith Collection, Smith College (Northampton, Massachusetts).

85. Elderton, *Case Studies of Unemployment,* 207, and also 322; and Roger Cooley Angell, *The Family Encounters the Great Depression* (New York: Scribner's Sons, 1936), 48, 63.

86. Jessica Peixotto, *How Workers Spend a Living Wage—San Francisco Typographers* (Berkeley: University of California Press, 1929), 164.

87. Ibid.

88. Elderton, *Case Studies of Unemployment,* 337–38.

89. Angell, *The Family Encounters the Great Depression,* 171.

90. Elderton, *Case Studies of Unemployment,* 333.

91. Freund, folder #25 Survey Materials Home Visits [*sic*] Schedules (Chicago), box 12, Raw Data for Published Bulletins, Bulletin No. 25, Records of the Women's Bureau.

92. Schedule 7-2-167, box 98, Raw Data for Published Bulletins, Bulletin No. 74, Records of the Women's Bureau.

93. Mary Elizabeth Pidgeon, *The Employment of Women in Slaughtering and Meat Packing,* Bulletin of the Women's Bureau, no. 88 (Washington, DC: Government Printing Office, 1932), 133.

94. 3rd case, "Case Records from United Charities, St. Paul," folder "#88 Correspondence," box 117, Raw Data for Published Bulletins., Bulletin No. 88, Records of the Women's Bureau.

95. Ibid. 9th case, "Case Records from United Charities, St. Paul," folder "#88 Correspondence," box 117.

96. Schedule 42-21, box 123, Raw Data for Published Bulletins, Bulletin No. 88, Records of the Women's Bureau.

97. Schedule 221, box 63, Raw Data for Published Bulletins, Bulletin No. 60, Records of the Women's Bureau.

98. Manning, *The Immigrant Woman and Her Job,* 50–51.

99. Schedule 43-8, box 123, Raw Data for Published Bulletins, Bulletin No. 88, Records of the Women's Bureau.

100. Ibid. Schedule 11-39, box 120.

101. Ibid. Schedule 31-37, box 122.

102. Ibid. Schedule 32-51.

103. Ibid. Schedule 36-10

104. Ibid. Schedule 17-120, box 121.

105. Ibid. Schedule 21-Taylor, box 123.

106. Ibid. Schedule 42-16.

107. Ibid. Schedule 42-77.

108. Ibid. Schedule 42-127.

109. Schedule 74, Raw Data for Published Bulletins, *Women in Texas Industries: Hours, Wages, Working Conditions, and Home Work,* Bulletin No. 126 (1936), Records of the Women's Bureau.

110. Schedule 36-3, box 122, Raw Data for Published Bulletins, Bulletin No. 88, Records of the Women's Bureau.

111. Ibid. Schedule 36-30.

112. Ibid. Schedule 16-32, box 121.

113. Ibid. Schedule 16-33.

114. Ibid. Schedule 16-36.

115. Ibid. Schedule 36-2, box 122.

116. Pearson, box 25, , Raw Data for Published Bulletins, Bulletin No. 48, Records of the Women's Bureau.

117. Dennis, box 16, Raw Data for Published Reports, *Women in South Carolina Industries: A Study of Hours, Wages, and Working Conditions,* Bulletin No. 32, Records of the Women's Bureau.

118. Banks, box 31, Raw Data for Published Reports, Bulletin No. 56, Records of the Women's Bureau. For another case of illness so severe that a husband went to live with his parents, see Saunders, box 25, Raw Data for Published Bulletins, Bulletin No. 48, Records of the Women's Bureau.

119. Elderton, *Case Studies of Unemployment,* 127.

120. Schedule 7-2-244, box 98, Raw Data for Published Bulletins, Bulletin No. 74, Records of the Women's Bureau.

121. Ibid. Schedule 7-12-963, box 102.

122. Schedule 42-25, box 123, Raw Data for Published Bulletins, Bulletin No. 88, Records of the Women's Bureau.

123. Ibid. Schedule 24-16. See also schedule 16-47, box 121 (African American) and 37-22, box 122; and McKee, folder "Home Visit Schedules—Georgia—1," Raw Data for Published Bulletins, *Women in Georgia Industries: A Study of Hours, Wages, and Working Conditions,* Bulletin No. 22 (1922), Records of the Women's Bureau.

124. Schedule 21-6, box 123, Raw Data for Published Bulletins, Bulletin No. 88, Records of the Women's Bureau.

125. Schedule 7-2-115, box 97, Raw Data for Published Bulletins, Bulletin No. 74, Records of the Women's Bureau.

126. Schedule 11-107, box 120, Raw Data for Published Bulletins, Bulletin No. 88, Records of the Women's Bureau. See also schedule 16-44, box 121, for a similar statement by an African American mother of four.

127. Ibid. Schedule 26-44, box 123.

128. Ibid. Schedule 24-Dozoul, box 123; schedule 31-10, box 122.

129. Ibid. Schedule 16-50, box 121.

130. Ibid. Schedules 42-60 and 41-77, box 123.

131. Ibid. Schedule 17-114, box 121; see also Schedule 36-24, box 122; schedule 24-

Hlavek and 24-Zajac, box 123. See also Everett, box 3, Raw Data for Published Bulletins, Bulletin No. 10, Records of the Women's Bureau.

132. Schedules 42-12 and Ottumwa-16, box 123, Raw Data for Published Bulletins, Bulletin No. 88; Skee, folder "Home Visit Schedules—Georgia—2," box 9, Raw Data for Published Bulletins, Bulletin No. 22; Barrett, box 31, Raw Data for Published Bulletins, Bulletin No. 56; all in Records of the Women's Bureau.

133. Schedules 24-14 and 24-31, box 123, Raw Data for Published Bulletins, Bulletin No. 88, Records of the Women's Bureau.

134. Schedule 7-1-11, box 97, Raw Data for Published Bulletins, Bulletin No. 74, Records of the Women's Bureau.

135. Selected Cases Taken from Questionnaires Used as Basis of Report titled "Effects of Dismissing Married Persons from the Civil Service (Section 213)," folder "Effects of Dismissing Married Persons from the Civil Service (Section 213 of the Economy Act) 1932–1936," box 17, Division of Research, Unpublished Studies and Materials, 1919–1972, Records of the Women's Bureau.

136. Schedule 36-34, box 122, Raw Data for Published Bulletins, Bulletin No. 88, Records of the Women's Bureau; see also schedule 31-89.

137. "Why I Work," folder 1503, box 96, Mary Van Kleeck Papers. The document gives no demographic data about the writer.

138. Schedule 31-55, box 122, Raw Data for Published Bulletins, Bulletin No. 88, Records of the Women's Bureau.

139. Ibid. Schedule 26-29, box 123.

140. Stillwell, box 31, Raw Data for Published Bulletins, Bulletin No. 56, Records of the Women's Bureau.

141. Schedule 209, Raw Data for Published Bulletins, *Hours and Earnings in the Leather-Glove Industry,* Bulletin No. 119 (1934), Records of the Women's Bureau; see also schedule 14.

142. Wood, box 8, Raw Data for Published Bulletins, Bulletin No. 21, Records of the Women's Bureau.

143. Schedule 31-32, box 122, Raw Data for Published Bulletins, Bulletin No. 88, Records of the Women's Bureau. For other examples, see "Married Women in Industry (Stories from Aurora, Illinois)," folder 1503, box 96, Mary Van Kleeck Papers; Ellen Ryan, box 8, Raw Data for Published Bulletins, Bulletin No. 21, Records of the Women's Bureau; Mrs. Rose P., folder 5, box 31, YWCA Papers, Sophia Smith Collection. The account of Rose P. was one of the case histories collected by the YWCA's Commission on the Study of the Second Generation Girl, later the Commission on First Generation Americans, during the late 1920s and early 1930s.

144. Schedules 41-6 (Croatian), and 32-20 (African American), box 123, Raw Data for Published Bulletins, Bulletin No. 88, Records of the Women's Bureau.

145. "Married Women in Industry (Stories from Aurora Illinois)," folder 1503, box 96, Mary Van Kleeck Papers.

146. Vaughn, box 7, Raw Data for Published Bulletins, *Iowa Women in Industry, Bulletin No. 19* (1922), Records of the Women's Bureau.

147. Schedule 51-Whittington, box 123, Raw Data for Published Bulletins, Bulletin No. 88, Records of the Women's Bureau.

148. Ibid. Schedule 36-19, box 122.

149. Ibid. Schedule 17-53, box 121.

150. Ibid. Schedule 31-71, box 122.

151. Ibid. Schedule 36-2, box 122.

152. Ibid. Schedule South St. Paul A-4, box 123.

153. Pidgeon, *Employment of Women in Slaughtering and Meat Packing,* 126-27. The percentages in the following discussion are based on my tally of the responses on the home-visit forms. The basis for computation is the "634 women . . . who were not the sole support of themselves of others" (Pidgeon, *Employment of Women in Slaughtering and Meat Packing,* 126). Because the responses were often vague and unspecific, the counts are approximate and should be taken only as a general indication of the numbers of women in the various categories.

154. Schedule 36-1, box 122, Raw Data for Published Bulletins, Bulletin No. 88, Records of the Women's Bureau.

155. Ibid. Schedule 17-122, box 121.

156. Ibid. Schedule 17-Magier, box 121.

157. Ibid. Schedule 31-70, box 122.

158. Smith, folder "Home Visit Schedules—Atlanta," box 9, Raw Data for Published Bulletins, Bulletin No. 22, Records of the Women's Bureau.

159. Robinson, box 7, Raw Data for Published Bulletins, Bulletin No. 19, Records of the Women's Bureau.

160. Kahler, folder "#10 survey materials—home visits," box 3, Raw Data for Published Bulletin, Bulletin No. 10.

161. Mrs. Cordia Tennyson, box 18, folder "#35 Survey Materials—Home Visits Schedules (Mo.)," Raw Data for Published Bulletins, *Women in Missouri Industries: A Study of Hours and Wages,* Bulletin No. 35 (1924), Records of the Women's Bureau.

162. Ibid. Elizabeth Dubark.

163. Ibid. Mrs. Cordia Tennyson and Elizabeth Dubark; see also schedules 36-7 and 32-42, box 122; and schedule 42-129, box 123, both in Raw Data for Published Bulletins, Bulletin No. 88; Sanders, box 16, Raw Data for Published Bulletins, Bulletin No. 32; M. Smith, box 219, Raw Data for Published Bulletins, *Women in Arkansas Industries,* Bulletin No. 124 (1935); all in Records of the Women's Bureau. In addition, see "Married Women in Industry, Danville, Illinois," folder 1503, box 96, Mary Van Kleeck Papers. For a partial account of a family's financial division of labor, see Elderton, *Case Studies of Unemployment,* 354–55.

164. Schedule 42-129, box 123, Raw Data for Published Bulletins, Bulletin No. 88, Records of the Women's Bureau.

165. Ibid. Schedule 36-7, box 122.

166. Ibid. Schedule South St. Paul A-11, box 123; see also Schedule 32-17, box 122.

167. "Richmond," folder 1503, box 96, Mary Van Kleeck Papers.

168. "Woman Taking Comptometer Course," folder 1503, box 96, Mary Van Kleeck Papers.

169. "Some Reasons for Married Women Working," folder 1503, box 96, Mary Van Kleeck Papers. See also Ruth Schwartz Cowan, *More Work for Mother: The Ironies of Household Technology from the Open Hearth to the Microwave* (New York: Basic Books, 1983).

170. Howe, box 8, Raw Data for Published Bulletins, Bulletin No. 21, Records of the Women's Bureau.

171. Schedule 16-12, box 121, Raw Data for Published Bulletins, Bulletin No. 88, Records of the Women's Bureau.

172. Ingram and Martin schedules, box 16, Raw Data for Published Bulletins, Bulletin No. 32, Records of the Women's Bureau.

173. Howe, box 8, Raw Data for Published Bulletins, Bulletin No. 21, Records of the Women's Bureau.

174. Schedule 7-12-973, box 102, Raw Data for Published Bulletins, Bulletin No. 74, Records of the Women's Bureau.

175. Ibid. Schedule 7-9-778, box 101.

176. Ibid. Schedule 7-9-723; see also 7-9-785.

177. Deysch, box 12, folder "#25 survey materials—home visits schedules (Chicago)," Raw Data for Published Bulletins, Bulletin No. 25, Records of the Women's Bureau.

178. Ibid. Hawkenson, box 12, folder #25 survey materials—home visits schedules (Chicago)."

179. Schedule South St. Paul S-12, box 123, Raw Data for Published Bulletins, Bulletin No. 88; Dingley, box 31, Raw Data for Published Bulletins, Bulletin No. 56; both in Records of the Women's Bureau.

180. Peixotto, *How Workers Spend a Living Wage,* 177.

181. John Mack Faragher has made this argument; see his *Sugar Creek: Life on the Illinois Prairie* (New Haven: Yale University Press, 1988), 101; and *Women and Men on the Overland Trail,* 2nd ed. (New Haven: Yale University Press, 2001), 80–87, 108–9.

182. The determinations of ethnicity should be viewed as approximate because of the imprecise reporting on the forms. No questions were asked about husbands' ethnicity. The forms contained blanks for wife's race and country of birth. Ethnicity was often recorded in the race blank, but this blank was also frequently left unfilled. I included in the category "central European" the wives whose birthplace or race was listed as Poland, Croatia, Serbia, Estonia, Yugoslavia, Hungary, Lithuania, Russia, Austria, Rumania, Czechoslovakia, Slovakia, and the Ukraine. Also included were thirty-five women whose surnames were clearly of one of these ethnicities even though they themselves were listed as native-born. Those identified as "colored" on the forms are counted as African American; native-born people with surnames that appear to be English, Irish, Scandinavian, or German were counted as being of northern or western European origin. I assumed that there

were no interracial marriages. The necessity of relying on both the wife's ethnicity and the husband's surname to categorize ethnicity inevitably creates imprecision. The major source of error in assigning ethnicity results from putting native-born non-African Americans with surnames of indeterminate ethnicity into the northern or western European category; it should therefore be considered something of a residual category. The errors are unavoidable given the nature of the data, but the differences between the central Europeans and all others are much larger than the probable degree of error.

183. Elderton, *Case Studies of Unemployment,* 139, 230, 343. For additional evidence, see Barrett, box 18, Raw Data for Published Bulletins, Bulletin No. 35; Jasper, box 8, Raw Data for Published Bulletins, Bulletin No. 21; Bright, box 7, Raw Data for Published Bulletins, Bulletin No. 19; Edwards, box 16, Raw Data for Published Bulletins, Bulletin No. 32; all in Records of the Women's Bureau; and Komarovsky, *The Unemployed Man and His Family,* 44, 45, 76, 78–79. Barrett and Jasper are cases where husbands did housework in the absence of a mother.

184. For examples of each, Schedules 11-80 and 11-48, box 120, schedule 17-105, box 121, Raw Data for Published Bulletins, Bulletin No. 88, Records of the Women's Bureau.

185. Komarovsky, *The Unemployed Man and His Family,* 45, 78–79; schedule Ottumwa-6, box 123, Raw Data for Published Bulletins, Bulletin No. 88, Records of the Women's Bureau.

186. Elderton, *Case Studies of Unemployment,* 100; Komarovsky, *The Unemployed Man and His Family,* 44.

187. Schedule 7-3-284, box 98, and schedule 7-7-476, box 99, Raw Data for Published Bulletins, Bulletin No. 74, Records of the Women's Bureau.

188. Schedule 2941, box 33, Raw Data for Published Bulletins, Bulletin No. 60, Records of the Women's Bureau.

189. Ibid. Schedule 1101.

190. Louise Lamphere, *From Working Daughters to Working Mothers: Immigrant Women in a New England Industrial Community* (Ithaca: Cornell University Press, 1987), 278–88, 366–69.

191. Schedule 11-79, box 120, Raw Data for Published Bulletins, Bulletin No. 88, Records of the Women's Bureau.

192. "Ilona vs. Gizella," Folder #5, Box 31, YWCA Papers, Sophia Smith Collection, Smith College.

193. Elderton, *Case Studies of Unemployment,* 138.

194. Schedules 31-17 and 31-70, box 122, schedule 24-14, box 123, Raw Data for Published Bulletins, Bulletin No. 88, Records of the Women's Bureau.

195. Schedule 7-5-441, box 99, Raw Data for Published Bulletins, Bulletin No. 74, Records of the Women's Bureau.

196. Arlie Russell Hochschild, *The Second Shift* (New York: Avon Books, 1989), 59–74.

197. Schedule 87, Raw Data for Published Bulletins, Bulletin No. 126, Records of the Women's Bureau.

198. Schedule 7-1-9, box 97; schedules 7-8-686 and 7-8-705, box 101; all in Raw Data for Published Bulletins, Bulletin No. 74, Records of the Women's Bureau.

199. Ibid. Schedule 7-6-451, box 99.

200. Lamb, folder "#11—Survey Materials—Questionnaires," box 4, Raw Data for Published Bulletins, *Women Street Car Conductors and Ticket Agents,* Bulletin No. 11 (1921), Records of the Women's Bureau.

201. Schedule 32-35, box 122, Raw Data for Published Bulletins, Bulletin No. 88, Records of the Women's Bureau.

202. Ibid. Schedule 37-5.

203. Ibid. Schedule 56-14, box 123.

204. Schedule 7-8-687, box 101, Raw Data for Published Bulletins, Bulletin No. 74, Records of the Women's Bureau.

205. Schedule 41-23, box 123, Raw Data for Published Bulletins, Bulletin No. 88, Records of the Women's Bureau.

206. Ibid. Schedule 56-18, box 123; schedule 16-51, box 121.

207. Schedule 7-8-708, box 101, Raw Data for Published Bulletins, Bulletin No. 74, Records of the Women's Bureau .

208. Ibid. Schedule 7-8-560, box 100.

209. Levini family case study, folder 12, box 43, Helen Hall Papers.

210. Schedule 56-67, box 123, and schedule 37-5, box 122, Raw Data for Published Bulletins, Bulletin No. 88, Records of the Women's Bureau.

211. Schedule 7-6-452, box 99, Raw Data for Published Bulletins, Bulletin No. 74, Records of the Women's Bureau.

212. Susan A. Glenn, *Daughters of the Shtetl: Life and Labor in the Immigrant Generation* (Ithaca: Cornell University Press, 1990), 238–39.

213. Osborn, box 7, Raw Data for Published Bulletins, Bulletin No. 19, Records of the Women's Bureau.

214. Schedule 7-2-115, box 97, Raw Data for Published Bulletins, Bulletin No. 74, Records of the Women's Bureau.

215. Ibid. Schedule 7-8-617, box 100.

216. Koos, box 25, Raw Data for Published Bulletins, Bulletin No. 48, Records of the Women's Bureau.

217. Schedule 24-26, box 123, Raw Data for Published Bulletins, Bulletin No. 88, Records of the Women's Bureau.

218. Heller Committee for Research on Social Economics, University of California, *Spending Ways of a Semi-Skilled Group: A Study of the Incomes and Expenditures of Ninety-Eight Street-Car Men's Families in the San Francisco East Bay Region,* vol. 4 of *Cost of Living Studies* (Berkeley: University of California Press, 1931), 344.

219. Elderton, *Case Studies of Unemployment,* 218.

220. Glenn, *Daughters of the Shtetl.* 240.

221. Schedule 11, Raw Data for Published Bulletins, Bulletin No. 126, Records of the Women's Bureau.

222. Ibid. Schedule 45.

223. Ibid. Schedule 48.

224. Elderton, *Case Studies of Unemployment,* 109.

225. E. Wight Bakke, *Citizens without Work: A Study of the Effects of Unemployment upon the Workers' Social Relations and Practices,* Institute of Human Relations (New Haven: Yale University Press, 1940), 110–119.

226. Angell, *The Family Encounters the Great Depression,* 111–13.

227. Ibid., 200.

228. Ferranza, box 18, Raw Data for Published Bulletins, Bulletin No. 35, Records of the Women's Bureau.

229. Schedule 7-4-341, box 99, Raw Data for Published Bulletins, Bulletin No. 74, Records of the Women's Bureau.

230. "My Ideas on Married Women in Industry," folder 1503, box 96, Mary Van Kleeck Papers.

231. Day, folder "Home visit schedules—Georgia," box 9, Raw Data for Published Bulletins, Bulletin No. 22, Records of the Women's Bureau.

232. Schedule 11-46, box 120, Raw Data for Published Bulletins, Bulletin No. 88, Records of the Women's Bureau.

233. For a similar case, see ibid., schedule 41-23, box 123.

234. Ibid. Schedule 37-30, box 122.

235. Ibid. Schedule 24-16, box 123.

236. See, for example, ibid., schedule 36-38, box 122.

237. Ibid. Schedule 11-16, box 120.

238. Ibid. Schedule 56-96, box 123; Schedule 7-2-112, box 97, and schedule 7-9-722, box 101, Raw Data for Published Bulletins, Bulletin No. 74, Records of the Women's Bureau.

239. Schedule 7-8-616, box 100, Raw Data for Published Bulletins, Bulletin No. 74, Records of the Women's Bureau.

240. Ibid. Schedule 7-2-178, box 98.

241. Ibid. Schedule 7-3-297, box 98.

242. "Why I Went to Work so Young," folder 1503, box 96, Mary Van Kleeck Papers.

243. Lofton, folder "Home Visit Schedules—Georgia—1," box 9, Raw Data for Published Bulletins, Bulletin No. 22, Records of the Women's Bureau. See also Dill schedule in the same folder.

244. Lowrie, folder "#10 survey materials—home visits," box 3, Raw Data for Published Bulletins, Bulletin No. 10, Records of the Women's Bureau.

245. Lovich, folder "Home Visit Schedules—Georgia—2," box 9, Raw Data for Published Bulletins, Bulletin No. 22, Records of the Women's Bureau. See also Dill in "Home Visit Schedules—1."

246. Schedule 37-30, box 122, Raw Data for Published Bulletins, Bulletin No. 88, Records of the Women's Bureau.

247. Ibid. Schedule 36-38; for almost identical statements, see also "Mothers' Pensions 1925–26," Nos. 45 and 58, box 3, Unpublished Studies and Materials, Records of the Women's Bureau.

248. Schedule 21-10, box 123, Raw Data for Published Bulletins, Bulletin No. 88, Records of the Women's Bureau.

249. Haney family case study, folder 9, box 105, Helen Hall Papers.

250. Schedule 7-2-112, box 97, Raw Data for Published Bulletins, Bulletin No. 74, Records of the Women's Bureau.

251. Ibid. Schedule 7-3-321, box 98.

252. Ibid. Schedule 7-12-949, box 102, and schedule 7-2-123, box 97; Manning, *The Immigrant Woman and Her Job,* 91.

253. Schedule 7-2-187, box 98, Raw Data for Published Bulletins, Bulletin No. 74, Records of the Women's Bureau.

2. "Cooperative Conflict"

1. Susan Porter Benson, "Living on the Margin: Working-Class Marriage and Family Survival Strategies in the United States, 1919–1941," in *The Sex of Things: Gender and Consumption in Historical Perspective,* ed. Victoria De Grazia with Ellen Furlough (Berkeley: University of California Press, 1996), 212–43.

2. David Nasaw, *Children of the City: At Work and at Play* (New York: Oxford University Press, 1985).

3. David Nasaw, "Children and Commercial Culture: Moving Pictures in the Early Twentieth Century," in *Small Worlds: Children & Adolescents in America, 1850–1950,* ed. Elliott West and Paula Petrik (Lawrence: University Press of Kansas, 1992), 18.

4. See T. J. Woofter, *Races and Ethnic Groups in American Life* (New York: McGraw-Hill, 1933), 164–66; Jeremiah W. Jenks and W. Jett Lauck, *The Immigration Problem: A Study of American Immigration Conditions and Needs,* ed. Rufus D. Smith, rev. ed. (New York: Funk & Wagnalls, 1926), 349–57; David B. Tyack, *The One Best System: A History of American Urban Education* (Cambridge: Harvard University Press, 1974), 182–83.

5. The Heller Committee for Research in Social Economics of the University of California and Constantine Panunzio, *How Mexicans Earn and Live: A Study of the Incomes and Expenditures of One Hundred Mexican Families in San Diego, California,* University of California Publication in Economics 13.1, May 17, 1933 (Berkeley: University of California Press, 1933), 7, 50; Emily H. Huntington and Mary Gorringe Luck, *Living on a Moderate Income: The Incomes and Expenditures of Street-Car Men's and Clerks' Families in the San Francisco Bay Region* (Berkeley: University of California Press, 1937), 29, 87, 117, 164.

6. Heller Committee and Panunzio, *How Mexicans Earn and Live,* 52.

7. Ibid., 51; Huntington and Luck, *Living on a Moderate Income,* 164.

8. Gwendolyn Salisbury Hughes, *Mothers in Industry: Wage-Earning by Mothers in Philadelphia* (New York: New Republic, 1925), 195–96 similarly found the "little mother" to be a thing of the past. See also 30. The two cases discussed are Schedule 33-4, Raw Data for Published Bulletins, *Women in Georgia Industries: A Study of Hours, Wages, and Working Conditions,* Bulletin No. 22 (1922); and Schedule 89, Raw Data for Published Bulletins, *Women in Texas Industries: Hours, Wages, Working Conditions, and Home Work,* Bulletin No. 126 (1936); both in Records of the Women's Bureau, RG 86 (National Archives, College Park). For a representation of the "little mother" by Riis, see Jacob Riis, *How the Other Half Lives* (New York: Dover, 1971), 120.

9. Schedule 7-5-418, box 99, Raw Data for Published Bulletins, *The Immigrant Woman and Her Job,* Bulletin No. 74 (1930), Records of the Women's Bureau.

10. Ibid. Schedule 7-8-695, box 101.

11. Ibid. Schedule 7-8-696, box 101; see also schedule 7-12-868, box 102.

12. Ibid. Schedule 7-9-715, box 101.

13. Ibid. Schedule 7-9-748.

14. Ibid. Schedule 7-9-799.

15. Ibid. Schedule 7-9-723.

16. Ibid. Schedule 7-12-901, box 102.

17. Ibid. Schedule 7-1-42, box 97.

18. Ibid. Schedule 7-12-907, box 102.

19. Ibid. Schedule 7-8-648, box 100.

20. Ibid. Schedule 7-9-786, box 101.

21. Ibid. Schedule 7-2-123, box 97. See Ileen A. DeVault, *Sons and Daughters of Labor: Class and Clerical Work in Turn-of-the-Century Pittsburgh* (Ithaca: Cornell University Press, 1991), 73–104.

22. Schedule 7-12-915, box 102, Raw Data for Published Bulletins, Bulletin No. 74, Records of the Women's Bureau.

23. Ibid. Schedule 7-2-113, box 97.

24. Ibid. Schedules 7-1-20 (Polish), 7-2-70 (Jewish), and 7-2-121 (Hungarian), box 97; schedule 7-4-371, box 99 (Italian); schedule 7-8-623, box 100 (Polish).

25. Ibid. Schedule 7-2-131, box 97.

26. Ibid. Schedule 7-2-138.

27. Ibid. Schedule 7-8-657, box 101; see also schedule 7-12-901, box 102.

28. Ibid. Schedule 7-1-9, box 97.

29. Ibid. Schedule 7-2-232, box 98.

30. Ibid. Schedule 7-12-930, box 102.

31. Schedule 17-7-8721, box 121, Raw Data for Published Bulletins, *The Employment of Women in Slaughtering and Meat Packing,* Bulletin No. 88 (1932), Records of the Women's Bureau.

32. Ibid. Schedule 36-6-9, box 122.

33. Schedule 7-2-115, box 97, Raw Data for Published Bulletins, Bulletin No. 74, Records of the Women's Bureau.

34. Ibid. Schedule 7-2-187, box 98.

35. Schedule 36-6-10, box 122, Raw Data for Published Bulletins, Bulletin No. 88, Records of the Women's Bureau.

36. Schedule 7-12-863, box 102, Raw Data for Published Bulletins, Bulletin No. 74, Records of the Women's Bureau.

37. Ibid. Schedule 7-12-925, box 102.

38. Irvin Child, *Italian or American? The Second Generation Conflict* (New Haven, 1943), 106.

39. Ruth Shonle Cavan and Katherine Howland Ranck, *The Family and the Depression: A Study of One Hundred Chicago Families* (Chicago: University of Chicago Press, 1938), 92. At least two-thirds of the families in this study were working class.

40. Ibid., 92.

41. Schedule 31-25, box 122, Raw Data for Published Bulletins, Bulletin No. 88; Hazel Hall, box 7, Raw Data for Published Bulletins, *Iowa Women in Industry, Bulletin No. 19* (1922); both in Records of the Women's Bureau.

42. Schedule 25-7, box 8, Raw Data for Published Bulletins, *Women in Rhode Island Industries: A Study of Hours, Wages, and Working Conditions,* Bulletin No. 21 (1922), Records of the Women's Bureau.

43. Schedule 46-5, box 123, Raw Data for Published Bulletins, Bulletin No. 88, Records of the Women's Bureau.

44. Falls, box 3, Raw Data for Published Bulletins, *Hours and Conditions of Work for Women in Industry in Virginia,* Bulletin No. 10 (1920), Records of the Women's Bureau.

45. Schedule 31-2, box 8, Raw Data for Published Bulletins, Bulletin No. 21, Records of the Women's Bureau.

46. Schedule 51-Pankau, box 123, Raw Data for Published Bulletins, Bulletin No. 88, Records of the Women's Bureau.

47. Crowley, box 9, folder "Home visit schedules—Atlanta," Raw Data for Published Bulletins, Bulletin No. 22, Records of the Women's Bureau.

48. Mirra Komarovsky, *The Unemployed Man and His Family* (New York; Dryden Press for the Institute of Social Research, 1940), 99.

49. Cavan and Ranck, *The Family and the Depression,* 142.

50. Roger Angell, *The Family Encounters the Depression* (New York: C. Scribner's Sons, 1936), 108.

51. Profile of John, folder 1, box 44, Helen Hall Papers, Social Welfare History Archives, University of Minnesota, Minneapolis.

52. Schedule 3185, box 33, Raw Data for Published Bulletins, *Industrial Accidents to Women in New Jersey, Ohio, and Wisconsin,* Bulletin No. 60 (1927), Records of the Women's Bureau.

53. Schedule Sioux City A-4, box 122, Raw Data for Published Bulletins, Bulletin No. 88, Records of the Women's Bureau.

54. Uherka, box 7, Raw Data for Published Bulletins, Bulletin No. 19, Records of the Women's Bureau.

55. Dorn, box 16, Raw Data for Published Bulletins, *Women in South Carolina Industries: A Study of Hours, Wages, and Working Conditions,* Bulletin No. 32 (1923), Records of the Women's Bureau.

56. Schedule 32-9, box 122, Raw Data for Published Bulletins, Bulletin No. 88, Records of the Women's Bureau.

57. Schedule St. Louis-Seeger, box 12, Raw Data for Published Bulletins, *Women in the Candy Industry in Chicago and St. Louis: A Study of Hours, Wages, and Working Conditions in 1920–1921,* Bulletin No. 25 (1923), Records of the Women's Bureau.

58. Schedule 14-4, box 8, Raw Data for Published Bulletins, Bulletin No. 21, Records of the Women's Bureau.

59. Schedule Chicago-Rychlechi, box 12, Raw Data for Published Bulletins, Bulletin No. 25, Records of the Women's Bureau.

60. Schedule 12, box 25, Raw Data for Published Bulletins, *Women in Oklahoma Industries: A Study of Hours, Wages, and Working Conditions,* Bulletin No. 48 (1926), Records of the Women's Bureau.

61. Schedule 51, box 3, Raw Data for Published Bulletins, Bulletin No. 10, Records of the Women's Bureau.

62. Frances R. Whitney, *What Girls Live On—and How: A Study of the Expenditures of a Sample Group of Girls Employed in Cincinnati in 1929* (Cincinnati, 1930), 13; see also 19.

63. Schedule 42-123, box 123, Raw Data for Published Bulletins, Bulletin No. 88, Records of the Women's Bureau.

64. Kathy Peiss, *Cheap Amusements: Working Women and Leisure in New York City, 1880–1920* (Philadelphia: Temple University Press, 1986), 62–67. See also Nan Enstad, *Ladies of Labor, Girls of Adventure: Working Women, Popular Culture, and Labor Politics at the Turn of the Twentieth Century* (New York: Columbia University Press, 1999), 17–83.

65. Schedule 61-1, folder "Home visit schedules—Georgia," box 9, Raw Data for Published Bulletins, Bulletin No. 22, Records of the Women's Bureau.

66. Schedule 59-14, box 8, Raw Data for Published Bulletins, Bulletin No. 21, Records of the Women's Bureau.

67. Schedule 31-22, box 122, Raw Data for Published Bulletins, Bulletin No. 88, Records of the Women's Bureau; see also schedule 42-53, box 123.

68. Schedule 2336, box 33, Raw Data for Published Bulletins, Bulletin No. 60, Records of the Women's Bureau.

69. Ibid. Schedule 1776.

70. Ibid. Schedule 2535.

71. Marion Elderton, ed., *Case Studies of Unemployment Compiled by the Unemployment Committee of the National Federation of Settlements* (Philadelphia: University of Pennsylvania Press, 1931), 22–23.

72. Christine Stansell, *City of Women: Sex and Class in New York, 1789–1860* (Urbana: University of Illinois Press, 1987), 89–100.

73. Thanks to Sharon Strom for suggesting this point to me.

74. Hennings, box 7, Raw Data for Published Bulletins, Bulletin No. 19, Records of the Women's Bureau.

75. Helen Howard, folder "Home visit schedules—Atlanta," box 9, Raw Data for Published Bulletins, Bulletin No. 22, Records of the Women's Bureau.

76. Schedule 61-G, box 16, Raw Data for Published Bulletins, Bulletin No. 32, Records of the Women's Bureau.

77. Whitney, *What Girls Live On*, 11–12.

78. Schedule Sioux City-A-3, box 122, Raw Data for Published Bulletins, Bulletin No. 88, Records of the Women's Bureau.

79. Ibid., Schedule 32-3.

80. Poss, folder "Home visit schedules—Atlanta," box 9, Raw Data for Published Bulletins, Bulletin No. 22, Records of the Women's Bureau.

81. Elderton, *Case Studies of Unemployment*, 166.

82. Osborn, box 7, Raw Data for Published Bulletins, Bulletin No. 19, Records of the Women's Bureau.

83. Schedule 31-4, box 122; schedules 42-21 and 56-15, box 123; all in Raw Data for Published Bulletins, Bulletin No. 88, Records of the Women's Bureau.

84. Ibid. Schedule 36-10, box 122; schedule 51-37, box 123; schedules 36-20 and 32-46, box 122.

85. Elderton, *Case Studies of Unemployment*, 326.

86. Ibid., 322.

87. Cavan and Ranck, *The Family and the Depression*, 142.

88. Schedules 5 and 104, folder "Housing Survey 1933 District of Columbia—Schesdules," box 14, Division of Research, Unpublished Studies and Materials, Records of the Women's Bureau.

89. Kernahan, box 7, Raw Data for Published Bulletins, Bulletin No. 19, Records of the Women's Bureau.

90. Schedule 46-3, folder "Home visit schedules—Georgia," box 9, Raw Data for Published Bulletins, Bulletin No. 22, Records of the Women's Bureau.

91. Schedule 84, folder "Housing Survey 1933 District of Columbia—Schedules," box 14, Unpublished Studies and Materials, Records of the Women's Bureau; see also schedule 101.

92. Dorn, box 16, Raw Data for Published Bulletins, Bulletin No. 32, Records of the Women's Bureau.

93. Schedule 41-53, box 123, Raw Data for Published Bulletins, Bulletin No. 88, Records of the Women's Bureau.

94. Ibid. Schedules 42-135 and 42-36, box 123; schedule 17-83, box 120.

95. Schedule St. Louis-Rose Miller/Elizabeth Miller, box 12, Raw Data for Published Bulletins, Bulletin No. 25, Records of the Women's Bureau.

96. See, for example, E. Wight Bakke, *Citizens without Work: A Study of the Ef-*

fects of Unemployment upon the Workers' Social Relations and Practices (New Haven: Yale University Press, 1940), 125–26.

97. Cavan and Ranck, *The Family and the Depression*, 163–64; quotation from 164. See also 92–94.

98. Sadie Tanner Mossell, *The Standard of Living among One Hundred Negro Migrant Families in Philadelphia*, appendix to *Annals of the American Academy of Political and Social Sciences* 98 (November 1921): 186.

99. Elderton, *Case Studies of Unemployment*, 97.

100. Whitney, *What Girls Live On*, 22.

101. Schedules 56-11 and 56-12, box 123, Raw Data for Published Bulletins, Bulletin No. 88, Records of the Women's Bureau.

102. Elderton, *Case Studies of Unemployment*, 335–36.

103. Schedule 24-50, box 123, Raw Data for Published Bulletins, Bulletin No. 88, Records of the Women's Bureau.

104. Ibid. Schedule 21-23.

105. Schedule Chicago-Annuzzio, box 12, Raw Data for Published Bulletins, Bulletin No. 25, Records of the Women's Bureau.

106. Jeanne Boydston, chap. 7 in *Home and Work: Housework, Wages, and the Ideology of Labor in the Early Republic* (New York: Oxford University Press, 1990).

3. The Mutuality of Shared Spaces

1. Judith M. Bennett, *Ale, Beer, and Brewsters in England: Women's Work in a Changing World, 1300–1600* (New York: Oxford University Press, 1996); Steve J. Stern, *The Secret History of Gender: Women, Men, and Power in Late Colonial Mexico* (Chapel Hill: University of North Carolina Press, 1995); and Gracia Clark, *Onions Are My Husband: Survival and Accumulation by West African Market Women* (Chicago: University of Chicago Press, 1994).

2. Eric Hobsbawm, "Introduction: Inventing Traditions," in *The Invention of Tradition*, ed. Hobsbawm and Terence Ranger (Cambridge, UK: Cambridge University Press, 1983), 1–14. I thank Charles McGraw for suggesting this point to me.

3. Judith E. Smith, *Family Connections: A History of Italian and Jewish Immigrant Lives in Providence, Rhode Island, 1900–1940* (Albany: State University of New York Press, 1985); and Carol B. Stack, *All Our Kin: Strategies for Survival in the Black Community* (New York: Harper and Row, 1974).

4. E. Wight Bakke, *Citizens without Work: A Study of the Effects of Unemployment upon the Workers' Social Relations and Practices*, Institute for Human Relations (New Haven: Yale University Press, 1940), 186.

5. Schedule 7-2-87, box 97, Raw Data from Published Bulletins, *The Immigrant Woman and Her Job*, Bulletin No. 74 (1930), Records of the Women's Bureau, RG 86 (National Archives, College Park).

6. Ibid. Schedule 7-2-209, box 98.

7. Caroline Manning, *The Immigrant Woman and Her Job*, Bulletin of the Women's Bureau, No. 74 (Washington, DC: Government Printing Office, 1930); Mary Elizabeth Pidgeon, *The Employment of Women in Slaughtering and Meat Packing*, Bulletin of the Women's Bureau, No. 88 (Washington, DC: Government Printing Office, 1932); Mary Loretta Sullivan and Bertha Blair, *Women in Texas Industries: Hours, Wages, Working Conditions, and Home Work*, Bulletin of the Women's Bureau, No. 126 (Washington, DC: Government Printing Office, 1936). The research on which these Bulletins is based was conducted, respectively, in 1925, from July 1928 through January 1929, and in 1932.

8. *Women in Georgia Industries: A Study of Hours, Wages, and Working Conditions*, Bulletin of the Women's Bureau, No. 22 (Washington, DC: Government Printing Office, 1922); *Case Studies of Unemployment Compiled by the Unemployment Committee of the National Federation of Settlements*, ed. Marion Elderton (Philadelphia: University of Pennsylvania Press, 1931); Gwendolyn Salisbury Hughes, *Mothers in Industry: Wage-Earning by Mothers in Philadelphia* (New York: New Republic, 1925), 92. The Elderton profiles are sometimes composites, but the whole was assembled to be representative of the cases submitted by settlement houses. The figure from Hughes is from the whole population of houses visited, not from those where fuller interviews were conducted; 300 out of the 728 in the latter category were expanded.

9. Manning, *The Immigrant Woman and Her Job*, 64–65. I have excluded the data from the Lehigh Valley from this book because it overlapped with that from Philadelphia in the same Bulletin (No. 74) and that from Bulletin No. 88.

10. These and figures for East St. Louis, Kansas City, and Omaha come from Pidgeon, *The Employment of Women in Slaughtering and Meat Packing*, Table 44, 190–91.

11. Ibid.

12. Schedule 7-8-627, box 100, Raw Data for Published Bulletins, Bulletin No. 74, Records of the Women's Bureau.

13. Ruth Shonle Cavan and Katherine Howland Ranck, *The Family and the Depression: A Study of One Hundred Chicago Families* (Chicago: University of Chicago Press, 1938), 90.

14. Computed from Table 44 in Pidgeon, *The Employment of Women in Slaughtering and Meat Packing*, 190–91.

15. Schedule 11-1-34, box 120, Raw Data for Published Bulletins, *The Employment of Women in Slaughtering and Meat Packing*, Bulletin No. 88 (1932), Records of the Women's Bureau.

16. The home visit forms for Ottumwa are dated January 10–13, 1928, all by the same agent. Given that it is unlikely that the Ottumwa home visits would have been done so long before those in other cities, I assume that the agent made the common mistake of using the last year's date in the early days of the new year.

17. Schedule 5.2.3, Raw Data for Published Bulletins, Industrial Homework in Rhode Island, Bulletin No. 131 (1935), Records of the Women's Bureau.

18. Schedule 11-19, box 120, Raw Data for Published Bulletins, Bulletin No. 88, Records of the Women's Bureau.

19. Schedule 7-2-206, box 98; schedule 7-5-418, box 99; and schedule 7-3-316, box 98; all in Raw Data for Published Bulletins, Bulletin No. 74, Records of the Women's Bureau. For a similar arrangement, by coincidence also in Philadelphia, see Elderton, *Case Studies of Unemployment,* 26–27: a couple with six young children were splitting the mortgage and taxes on a house with the wife's "real old" mother, her sister, and brother.

20. Schedule 7-2-206, box 98, Raw Data for Published Bulletins, Bulletin No. 74, Records of the Women's Bureau.

21. Ibid. Schedule 7-1-27, box 97.

22. Ibid. Schedule 7-2-224, box 98.

23. Ibid. Schedule 7-2-240.

24. Ibid. Schedule 7-4-334, box 99.

25. Wood, Raw Data for Published Bulletins, *Women in Arkansas Industries,* Bulletin No. 124, Records of the Women's Bureau.

26. Schedule 7-2-158, box 98, Raw Data for Published Bulletins, Bulletin No. 74, Records of the Women's Bureau.

27. The preceding paragraph is based on the following classifications:

Table 1. Each category as percent of total in study

House-sharing	WB 22— GA&Atl 1920–21 n = 273		WB 74— Phila 1925 n = 988		WB 88— Meat 7/28–1/29 n = 897		WB 126— Texas 1932 n = 119	
	#	%	#	%	#	%	#	%
Any	56	20.5	157	15.9	146	16.2	20	16.8
With kin	50	18.3	133	13.5	111	12.4	17	14.3
With woman's parents	26	9.5	50	5.1	59	6.6	6	5.0
Among female kin	41	15.0	98	9.9	84	9.4	15	12.6
Among different generations of female kin	30	9.5	62	6.3	72	8.0	8	6.7
Among same generation of female kin	17	6.2	37	3.7	17	1.9	7	5.9
With husband's parents	5	1.8	10	1.0	11	1.2	1	0.8
With male kin not husband's parents	4	1.5	25	2.5	2	0.2	1	0.8
With male kin of different generation	3	1.1	9	0.9	1	0.1	—	—
With male kin of same generation	1	0.3	16	1.6	1	0.1	1	0.8

Table 2. Each category as percent of house-sharing

House-sharing	WB 22—GA&Atl 1920–21 n = 273		WB 74—Phila 1925 n = 988		WB 88—Meat 7/28–1/29 n = 897		WB 126—Texas 1932 n = 119	
	#	%	#	%	#	%	#	%
Any	56	—	157	—	146	—	20	—
With kin	50	89.3	133	84.7	111	76.0	17	85.0
With woman's parents	26	46.4	50	31.8	59	40.4	6	30.0
Among female kin	41	73.2	98	62.4	84	57.5	15	75.0
Among different generations of female kin	30	53.6	62	39.5	72	49.3	8	40.0
Among same generation of female kin	17	30.3	37	23.6	17	11.6	7	35.0
With husband's parents	5	8.9	10	6.4	11	7.5	1	5.0
With male kin not husband's parents	4	7.1	25	15.9	2	1.4	1	5.0
With male kin of different generation	3	5.4	9	5.7	1	0.7	—	—
With male kin of same generation	1	1.8	16	10.2	1	0.7	1	5.0

Table 3. All four WB reports as percent of house-sharing (overall N = 2277, with 379 sharing = 16.6%)

House-sharing	WB Reports 22, 74, 88, and 126	
	#	%
Any	379	
With kin	311	82.1
With woman's parents	141	37.2
Among female kin	238	62.8
Among different generations of female kin	172	45.4
Among same generation of female kin	78	20.6
With husband's parents	27	7.1
With male kin not husband's parents	32	8.4
With male kin of different generation	13	3.4
With male kin of same generation	9	5.0

The incidence of parents living with daughters is slightly lower than that found by Judith Smith for Providence Jews and Italians, and that of parents living with sons is dramatically lower. This difference could be due to a number of factors: Smith considers only immigrant families with both parents and children in Providence (although the highest incidence of parent-daughter co-residence in the Women's Bureau studies was in the almost exclusively non-immigrant group in the Georgia study) and the peculiar residential stock of Providence (triple-decker tenements) may have produced more parent-child co-residence, but as I argue below, my guess is that the Women's Bureau pivot of wage-earning women made the difference.

28. Hughes, *Mothers in Industry*, 97, also finds a preponderance of female kin, with women living with female kin three times as often as with male kin. This is an imperfect measure, however, since her categories do not separate natal kin from kin by marriage and do not separate cousins, nephews and nieces, and grandchildren by sex.

29. There is, of course, not a simple relationship between age and generation: given larger families and longer periods of childbearing, aunts and nieces could be close in age, just as there could be many years' age difference between cousins and between sisters.

30. Schedule 19 (Bertha Smith), Raw Data for Published Bulletins, *Women in Oklahoma Industries: A Study of Hours, Wages, and Working Conditions*, Bulletin No. 48 (1926), Records of the Women's Bureau.

31. Tillie Warren, Raw Data for Published Bulletins, *Women in Maryland Industries*, Bulletin No. 24 (1922), Records of the Women's Bureau.

32. Schedule 31-9, box 122, Raw Data for Published Bulletins, Bulletin No. 88, Records of the Women's Bureau.

33. Hughes, *Mothers in Industry*, 30.

34. Schedules 38-2 and 46-5, Raw Data for Published Bulletins, *Women in Rhode Island Industries: A Study of Hours, Wages, and Working Conditions*, Bulletin No. 21 (1922) Records of the Women's Bureau. This family was not the only one that tried to make up for a deserting son or brother; a spooler in a Georgia cotton mill had moved from Oklahoma with her husband in order to be near his family. He shortly went back to Oklahoma, never making good on his promise to send for his wife and four children. The agent recorded her comments: "Said the husband's family are very good to her and help her some now and then. They want her to come and live with them, but she feels that she wants to raise her children herself." She kept a "very clean and tidy" house with a garden. See Schedule 31-1, Raw Data for Published Bulletins, *Women in Georgia Industries: A Study of Hours, Wages, and Working Conditions*, Bulletin No. 22 (1922), Records of the Women's Bureau.

35. K.W. [Kate White], Raw Data for Published Bulletins, Bulletin No. 124, Records of the Women's Bureau.

36. Schedule 7-3-321, box 98, Raw Data for Published Bulletins, Bulletin No. 74, Records of the Women's Bureau.

37. Schedule 38-2, Raw Data for Published Bulletins, Bulletin No. 21, Records of the Women's Bureau.

38. WB #74, 7-1-58, box 97, Raw Data for Published Bulletins, Bulletin No. 74, Records of the Women's Bureau.

39. Ibid. Schedule 7-8-596, box 100.

40. Ibid. Schedule 7-4-399, box 99.

41. Ibid. Schedule 7-9-717, box 101.

42. N.G. [Nellie Golovack], Raw Data for Published Bulletins, *Women in the Candy Industry in Chicago and St. Louis: A Study of Hours, Wages, and Working Conditions in 1920–1021*, Bulletin No. 25 (1923), Records of the Women's Bureau.

43. Schedule 42-2-108, box 123, Raw Data for Published Bulletins, Bulletin No. 88, Records of the Women's Bureau.

44. Schedule 50, Raw Data for Published Bulletins, *Women in Texas Industries: Hours, Wages, Working Conditions, and Home Work,* Bulletin No. 126 (1936), Records of the Women's Bureau.

45. Schedule 25-5, Raw Data for Published Bulletins, Bulletin No. 21, Records of the Women's Bureau.

46. Schedule 7-2-94, box 97, Raw Data for Published Bulletins, Bulletin No. 74, Records of the Women's Bureau.

47. Ibid. Schedule 7-4-376, box 99.

48. Schedule 41-77, box 123, Raw Data for Published Bulletins, Bulletin No. 88, Records of the Women's Bureau.

49. Schedule 7-8-561, box 100, Raw Data for Published Bulletins, Bulletin No. 74, Records of the Women's Bureau.

50. Ibid. Schedule 7-8-635. For a similar case, this one in a German family, see schedule 7-9-785, box 101.

51. Schedule 2535, Raw Data for Published Bulletins, *Industrial Accidents to Women in New Jersey, Ohio, and Wisconsin,* Bulletin No. 60 (1927), Records of the Women's Bureau.

52. Ibid. Gerosick.

53. Ibid. Schedule 792.

54. Ibid. Schedule 667.

55. Ibid. Schedule 2689.

56. Ibid. Schedule 1994.

57. Ibid. Schedule 2284.

58. Ibid. Schedule 2854.

59. Ibid. Schedule 3309.

60. B.G. [Belle Griffiths], Raw Data for Published Bulletins, Bulletin No. 25, Records of the Women's Bureau.

61. Schedules 43 (mother's and daughter's schedules both numbered 43), Georgia file #1, Raw Data for Published Bulletins, Bulletin No. 22, Records of the Women's Bureau.

62. Schedule 43-5, box 123, Raw Data for Published Bulletins, Bulletin No. 88, Records of the Women's Bureau.

63. Ibid. Schedule 16-23, box 121.

64. Schedule 7-2-235, box 98, Raw Data for Published Bulletins, Bulletin No. 74, Records of the Women's Bureau.

65. Ibid. Schedule 7-4-373, box 99.

66. Ibid. Schedule 7-2-190, box 98.

67. Ibid. Schedule 7-1-27, box 97.

68. For another family in which a daughter paid "all bills" in exchange for living in a house owned by her ailing mother, see Schedule 42-108, box 123, Raw Data for Published Bulletins, Bulletin No. 88, Records of the Women's Bureau.

69. Elderton, *Case Studies of Unemployment*, 336.

70. Ibid., 80.

71. Ibid., 70–71, quotation from 71. A similar proportion of families doubling up on housing as a result of the Depression were found in a study of Houston (eight of forty electricians' families); Ruth Alice Allen and Sam B. Barton, *Wage Earners Meet the Depression*, The University of Texas Bulletin No. 3545 (December 1, 1935), Bureau of Research in the Social Sciences Study No. 15, 27.

72. Schedule 7-8-501, box 100, Raw Data for Published Bulletins, Bulletin No. 74, Records of the Women's Bureau.

73. Ibid. Schedule 7-8-699, box 101.

74. Schedule 31-63, box 122, Raw Data for Published Bulletins, Bulletin No. 88, Records of the Women's Bureau.

75. Ibid. Schedule 32-31.

76. Ibid. Schedule 17-76, box 121.

77. "Housing Survey 1933 District of Columbia—Schedules," No. 94, box 14, Division of Research, Unpublished Studies and Materials, 1919–1972, Records of the Women's Bureau.

78. Family Society of Philadelphia, *Family Life and National Recovery: The Effect of Economic Unemployment on Family Life* (New York: Family Welfare Association of America, 1934), 7.

79. Cavan and Ranck, *The Family and the Depression*, 91.

80. J.B. (Josephine Banks), Raw Data for Published Bulletins, *Women in Tennessee Industries: A Study of Hours, Wages, and Working Conditions*, Bulletin No. 56 (1927), Records of the Women's Bureau. See also Gerosick, Raw Data for Published Bulletins, Bulletin No. 60, Records of the Women's Bureau. Although the pattern of spouses splitting up was most common during the Depression, it could be the result of personal misfortune. In 1925, for example, a Tennessee couple went to live with their respective parents because of the husband's illness and multiple surgeries; the wife worked at a candy factory in her desperate effort to pay medical bills and debt from the six weeks she took off from work to care for him. Her load at home was heavy, since her mother was elderly and needed help with the housework and laundry.

81. Schedule 5.1.29, Raw Data for Published Bulletins, Bulletin No. 131, Records of the Women's Bureau.

82. See especially "Housing Survey 1933 District of Columbia—Schedules," box 14, Division of Research, Unpublished Studies and Materials, 1919–1972, Records of the Women's Bureau. Good examples are schedules numbered 6, 11, 12, 15, 24, 25, 29, 33, 55, 101, and 108.

83. Schedule 6-1, Raw Data for Published Bulletins, Bulletin No. 22, Records of the Women's Bureau.

84. M.R. [Mollie Richardson] and C.B. [Cora Baerer], Raw Data for Published Bulletins, *Women in Missouri Industries: A Study of Hours and Wages,* Bulletin No. 35 (1924), Records of the Women's Bureau.

85. Schedule 6.2.16, Raw Data for Published Bulletins, Bulletin No. 131, Records of the Women's Bureau.

86. Elderton, *Case Studies of Unemployment,* 177.

87. Schedule 32, Raw Data for Published Bulletins, Bulletin No. 126, Records of the Women's Bureau.

88. Ibid. Schedule 87.

89. Schedule 2.1.11, Raw Data for Published Bulletins, Bulletin No. 131, Records of the Women's Bureau.

90. Schedule 7-2-183, box 98, Raw Data for Published Bulletins, Bulletin No. 74, Records of the Women's Bureau.

91. Schedule 63-3, Raw Data for Published Bulletins, Bulletin No. 22, Records of the Women's Bureau.

92. Schedule 5.1.31, Raw Data for Published Bulletins, Bulletin No. 131, Records of the Women's Bureau. Similar examples of flexible rent: Schedule 81, Raw Data for Published Bulletins, Bulletin No. 126; Mrs. Scott, Raw Data for Published Bulletins, Bulletin No. 22; both in Records of the Women's Bureau. Mrs. Scott paid "what she can spare."

93. Schedule 42-25, box 123, Raw Data for Published Bulletins, Bulletin No. 88, Records of the Women's Bureau.

94. Schedule 7-2-149, box 97; schedules 7-2-186 and 7-2-197, box 98; Raw Data for Published Bulletins, Bulletin No. 74, Records of the Women's Bureau.

95. Ibid. 7-11-818, box 102.

96. Schedule 115, Raw Data for Published Bulletins, Bulletin No. 126, Records of the Women's Bureau.

97. Schedule 7-2-163, box 98, Raw Data for Published Bulletins, Bulletin No. 74, Records of the Women's Bureau.

98. Ibid. Schedule 7-3-320.

99. Ibid. Schedule 7-4-362, box 99.

100. Ibid. Schedule 7-2-236, box 98.

101. Schedule 31-84, box 122, Raw Data for Published Bulletins, Bulletin No. 88, Records of the Women's Bureau.

102. Schedules 40-2 and 46-1, Raw Data for Published Bulletins, Bulletin No. 21, Records of the Women's Bureau.

103. Schedules 31-4 and 31-5, Raw Data for Published Bulletins, Bulletin No. 22, Records of the Women's Bureau.

104. Schedule 41, Raw Data for Published Bulletins, Bulletin No. 10, Records of the Women's Bureau. Elderton, *Case Studies of Unemployment,* 247, includes a case in which an Italian immigrant's uncle bought a house for her but offers no other details. The woman had left Italy when her mother died, coming to the United States to join her father, who many years later was living with her. The case study

offers no hint as to whether the uncle was the brother of the woman's mother or father; if the latter, he may have wanted to secure a home for his brother in his old age.

105. Schedule 7-2-143, box 97, Raw Data for Published Bulletins, Bulletin No. 74, Records of the Women's Bureau.

106. Ibid. Schedule 7-2-220, box 98.

107. Ibid. Schedules 7-9-760 and 7-9-762, box 101.

108. Ibid., Schedule 7-8-523, box 100.

109. Manning, *The Immigrant Woman and Her Job*, 66–68; Midwestern percentages calculated from Pidgeon, *The Employment of Women in Slaughtering and Meat Packing*, tables 40 and 41, 182–84. It is not possible to calculate from Pidgeon's table the percentages living two or more to a room.

110. Family Life and National Recovery, 7–8, quotation from 8.

111. Schedule 7-8-603, box 100, Raw Data for Published Bulletins, Bulletin No. 74, Records of the Women's Bureau.

112. Ibid., Schedule 7-12-948, box 102.

113. Ticco family case study, folder 1, box 42, Helen Hall Papers, Social Welfare History Archives, University of Minnesota, Minneapolis.

114. Elderton, *Case Studies of Unemployment*, 234–36.

115. G.M. (Grace Mitchell), Raw Data for Published Bulletins, *Iowa Women in Industry*, Bulletin No. 19 (1922), Records of the Women's Bureau.

116. C.C. (Clara Craig), Raw Data for Published Bulletins, Bulletin No. 124, Records of the Women's Bureau .

117. Schedule 44-1, Raw Data for Published Bulletins, Bulletin No. 22, Records of the Women's Bureau.

118. Elderton, *Case Studies of Unemployment*, 172.

119. Ibid., 166–68.

120. Ibid., 115–19.

121. Schedule 7-2-107, box 97, Raw Data for Published Bulletins, Bulletin No. 74, Records of the Women's Bureau.

122. Ibid. Schedule 7-2-139. For an estimate of the cost of food in Philadelphia in the mid-1920s, see National Industrial Conference Board, *The Cost of Living in Twelve Industrial Cities* (New York: National Industrial Conference Board, 1928), 16–17.

123. Schedule 30-4, Raw Data for Published Bulletins, Bulletin No. 22, Records of the Women's Bureau.

124. Schedule 7-8-624, box 100, Raw Data for Published Bulletins, Bulletin No. 74, Records of the Women's Bureau.

125. Ibid. Schedule 11-14.

126. Ibid. Schedule 7-11-845, box 102.

127. Ibid., Schedule 7-8-667, box 101.

128. Schedule 6.2.7., Raw Data for Published Bulletins, Bulletin No. 131, Records of the Women's Bureau.

129. Schedules 7-1-10 and 7-1-39, box 97, Raw Data for Published Bulletins, Bulletin No. 74, Records of the Women's Bureau.

130. Schedules 11-19 and 11-20, box 120, Raw Data for Published Bulletins, Bulletin No. 88, Records of the Women's Bureau.

131. Ibid. Schedule 17-58, box 121.

132. Schedule 7-2-235, box 98, Raw Data for Published Bulletins, Bulletin No. 74, Records of the Women's Bureau.

133. Ibid. Schedules 7-8-551 and 7-8-558, box 100.

134. Ibid. Schedule 7-12-923, box 102.

135. Ibid. Schedule 7-9-795, box 101.

136. Schedule 21-213, box 123, Raw Data for Published Bulletins, Bulletin No. 88, Records of the Women's Bureau.

137. Schedule 7-2-224, box 98, Raw Data for Published Bulletins, Bulletin No. 74, Records of the Women's Bureau.

138. Ibid. Schedule 7-2-240.

139. Ibid. Schedule 7-9-730, box 101.

140. Ibid. Schedule 7-9-773.

141. Ibid. Schedule 7-8-627, box 100.

142. Ibid. Schedule 7-12-877, box 102.

143. Ibid. Schedule 7-1-118, box 97.

144. Schedule 21, Raw Data for Published Bulletins, Bulletin No. 10, Records of the Women's Bureau.

145. Schedule 7-4-399, box 99, Raw Data for Published Bulletins, Bulletin No. 74, Records of the Women's Bureau.

146. Ibid. Schedule 7-5-430.

147. Ibid. Schedule 7-4-356.

4. What Goes 'Round, Comes 'Round

1. Schedule 7-3-316, box 98, Raw Data for Published Bulletins, *The Immigrant Woman and Her Job,* Bulletin No. 74 (1930), Records of the Women's Bureau, RG 86 (National Archives, College Park).

2. On the pastoralization of housework, see Jeanne Boydston, *Home and Work: Housework, Wages, and the Ideology of Labor in the Early Republic* (New York: Oxford University Press, 1990).

3. Schedule 16-34, box 121, Raw Data for Published Bulletins, *The Employment of Women in Slaughtering and Meat Packing,* Bulletin No. 88 (1932), Records of the Women's Bureau.

4. Schedule 7-12-870, box 102, Raw Data for Published Bulletins, Bulletin No. 74, Records of the Women's Bureau.

5. P.L. [Pauline Lipke], Raw Data for Published Bulletins, *Women in the Candy Industry in Chicago and St. Louis: A Study of Hours, Wages, and Working Conditions in 1920–1921,* Bulletin No. 25 (1923), Records of the Women's Bureau.

6. Schedule 7-4-366, box 99, Raw Data for Published Bulletins, Bulletin No. 74, Records of the Women's Bureau.

7. Ibid. Schedule 7-2-174, box 97.

8. Schedule 52-4, Raw Data for Published Bulletins, *Women in Rhode Island Industries: A Study of Hours, Wages, and Working Conditions,* Bulletin No. 21 (1922), Records of the Women's Bureau.

9. N.R. [Nelle Rule], Raw Data for Published Bulletins, *Iowa Women in Industry,* Bulletin No. 19 (1922), Records of the Women's Bureau.

10. In four cases, two people shared the role of housekeeper: the wage-earner's mother and sister, mother and sister-in-law, mother and father, and daughter and daughter-in-law.

11. Schedule 17-7-53, box 121, Raw Data for Published Bulletins, Bulletin No. 88, Records of the Women's Bureau.

12. Schedule 7-4-376, box 99, Raw Data for Published Bulletins, Bulletin No. 74, Records of the Women's Bureau.

13. Ibid. Schedule 7-4-334. For a similar case of the oldest daughter being the housekeeper, see schedule 7-2-182, box 98. On telephone workers, see Stephen Norwood, *Labor's Flaming Youth: Telephone Operators and Labor Militancy, 1878–1923* (Urbana: University of Illinois Press, 1990), 193, 197, 204, 305–6.

14. Gwendolyn Salisbury Hughes, *Mothers in Industry: Wage-Earning by Mothers in Philadelphia* (New York: New Republic, 1925), 167–68.

15. Schedule 2-13, Raw Data for Published Bulletins, Bulletin No. 88, Records of the Women's Bureau.

16. Ibid. Schedule 2-20.

17. Schedule 7-2-92, box 97, Raw Data for Published Bulletins, Bulletin No. 74, Records of the Women's Bureau.

18. Ibid. Schedule 7-9-742, box 101.

19. Ibid. Schedule 7-1-27, box 97.

20. Schedule 32-44, box 122, Raw Data for Published Bulletins, Bulletin No. 88, Records of the Women's Bureau.

21. Schedule 7-8-704, box 101, Raw Data for Published Bulletins, Bulletin No. 74, Records of the Women's Bureau.

22. Schedule 2-29, Raw Data for Published Bulletins, Bulletin No. 88, Records of the Women's Bureau.

23. Susan Porter Benson, "Living on the Margin: Working-Class Marriage and Family Survival Strategies in the United States, 1919–1941," in *The Sex of Things: Gender and Consumption in Historical Perspective,* ed. Victoria De Grazia with Ellen Furlough (Berkeley: University of California Press, 1996), 232–34.

24. Schedule 7-2-105, box 97, Raw Data for Published Bulletins, Bulletin No. 74, Records of the Women's Bureau.

25. Ibid. Schedule 7-4-380, box 99.

26. Ibid. Schedule 7-3-272, box 98.

27. Ibid. Schedule 7-3-299.

28. Ibid. Schedule 7-5-433, box 99.

29. Hughes, *Mothers in Industry*, 98, 103–4. In this book, Gwendolyn Hughes argued that the pattern of trading very low rent for household services was especially common among immigrants.

30. Ibid., 172, 194. For children under five, the proportions in day nurseries and at others' homes were about equal, 12 percent and 11 percent respectively.

31. Approximately 9 percent of mothers working in slaughtering and meat-packing and 19 percent of Philadelphia immigrant women.

32. B.H. (Bedie Hale), Raw Data for Published Bulletins, *Women in Tennessee Industries: A Study of Hours, Wages, and Working Conditions*, Bulletin No. 56 (1927), Records of the Women's Bureau.

33. See, for example, schedules 7-2-69, 7-2-82, and 7-2-142, box 97, Raw Data for Published Bulletins, Bulletin No. 74, Records of the Women's Bureau.

34. Ibid. Schedules 7-8-522 and 7-8-578, box 100.

35. Ibid. Schedule 7-9-722, box 101.

36. Elizabeth Rose, chap. 1 in A *Mother's Job: The History of Day Care, 1890–1960* (New York: Oxford University Press, 1999), quotation, 30.

37. Schedules 7-4-342 and 7-7-464, box 99, Raw Data for Published Bulletins, Bulletin No. 74, Records of the Women's Bureau.

38. Ibid. Schedule 7-3-321, box 98.

39. Marion Elderton, ed., *Case Studies of Unemployment Compiled by the Unemployment Committee of the National Federation of Settlements* (Philadelphia: University of Pennsylvania Press, 1931), 261; for a similar case, see schedule 46-2, Raw Data for Published Bulletins, Bulletin No. 21, Records of the Women's Bureau.

40. Elderton, *Case Studies of Unemployment*, 229.

41. Mrs. C. (Crompton), Raw Data for Published Bulletins, *Women in South Carolina Industries: A Study of Hours, Wages, and Working Conditions*, Bulletin No. 32 (1923), Records of the Women's Bureau. Rose found evidence in day-nursery case records of mothers' appreciation for institutional reliability and quality of care (*A Mother's Job*, 50).

42. Schedule 7-4-397, box 99, Raw Data for Published Bulletins, Bulletin No. 74, Records of the Women's Bureau.

43. See Rose, *A Mother's Job*, especially 54–55, 63–64, 97.

44. Schedules 7-2-82 and 7-2-142, box 97, Raw Data for Published Bulletins, Bulletin No. 74, Records of the Women's Bureau.

45. Ibid. Schedule 7-2-119.

46. Rose, *A Mother's Job*, 55.

47. Elderton, *Case Studies of Unemployment*, 306–7.

48. Schedule 7-4-341, box 99, Raw Data for Published Bulletins, Bulletin No. 74, Records of the Women's Bureau.

49. Hughes, *Mothers in Industry*, 195.

50. Schedule 7-1-27, box 97, Raw Data for Published Bulletins, Bulletin No. 74, Records of the Women's Bureau.

51. Ibid. Schedule 7-8-629, box 100.

52. Ibid. Schedules 7-8-524 and 7-8-629.

53. Ibid. Schedules 7-2-107, box 97.

54. Ibid. Schedule 7-2-235, box 98.

55. Ibid. Schedule 7-12-895, box 102.

56. Ibid. Schedule 7-3-279, box 98.

57. Ibid. Schedule 7-2-224, box 98.

58. Schedule 42-2-64, box 123, Raw Data for Published Bulletins, Bulletin No. 88, Records of the Women's Bureau.

59. Ibid. Schedules 42-2-64 and 41-1-77.

60. Schedule 7-8-685, box 101; schedule 7-1-27, box 97; Raw Data for Published Bulletins, Bulletin No. 74; Schedules 41-1-1 and 41-1-77, box 123, Raw Data for Published Bulletins, Bulletin No. 88; all in Records of the Women's Bureau. A fifth cared for children 5 and 7, both in school but probably cared for them before they started school as well and the sixth may have had the care of a six-year-old before he started school . See Schedule 7-8-629, box 100, Raw Data for Published Bulletins, Bulletin No. 74; and Schedule 3-6-13, Raw Data for Published Bulletins, Bulletin No. 88.

61. Schedule 7-3-279, box 98, Raw Data for Published Bulletins, Bulletin No. 74, Records of the Women's Bureau.

62. This analysis of child care furnished by those living outside the household excludes those children who were cared for in day nurseries.

63. Schedule 51-104, box 123, Raw Data for Published Bulletins, Bulletin No. 88, Records of the Women's Bureau.

64. Ibid. Schedule 56-6-5.

65. Schedule 7-12-895, box 102, Raw Data for Published Bulletins, Bulletin No. 74, Records of the Women's Bureau.

66. Ibid. Schedule 7-12-951.

67. Ibid. Schedule 7-8-688, box 101.

68. Hughes, *Mothers in Industry,* 197.

69. "Mothers' Pensions 1925–26," 4, box 3, Unpublished Studies and Materials, Records of the Women's Bureau.

70. Schedule 7-1-39, box 97, Raw Data for Published Bulletins, Bulletin No. 74, Records of the Women's Bureau.

71. Schedule 21-9, box 123, Raw Data for Published Bulletins, Bulletin No. 88, Records of the Women's Bureau.

72. Schedule 7-6-456, box 99, Raw Data for Published Bulletins, Bulletin No. 74, Records of the Women's Bureau.

73. Ibid. Schedule 7-4-342.

74. Ibid. Schedule 7-4-372.

75. Ibid. Schedule 7-3-298, box 98.

76. Ibid. Schedule 7-1-27, box 97.

77. Ibid. Schedule 7-8-598, box 100.

78. Ibid. Schedule 7-8-658, box 101.

79. Ibid. Schedule 7-8-710.

80. Schedule 41-1, box 123, Raw Data for Published Bulletins, Bulletin No. 88, Records of the Women's Bureau.

81. Ibid. Schedule Ottumwa-12.

82. See, for example, Hodgen, Raw Data for Published Bulletins, *Women in Mississippi Industries,* Bulletin No. 55 (1926); and "Mothers' Pensions 1925–26," Cases 62 and 125, box 3, Unpublished Studies and Materials; all in Records of the Women's Bureau.

83. Elderton, *Case Studies of Unemployment,* 177–78.

84. Schedule 43-26, box 123, Raw Data for Published Bulletins, Bulletin No. 88, Records of the Women's Bureau.

85. Ibid. Schedule 42-66.

86. Ibid. Schedule 43-9.

87. Schedule 7-9-733, box 101.

88. Schedule 28-5, Raw Data for Published Bulletins, *Women in Georgia Industries: A Study of Hours, Wages, and Working Conditions,* Bulletin No. 22 (1922), Records of the Women's Bureau.

89. Schedule 36, box 25, Raw Data for Published Bulletins, *Women in Oklahoma Industries: A Study of Hours, Wages, and Working Conditions,* Bulletin No. 48 (1926), Records of the Women's Bureau.

90. Huggins, Raw Data for Published Bulletins, Bulletin No. 32, Records of the Women's Bureau.

91. Pearl Brown, Raw Data for Published Bulletins, Bulletin No. 19, Records of the Women's Bureau.

92. See, for example, Schedule 46, box 25, Raw Data for Published Bulletins, Bulletin No. 48; schedules 42-1, 43-1, 35-4, and 37-2, box 9, Raw Data for Published Bulletins, Bulletin No. 22; all in Records of the Women's Bureau.

93. Schedule 42-1, box 9, Raw Data for Published Bulletins, Bulletin No. 22, Records of the Women's Bureau.

94. "Housing Survey 1933 District of Columbia—Schedules," Nos. 69 and 93, box 14, Division of Research, Unpublished Studies and Materials, 1919–1972, Records of the Women's Bureau.

95. Elderton, *Case Studies of Unemployment,* 15–16, quotation from 16.

96. Schedule M. S. (Marie Schlitz), Raw Data for Published Bulletins, Bulletin No. 25, Records of the Women's Bureau.

97. Elderton, *Case Studies of Unemployment,* 58.

98. Ruth Shonle Cavan and Katherine Howland Ranck, *The Family and the Depression: A Study of One Hundred Chicago Families* (Chicago: University of Chicago Press, 1938), 118.

99. Schedule 1, Raw Data for Published Bulletins, Bulletin No. 48, Records of the Women's Bureau.

100. Elderton, *Case Studies of Unemployment,* 4.

101. Schedule 78, Raw Data for Published Bulletins, *Hours and Earnings in the Leather-Glove Industry,* Bulletin No. 119 (1934), Records of the Women's Bureau.

102. Kathleen B. Jennison Lowrie, *Industrial Accidents to Women in New Jersey, Ohio, and Wisconsin,* Bulletin of the Women's Bureau No. 60 (Washington: Government Printing Office, 1927). The interviews were conducted from June 1923 through March 1924.

103. Hughes, *Mothers in Industry.* Hughes's interviews began on November 20, 1918, and continued through the following August.

104. Hughes, *Mothers in Industry,* 170–71. Hughes's categorization of work is too confusing to permit further analysis.

105. Schedule 2383, Raw Data for Published Bulletins, *Industrial Accidents to Women in New Jersey, Ohio, and Wisconsin,* Bulletin No. 60 (1927), Records of the Women's Bureau.

106. Ibid. Schedule 1777.

107. Ibid. Schedule 2010.

108. Ibid. Schedule 1786.

109. Ibid. Schedules 310 and 318.

110. Ibid. Schedules 341 and 2953.

111. Ibid. Schedules 2621, Schroeder, and Carter.

112. Schedule 31-44, box 122, Raw Data for Published Bulletins, Bulletin No. 88, Records of the Women's Bureau.

113. Cushing, Raw Data for Published Bulletins, Bulletin No. 19, Records of the Women's Bureau.

114. Schedule 7-8-556, box 100, Raw Data for Published Bulletins, Bulletin No. 74, Records of the Women's Bureau.

115. T. S. (Steward), Raw Data for Published Bulletins, Bulletin No. 25, Records of the Women's Bureau.

116. Schedule 2953, Raw Data for Published Bulletins, Bulletin No. 60, Records of the Women's Bureau.

117. Schedule 17, box 25, Raw Data for Published Bulletins, Bulletin No. 48, Records of the Women's Bureau.

118. Schedule 7-9-731, box 101, Raw Data for Published Bulletins, Bulletin No. 74, Records of the Women's Bureau.

119. Ibid. Schedule 7-4-342, box 99.

120. Ibid. Schedule 7-2-240, box 98.

121. Schedules 11-1-109, 11-1-103, and 11-1-117, box 120, Raw Data for Published Bulletins, Bulletin No. 88, Records of the Women's Bureau.

122. Schedule 7-1-7, box 97, Raw Data for Published Bulletins, Bulletin No. 74, Records of the Women's Bureau.

123. Schedule 341, Raw Data for Published Bulletins, Bulletin No. 60, Records of the Women's Bureau.

124. Schedule 7-3-291, box 98, Raw Data for Published Bulletins, Bulletin No. 74, Records of the Women's Bureau.

125. Schedule 11-1-109, box 120, Raw Data for Published Bulletins, Bulletin No. 88, Records of the Women's Bureau.

126. Alvin W. Gouldner, *Patterns of Industrial Bureaucracy* (Glencoe, IL: Free Press, 1954), 51; Jason Ditton, "Pots, Pilferage, and the Fiddle: The Historical Structure of Invisible Wages," *Theory and Society* 4, 1 (1997), 39–71.

127. Mirra Komarovsky, *The Unemployed Man and His Family: The Effect of Unemployment upon the Status of the Man in Fifty-Nine Families* (New York: Dryden Press for the Institute of Social Research, 1940), 78–79. The families interviewed lived "in a large industrial city just outside New York City," 4.

128. Komarovsky, *The Unemployed Man and His Family,* 79.

129. Elderton, *Case Studies of Unemployment,* 321.

130. Case 5, folder "Mothers' Pensions 1925–26," box 3, Unpublished Studies and Materials, 1919–1972, Records of the Women's Bureau.

131. Elderton, *Case Studies of Unemployment.* 293.

132. Ibid., 211.

133. Lorance, Raw Data for Published Bulletins, *Women in Arkansas Industries,* Bulletin No. 124 (1935); Records of the Women's Bureau.

134. 5-22-11, box 131, Bulletin 131, Records of the Division of Special Services and Publications, Records of the Women's Bureau.

135. Robert Cooley Angell, *The Family Encounters the Depression* (New York: Scribner's Sons, 1936), 144.

136. Elderton, 145; see also Chesnough, 3a, folder 11, box 45, Helen Hall Papers, Social Welfare History Archives, University of Minnesota, Minneapolis.

137. Elderton, *Case Studies of Unemployment,* 173, 145, and 148.

138. Schedule 7-12-923, box 102, Raw Data for Published Bulletins, Bulletin No. 74, Records of the Women's Bureau.

139. Chesnough, 9, folder 11, box 45, Helen Hall Papers.

140. Cavan and Ranck, *The Family and the Depression,* 119.

141. Ibid.

142. Elderton, *Case Studies of Unemployment,* 316; see also 348, and 173; and Lorance, box 219, Bulletin 124, Records of the Division of Special Services and Publications, Records of the Women's Bureau.

143. Elderton, *Case Studies of Unemployment,* 58.

144. Ibid., 145.

145. Ibid., 287.

146. Ibid., 62.

147. E. Wight Bakke, *The Unemployed Worker: A Study of the Task of Making a Living without a Job* (New Haven: Yale University Press, 1940), 272.

148. Elderton, *Case Studies of Unemployment,* 240.

149. Cushing, Raw Data for Published Bulletins, Bulletin No. 19, Records of the Women's Bureau.

150. Elderton, *Case Studies of Unemployment,* 98. For gifts of clothing from another teacher, these apparently secondhand, see 117.

151. Marrow family case study, folder 5, box 43, Helen Hall Papers.

152. Gilbraith, Raw Data for Published Bulletins, Bulletin No. 124, Records of the Women's Bureau.

153. Elderton, *Case Studies of Unemployment*, 81.

154. Merrick House case, folder 1, box 45, Helen Hall Papers.

155. Ibid.

156. Ibid.

157. Ibid., 45-11, Balletto.

158. Elderton, *Case Studies of Unemployment*, 13.

159. Taber family case study, folder 9, box 43, Helen Hall Papers.

160. Peralta family case study, folder 1, box 44, Helen Hall Papers.

161. Other examples of families receiving food from families include Elderton, *Case Studies of Unemployment, 78, 107, 109, and 135.* Case 35 is from the wife's brother; case 37 is from the husband's mother; case 68 is from the wife's mother; and case 25 is from an unspecified relative.

162. Elderton, *Case Studies of Unemployment*, 293.

163. "Housing Survey 1933 District of Columbia—Schedules," No. 29, box 14, Division of Research, Unpublished Studies and Materials, 1919–, Records of the Women's Bureau.

164. Schedule 36, Raw Data for Published Bulletins, *Women in Texas Industries: Hours, Wages, Working Conditions, and Home Work,* Bulletin No. 126 (1936), Records of the Women's Bureau.

165. Ibid. Schedule 44.

166. Havenner, Raw Data for Published Bulletins, Bulletin No. 25, Records of the Women's Bureau .

167. Skipper, Raw Data for Published Bulletins, Bulletin No. 10, Records of the Women's Bureau.

168. O'Dowd family case study, folder 7, box 43, Helen Hall Papers.

169. Schedule 41-19, box 123, Raw Data for Published Bulletins, Bulletin No. 88, Records of the Women's Bureau.

170. Elderton, *Case Studies of Unemployment*, 307.

171. No. 76, box 226, Bulletin 126, Records of the Division of Special Services and Publications, Records of the Women's Bureau.

172. Bakke, *Unemployed Worker*, 278.

173. Schedule 42-66, box 123, Raw Data for Published Bulletins, Bulletin No. 88, Records of the Women's Bureau.

174. Elderton, *Case Studies of Unemployment*, 186–87.

175. Ibid., 81.

176. O'Dowd family case study, folder 7, box 43, Helen Hall Papers.

177. Ibid., Hinchman family case study, folder 14, box 43, Helen Hall Papers. For another example of a family whose move to a larger community worsened instead of bettered their conditions, see Dwyer family case study, folder 14, box 43, Helen Hall Papers.

178. Schedule 195, Raw Data for Published Bulletins, Bulletin No. 119, Records of the Women's Bureau.

179. Schedule 115, Raw Data for Published Bulletins, Bulletin No. 126, Records of the Women's Bureau.

180. Ibid. Schedule 84.

181. Susan Porter Benson, "What Goes 'Round, Comes 'Round: Second-Hand Clothing, Furniture, and Tools in Working-Class Lives in the Interwar USA," *Journal of Women's History* 19, 1 (2007).

182. Schedule 68, Raw Data for Published Bulletins, Bulletin No. 126, Records of the Women's Bureau.

183. Ibid. Schedule 59. .

184. Ruth Alice Allen and Sam B. Barton, *Wage Earners Meet the Depression*, Bureau of Research in the Social Sciences Study No. 15, University of Texas Bulletin No. 3545, December 1, 1935 (Austin, 1935), 22.

185. Allen and Barton, *Wage Earners Meet the Depression*, 22.

186. Ibid., 52.

187. Capella family case study, folder 2, box 43, Helen Hall Papers.

188. Elderton, *Case Studies of Unemployment*, 172.

189. Ibid., 389.

190. Cases 66, 43, 36, 72, "Housing Survey 1933 District of Columbia—Schedules," Division of Research, Unpublished Studies and Materials, 1919–1972, Records of the Women's Bureau.

191. Elderton, *Case Studies of Unemployment*, 312.

192. Ibid., 321.

193. Ibid., 251.

194. "Housing Survey 1933 District of Columbia—Schedules," Division of Research, Unpublished Studies and Materials, 1919–1972, Records of the Women's Bureau.

195. Schedules 7-2-130, 7-2-132, and 7-2-143, box 97; schedules 7-2-158, 7-2-167, 7-2-172, 7-2-185, 7-2-220, 7-2-236, 7-2-240, 7-2-262, and 7-3-306, box 98; schedules 7-4-337 and 7-4-362; box 99; schedules 7-8-661, 7-9-724, 7-9-727, 7-9-751, 7-9-756, 7-9-760, and 7-9-762, box 101; 7-12-875 and 7-12-955, box 102, Raw Data for Published Bulletins, Bulletin No. 74, Records of the Women's Bureau.

196. Ibid. Schedule 7-2-167, box 98.

197. Schedules 103, 82, 31, 24, Raw Data for Published Bulletins, Bulletin No. 126, Records of the Women's Bureau.

198. Schedule 11-35, box 120, Raw Data for Published Bulletins, Bulletin No. 88, Records of the Women's Bureau.

199. Ibid. Schedule 11-118.

200. Schedule 37, Raw Data for Published Bulletins, Bulletin No. 126, Records of the Women's Bureau.

201. Schedule 42-123, box 123, Raw Data for Published Bulletins, Bulletin No. 88, Records of the Women's Bureau.

202. Thornburg, Raw Data for Published Bulletins, *Women in Missouri Industries: A Study of Hours and Wages,* Bulletin No. 35 (1924), Records of the Women's Bureau; for other examples, see Olson, Raw Data for Published Bulletins, Bulletin No. 19; Hall, Raw Data for Published Bulletins, Bulletin No. 10; Anthe, Raw Data for Published Bulletins, Bulletin No. 124; all in Records of the Women's Bureau.

203. Schedule 11-54, box 120, Raw Data for Published Bulletins, Bulletin No. 88, Records of the Women's Bureau.

204. Ibid. Schedule 31-42, box 122.

205. Elderton, *Case Studies of Unemployment,* 290–91 is an example of this.

206. Schedule 152, Raw Data for Published Bulletins, Bulletin No. 119, Records of the Women's Bureau.

207. Mary Merinka, 1938 Case Histories, box 1, Henry Street Settlement Records, Social Welfare History Archives, University of Minnesota, Minneapolis.

208. Elderton, *Case Studies of Unemployment,* 279, for both quotations. For other examples of people who repaid loans conscientiously, see Elderton, *Case Studies of Unemployment,* 35–36, 353, 160, 66; Cavan and Ranck, *The Family and the Depression,* 119.

209. Elderton, *Case Studies of Unemployment,* 270.

210. Ibid., 20. On the appeals and problems with Morris Plan loans, relatively available to the working poor, see Louis N. Robinson, "The Morris Plan," *American Economic Review* 21, 2 (1931): 222–35.

211. Ibid., 117.

212. Ibid., 247.

213. Case 42, "Housing Survey 1933 District of Columbia—Schedules," Division of Research, Unpublished Studies and Materials, 1919–1972, Records of the Women's Bureau.

214. Elderton, *Case Studies of Unemployment,* 309–10.

215. Cushing, Raw Data for Published Bulletins, Bulletin No. 19, Records of the Women's Bureau.

216. Schedule 7-7-485, box 99, Raw Data for Published Bulletins, Bulletin No. 74, Records of the Women's Bureau.

217. Schedule 209, Raw Data for Published Bulletins, Bulletin No. 119, Records of the Women's Bureau.

218. Elderton, *Case Studies of Unemployment,* 327; also 31–32.

219. Komarovsky, *The Unemployed Man and His Family,* 123.

220. Ibid.

221. Ibid.

222. Ibid., 124.

223. Ibid., 125.

224. Ibid., 129 (all citations).

225. Elderton, *Case Studies of Unemployment,* 205.

226. Ibid., 166–68, quotation 168. See 86–87 for another case of smoldering resentment among siblings.

5. The Family Economy in the Marketplace

1. Leila Houghteling, for example, in *The Income and Standard of Living of Unskilled Laborers in Chicago* (Chicago: University of Chicago Press, 1927), 120–21, 139–43.

2. Instructions for schedule 369, file "Correspondence," box 89, Raw Data for Published Bulletins, *The Immigrant Woman and Her Job*, Bulletin No. 74 (1930), Records of the Women's Bureau, RG 86, (National Archives, College Park).

3. Mary Elizabeth Pidgeon, *The Employment of Women in Slaughtering and Meat Packing*, Bulletin of the Women's Bureau, No. 88 (Washington, DC: Government Printing Office, 1932), 131–32, 203.

4. Susan Strasser, *Never Done: A History of American Housework* (New York: Pantheon, 1982), 23–24 and 34–36 on class, bread, and baking. See also Ruth Schwartz Cowan, *More Work for Mother: The Ironies of Household Technology from the Open Hearth to the Microwave* (New York: Basic Books, 1983), 49–53.

5. Raw Data for Published Bulletins, Bulletin No. 74, Records of the Women's Bureau; schedules 7-1-3 and 7-1-34, box 97, baked most of their bread; for women who baked some of it, see schedules 7-2-109, box 97; 7-3-302 and 7-3-312, box 98; and 7-9-787, box 101.

6. Ibid. Schedule 7-1-9A, box 97.

7. Ibid. Schedule 7-4-392, box 99.

8. Ibid. Schedules 7-2-84, box 97; 7-2-229, 7-2-230, and 7-3-314, box 98; 7-4-339, 7-4-374, 7-6-461, and 7-7-480, box 99; 7-8-506, 7-8-595, and 7-8-608, box 100; 7-12-897 and 7-12-975, box 102.

9. Ibid. Schedule 7-2-238, box 98.

10. Ibid. Schedule 7-5-428, box 99.

11. Ibid. Schedule 7-3-288, box 98.

12. Ibid. Schedule 7-3-310.

13. Ibid. Schedule 7-4-385, box 99.

14. Ibid. Schedule 7-8-565, box 100.

15. Ibid. Schedules 7-5-428, box 99; and 7-8-556, box 100.

16. Ibid. Schedules 7-3-307, box 98; and 7-6-446, box 99.

17. Ibid. Schedule 7-3-281, box 98. See also schedules 11-103, box 120; 17-102, 17-73, and 17-85, box 121; Raw Data for Published Bulletins, *The Employment of Women in Slaughtering and Meat Packing*, Bulletin No. 88 (1932), Records of the Women's Bureau.

18. Schedules 7-2-85, box 97; 7-3-310 and 7-3-312, box 98; and 7-7-464, box 99, Raw Data for Published Bulletins, Bulletin No. 74, Records of the Women's Bureau.

19. Ibid. Schedule 7-3-312, box 98.

20. Examples include schedules 7-1-60, box 97; 7-2-200 and 7-3-282, box 98; 7-4-346, box 99; and 7-9-716, box 101; Raw Data for Published Bulletins, Bulletin No. 74, Records of the Women's Bureau. See also schedules 11-48, box 120; 17-119, box

121; 31-3, box 122; 21-2 and 43-26, box 123; Raw Data for Published Bulletins, Bulletin No. 88, Records of the Women's Bureau.

21. Schedule 7-3-278, box 98, Raw Data for Published Bulletins, Bulletin No. 74, Records of the Women's Bureau.

22. Schedule Ottumwa-11, box 123, Raw Data for Published Bulletins, Bulletin No. 88, Records of the Women's Bureau.

23. Schedules 7-1-5, box 97; 7-2-190, 7-2-216, and 7-2-219, box 98; 7-4-365 and 7-4-386, box 99; and 7-8-606, box 100.

24. Ibid. Schedule 7-2-152, box 98.

25. Ibid. Schedule 7-5-420, box 99.

26. Ibid. Schedule 7-2-104, box 97.

27. Ibid. Schedule 7-8-682, box 101.

28. Ibid. Schedule 7-7-482, box 99. See also 7-4-340.

29. Ibid. Schedule 7-1-7, box 97.

30. Schedules 7-1-7, box 97; 7-8-682 and 7-8-697, box 101; Raw Data for Published Bulletins, Bulletin No. 74, Records of the Women's Bureau. See also schedules 17-135 and 17-70, box 121; and 21-20, box 123; Raw Data for Published Bulletins, Bulletin No. 88, Records of the Women's Bureau.

31. Schedules 7-2-104, box 97; and 7-4-340, box 99; Raw Data for Published Bulletins, Bulletin No. 74, Records of the Women's Bureau.

32. Ibid. Schedule 7-2-118, box 97.

33. Ibid. Schedule 7-2-136.

34. Ruth Alice Allen and Sam B. Barton, *Wage Earners Meet the Depression,* Bureau of Research in the Social Sciences Study No. 15, *The University of Texas Bulletin* 3545 (Austin, 1935), 21.

35. Gwendolyn Salisbury Hughes, *Mothers in Industry: Wage-Earning by Mothers in Philadelphia* (New York: New Republic, 1925), 172. The Hughes study does not discuss the frequency of home sewing as opposed to store-bought clothing. Allen and Barton also looked at expenditures for laundry, although less systematically, and found that between 20 and 45 percent of different groups used paid laundry services.

36. Heller Committee for Research in Social Economics of the University of California and Constantine Panunzio, *How Mexicans Earn and Live: A Study of the Incomes and Expenditures of One Hundred Mexican Families in San Diego, California,* vol. 5 of *Cost of Living Studies* (Berkeley: University of California Press, 1933), 44–45, quotation from 45.

37. Heller Committee and Panunzio, *How Mexicans Earn and Live,* 11.

38. Ibid., 42, Hughes, *Mothers in Industry,* 184. There was no systematic study of plumbing in the Philadelphia households visited for Caroline Manning's *The Immigrant Woman and Her Job,* Bulletin of the Women's Bureau, No. 74 (Washington, DC: Government Printing Office, 1930).

39. Arwen P. Mohun, *Steam Laundries: Gender, Technology, and Work in the*

United States and Great Britain, 1880–1940 (Baltimore: Johns Hopkins University Press, 1999), 161.

40. Heller Committee and Panunzio, *How Mexicans Earn and Live,* 43.

41. Ibid., 20.

42. Ibid., 45.

43. Schedule 1, box 25, Raw Data for Published Bulletins, *Women in Oklahoma Industries: A Study of Hours, Wages, and Working Conditions,* Bulletin No. 48 (1926), Records of the Women's Bureau.

44. Ibid. Schedule 4.

45. Ibid. Schedule 29. See also Hearnsberger, box 31, Raw Data for Published Bulletins, *Women in Tennessee Industries: A Study of Hours, Wages, and Working Conditions,* Bulletin No. 56 (1927), Records of the Women's Bureau.

46. Schedule 5, Raw Data for Published Bulletins, Bulletin No. 48, Records of the Women's Bureau.

47. Ibid. Schedule 2. Other women who stayed home from work to do laundry included Runes, Raw Data for Published Reports, *Women in South Carolina Industries: A Study of Hours, Wages, and Working Conditions,* Bulletin No. 32, Records of the Women's Bureau; Zawistowsky (Chicago), box 12, Raw Data for Published Bulletins, *Women in the Candy Industry in Chicago and St. Louis: A Study of Hours, Wages, and Working conditions in 1920–1021,* Bulletin No. 25 (1923), Records of the Women's Bureau; Glass, box 3, Raw Data for Published Bulletins, *Hours and Conditions of Work for Women in Industry in Virginia,* Bulletin No. 10 (1920), Records of the Women's Bureau.

48. *Case Studies of Unemployment Compiled by the Unemployment Committee of the National Federation of Settlements,* ed. Marion Elderton (Philadelphia: University of Pennsylvania Press, 1931), 299; a similar example is 270.

49. If we add in the sixteen Philadelphians and thirteen meatpackers who were entirely relieved of laundry duties by co-residents, we still find that only 5 percent of these hard-worked women were definitely spared the grueling tasks of laundry.

50. Mohun, *Steam Laundries,* 159.

51. Women who sent their laundry out in the winter included schedules 16-47 and 16-66, box 121; and 36-29, box 122; Raw Data for Published Bulletins, Bulletin No. 88, Records of the Women's Bureau.

52. Women who sent their laundry out when they were working full-time included schedules 7-8-605, box 100; 7-8-654 and 7-8-682, box 101; Raw Data for Published Bulletins, Bulletin No. 74, Records of the Women's Bureau. See also schedules 37-14, box 122; 41-27, and South St. Paul S-10, box 123; Raw Data for Published Bulletins, Bulletin No. 88, Records of the Women's Bureau. For a woman who sent out the laundry when her unemployed husband got a job, see schedule 7-5-437, box 99, Raw Data for Published Bulletins, Bulletin No. 74, Records of the Women's Bureau.

53. Women who sent laundry out for health reasons included schedules 17-8726, box 121; and 37-26, box 122; Raw Data for Published Bulletins, Bulletin No. 88,

Records of the Women's Bureau. See also schedules 16, 310, 318, 943, 1101, 1808, 2083, 2621, 2689, 2789, 2941, box 33, Raw Data for Published Bulletins, *Industrial Accidents to Women in New Jersey, Ohio, and Wisconsin,* Bulletin No. 60 (1927), Records of the Women's Bureau.

54. Mohun, *Steam Laundries,* 152–155, discusses women's many complaints about commercial laundries.

55. Schedule 7-8-521, box 100, Raw Data for Published Bulletins, Bulletin No. 74, Records of the Women's Bureau. See also 7-9-715, box 101, for a similar comment.

56. Ibid. Schedule 7-8-613, box 100.

57. Ibid. Schedules 7-3-319, box 98; 7-8-525, box 100; and 7-8-704, box 101; Raw Data for Published Bulletins, Bulletin No. 74, Records of the Women's Bureau.

58. Ibid. Schedule 7-4-355, box 99.

59. Although Mercie's wage is not given on the schedule, she probably earned about $20 per week; see tables 4 and 6 in Pidgeon, *The Employment of Women in Slaughtering and Meat Packing,* 77 and 145.

60. Schedule 11-48, box 120, Raw Data for Published Bulletins, Bulletin No. 88, Records of the Women's Bureau.

61. Strasser, *Never Done,* 119.

62. Schedule 16-29, box 121, Raw Data for Published Bulletins, Bulletin No. 88, Records of the Women's Bureau.

63. Cowan, *More Work for Mother,* 107, 185.

64. Ibid., 185; Mohun, *Steam Laundries,* 258. The drop in price resulted from Sears, Roebuck's determination to undersell its rivals.

65. Schedule 42-123, box 123, Raw Data for Published Bulletins, Bulletin No. 88, Records of the Women's Bureau. For another case of a washing machine replacing labor that a woman could no longer do, see schedule 1939, box 33, Raw Data for Published Bulletins, Bulletin No. 60, Records of the Women's Bureau; this woman had injured a hand in an industrial accident.

66. Elderton, *Case Studies of Unemployment,* 218.

67. Schedule 7-2-113, box 97, Raw Data for Published Bulletins, Bulletin No. 74, Records of the Women's Bureau. Another husband, a chronic deserter who had apparently disappeared for good a few years before the Women's Bureau's visit to his wife, may have been, as his wife described him, "lazy," but he may also have rigged up the water-powered motor for the washing machine she continued to use (WB #74, 44). These water-powered machines, while ingenious, were increasingly anachronistic, as 70 percent of new washing machines sold in 1921 were electric, as were 84 percent by 1929; see Strasser, *Never Done,* 118.

68. Schedule 7-4-358, box 99, Raw Data for Published Bulletins, Bulletin No. 74, Records of the Women's Bureau.

69. Schedule 31-14, box 122, Raw Data for Published Bulletins, Bulletin No. 88, Records of the Women's Bureau.

70. Ibid. Schedule 37-1.

71. Ibid. Schedule 42-77, box 123.

72. Ibid. Schedule 21-21-X, box 123.

73. Ruth Shonle Cavan and Katherine Howland Ranck, *The Family and the Depression: A Study of One Hundred Chicago Families* (Chicago: University of Chicago Press, 1938), 119. On teachers, see Elderton, *Case Studies of Unemployment*, 117, 98.

74. Schedule 5, folder "Mothers' Pensions 1925–26," box 3, Unpublished Studies and Materials, 1919–1972, Records of the Division of Research and Manpower Program Development, Records of the Women's Bureau.

75. E. Wight Bakke, *The Unemployed Worker: A Study of the Task of Making a Living without a Job* (New Haven: Yale University Press, 1940), 272.

76. Allen and Barton, *Wage Earners Meet the Depression*, 21.

77. Elderton, *Case Studies of Unemployment*, 321.

78. Perrywinkle family case study, folder 9, box 48, Helen Hall Papers, Social Welfare History Archives, University of Minnesota, Minneapolis.

79. Heller Committee and Panunzio, *How Mexicans Earn and Live*, 14, 36.

80. Elizabeth Clark-Lewis, *Living In, Living Out: African American Domestics in Washington, D.C., 1910–1940* (Washington, DC: Smithsonian Institution Press, 1994), 157.

81. "The Autobiography of a First Generation American Girl," box 31, YWCA Papers, Sophia Smith Collection, Smith College (Northampton, Massachusetts).

82. Bakke, *Unemployed Worker*, 272–73.

83. See, for example, Elderton, *Case Studies of Unemployment*, 173, 145, 148.

84. See, for example, schedule 7-2-90, box 97; 7-12-957, and 7-12-960, box 102; Raw Data for Published Bulletins, Bulletin No. 74, Records of the Women's Bureau; and schedule 32-20, box 122, Raw Data for Published Bulletins, Bulletin No. 88, Records of the Women's Bureau.

See also schedule 7-2-90, box 97; 7-12-957 and 7-12-960, box 102; Raw Data for Published Bulletins, *Bulletin No. 74*, Records of the Women's Bureau; and schedule 32-20, box 122, Raw Data for Published Bulletins, Bulletin No. 88, Records of the Women's Bureau.

85. "Second Generation Girl," Folder 5, box 31, YWCA Papers.

86. Elderton, *Case Studies of Unemployment*, 261–62.

87. Ibid., 287.

88. Ibid., 180–81.

89. Schedule 76, box 226, Raw Data for Published Bulletins, *Women in Texas Industries: Hours, Wages, Working Conditions, and Home Work*, Bulletin No. 126 (1936), Records of the Women's Bureau.

90. Bakke, *Unemployed Worker*, 278.

91. Schedule 37-9, box 122, Raw Data for Published Bulletins, Bulletin No. 88, Records of the Women's Bureau.

92. Heller Committee and Panunzio, *How Mexicans Earn and Live*, 53.

93. Elderton, *Case Studies of Unemployment*, 242–44.

94. Ibid., 38–41; quotation, 41.

95. Ibid., 121–122.

96. Schedule 45, box 33, Raw Data for Published Bulletins, Bulletin No. 60, Records of the Women's Bureau.

97. Elderton, *Case Studies,* pp. 127–128.

98. Ibid., 151.

99. Ibid., 17, 43, 51–52.

100. Bakke, *Unemployed Worker,* 260.

101. Elderton, *Case Studies of Unemployment,* 92–93.

102. Ibid., 296–97.

103. Schedule 38, box 25, Raw Data for Published Bulletins, Bulletin No. 48, Records of the Women's Bureau.

104. Elderton, *Case Studies of Unemployment,* 364.

105. Folders "#119 Schedules—Home Visits (Gloversville, NY)" and "#119 Schedules—Home Visits (Johnstown, NY)," box 207, Raw Data for Published Bulletins, *Hours and Earnings in the Leather-Glove Industry,* Bulletin No. 119 (1934), Records of the Women's Bureau.

106. Ibid. Schedule 199.

107. Ibid. Schedule 211.

108. Ibid. Schedule 206.

109. Ibid. Schedule 126.

110. Ibid. Schedule 160.

111. Bakke, *Unemployed Worker,* 229.

112. Elderton, *Case Studies of Unemployment,* 215.

113. See Lee Rainwater, Richard P. Coleman, and Gerald Handel, *Workingman's Wife* (1959; New York: Arno, 1979), and Lendol Glen Calder, *Financing the American Dream: A Cultural History of Consumer Credit* (Princeton: Princeton University Press, 1999).

114. Schedule 42-2-121, box 123, Raw Data for Published Bulletins, Bulletin No. 88, Records of the Women's Bureau.

115. Schedule 7-4-343, box 99, Raw Data for Published Bulletins, Bulletin No. 74, Records of the Women's Bureau.

116. Ibid. Schedule 7-3-298, box 98.

117. Ibid. Schedule 7-5-410, box 99.

118. Ibid. Schedule 7-11-836, box 102.

119. Ibid. Schedule 7-2-151, box 98.

120. Schedule 2336, box 33, Raw Data for Published Bulletins, Bulletin No. 60, Records of the Women's Bureau, which includes the intriguing comment from a mother to the agent: "We all help one another."

121. Schedule 31-1, box 122, Raw Data for Published Bulletins, Bulletin No. 88, Records of the Women's Bureau.

122. Ibid. Schedule South St. Paul A-9, box 123.

123. Schedule 341, box 33, Raw Data for Published Bulletins, Bulletin No. 60, Records of the Women's Bureau.

124. Schedule 41-13, box 123, Raw Data for Published Bulletins, Bulletin No. 88, Records of the Women's Bureau.

125. Ibid. Schedule 42-116.

126. David R. Roediger with James Barrett, "Inbetween Peoples: Race, Nationality, and the 'New-Immigrant' Working Class," in *Colored White: Transcending the Racial Past*, by Roediger (Berkeley: University of California Press, 2002), 138–68. For a similar case, see schedule 26-4, box 123, Raw Data for Published Bulletins, Bulletin No. 88, Records of the Women's Bureau.

127. Schedule 42-176, box 123, Raw Data for Published Bulletins, Bulletin No. 88, Records of the Women's Bureau.

128. Pidgeon, *The Employment of Women in Slaughtering and Meat Packing*, 77. (This is an estimate.)

129. Schedule 15-24, box 121, Raw Data for Published Bulletins, Bulletin No. 88, Records of the Women's Bureau.

130. Ibid. Schedule 31-70, box 122.

131. Ibid. Schedule 11-32, box 120.

132. Schedule 7-2-150, box 97, Raw Data for Published Bulletins, Bulletin No. 74, Records of the Women's Bureau.

133. Schedule 667, box 33, Raw Data for Published Bulletins, Bulletin No. 60, Records of the Women's Bureau.

134. Mattie, box 25, Raw Data for Published Bulletins, Bulletin No. 48, Records of the Women's Bureau.

135. Schedule 43-6, box 123, Raw Data for Published Bulletins, Bulletin No. 88, Records of the Women's Bureau.

136. Jordan, box 9, Raw Data for Published Bulletins, *Women in Georgia Industries: A Study of Hours, Wages, and Working Conditions*, Bulletin No. 22 (1922), Records of the Women's Bureau.

137. Schedules 11-10 and 11-131, box 120, Raw Data for Published Bulletins, Bulletin No. 88, Records of the Women's Bureau.

138. Folder "Housing Survey 1933 District of Columbia—Schedules," box 14, Division of Research, Unpublished Studies and Materials, 1919–1972, Records of the Women's Bureau.

139. Ibid. Schedule 4.

140. Ibid.

141. Ibid. Schedule 6.

142. Ibid. Schedule 5.

143. Ibid. Schedule 25.

144. Ibid. Schedule 76.

145. Ibid. Schedule 89.

146. Kenneth T. Jackson, *Crabgrass Frontier: The Suburbanization of the United States* (Oxford: Oxford University Press, 1985), 240–41.

147. Schedule 91, folder "Housing Survey 1933 District of Columbia—Sched-

ules," box 14, Division of Research, Unpublished Studies and Materials, 1919–1972, Records of the Women's Bureau.

148. Ibid. Schedule 94.

149. Ibid. Schedule 1.

150. Ibid. Schedule 6.

151. Clacknon (Atlanta), box 9, Raw Data for Published Bulletins, Bulletin No. 22, Records of the Women's Bureau.

152. Schedule 37-14, box 122, Raw Data for Published Bulletins, Bulletin No. 88, Records of the Women's Bureau.

153. Ibid. Schedule 42-115, box 123. See also schedule 43-10: USA-born, never paid, sometimes as much as $100.

154. Ibid. Sioux City S-3.

155. Yeomans, box 9, Raw Data for Published Bulletins, Bulletin No. 22, Records of the Women's Bureau.

156. Blaetz (St. Louis), box 12, Raw Data for Published Bulletins, Bulletin No. 25, Records of the Women's Bureau.

157. Arnold/Freeman/Burke (Atlanta), box 9, Raw Data for Published Bulletins, Bulletin No. 22, Records of the Women's Bureau.

158. Ibid. Carroll.

159. Schedule 2382, box 33, Raw Data for Published Bulletins, Bulletin No. 60, Records of the Women's Bureau.

160. Mrs. C.Poss (Atlanta), box 9, Raw Data for Published Bulletins, Bulletin No. 60, Records of the Women's Bureau.

161. Tennyson, box 18, Raw Data for Published Bulletins, *Women in Missouri Industries: A Study of Hours and Wages,* Bulletin No. 35 (1924), Records of the Women's Bureau.

162. Green (Atlanta), box 9, Raw Data for Published Bulletins, Bulletin No. 22, Records of the Women's Bureau.

163. Wilbanks, box 25, Raw Data for Published Bulletins, Bulletin No. 48, Records of the Women's Bureau.

164. Schedule 973, box 33, Raw Data for Published Bulletins, Bulletin No. 60, Records of the Women's Bureau.

165. Schedule 83, box 207, Raw Data for Published Bulletins, Bulletin No. 119, Records of the Women's Bureau.

166. Ibid. Schedule 60.

167. Schedule 17-52, box 121, Raw Data for Published Bulletins, Bulletin No. 88, Records of the Women's Bureau.

168. Ibid. Schedule 17-1538.

169. Ibid. Schedule 11-116, box 120.

170. Ibid. Schedule 16-1, box 121; see also schedule 24-31, box 123.

171. Ibid. Schedule 17-12.

172. Ibid. Schedule 32-6, box 122.

173. Ibid. Schedule 37-18.

174. Ibid. Schedule 36-7.

175. Ibid. Schedule 16-73, box 121.

176. Ibid. Schedule 32-6, box 122.

177. Schedule 55, folder "Housing Survey 1933 District of Columbia—Schedules," box 14, Division of Research, Unpublished Studies and Materials, 1919–1972, Records of the Women's Bureau.

178. Ibid. Schedule 85.

179. Schedule 11-4, box 120, Raw Data for Published Bulletins, Bulletin No. 88, Records of the Women's Bureau. See also schedule 17-47, box 121.

180. Ibid. Schedule 31-67, box 122.

181. Ibid. Schedule 11-12, box 120; see also schedules 11-17 and 11-128, box 120; 16-4 and 16-66, box 121; and 31-60 and 32-16, box 122.

182. Ibid. Schedule 17-98, box 121.

183. Ibid. Schedule 11-70, box 120.

184. Ibid. Schedule 17-76, box 121.

185. Ibid. Schedule 17-106.

186. Ibid. Schedule 31-2, box 122.

187. Ibid. Schedule 21-10, box 123.

188. Ibid. Schedule 37-5, box 122.

189. Ibid. Schedule South St. Paul S-13, box 123.

190. Ibid. Schedule 42-121.

191. Ibid. Schedule 11-27, box 120.

192. Ibid. Schedule 11-106.

193. Ibid. Schedule 11-113.

194. Ibid. Schedule 11-11; see also 16-36, box 121.

195. Ibid. Schedule 17-75, box 121.

196. Ibid. Schedule 17-105.

197. Ibid. Schedule 26-108, box 123.

198. Ibid. Schedule 31-46, box 122.

199. Ibid. Schedule 46-19, box 123.

200. Schedule 1877, box 33, Raw Data for Published Bulletins, Bulletin No. 60, Records of the Women's Bureau.

201. Schedule 11-103, box 120, Raw Data for Published Bulletins, Bulletin No. 88, Records of the Women's Bureau. For a similar case, see schedule 43-9, box 123 (USA-born).

202. Ibid. Schedule 17-137, box 121.

203. Ibid. Schedule South St. Paul S-10, box 123.

204. Ibid. Schedule 21-7, box 123.

205. Ibid. Schedule 43-6.

206. Ibid. Schedule 11-100, box 120.

207. Ibid. Schedule 37-26, box 122.

208. Ibid. Schedule 16-63, box 121.

209. Ibid. Schedule 16-33.

210. Ibid. Schedule 17-97.

211. Ibid. Schedule 16-2.

212. Ibid. Schedule 56-34, box 123.

213. Schedule 158, box 207, Raw Data for Published Bulletins, Bulletin No. 119, Records of the Women's Bureau.

214. Schedule 31-71, box 122, Raw Data for Published Bulletins, Bulletin No. 88, Records of the Women's Bureau; see also schedules 36-37, box 122; and 56-54, box 123.

215. Ibid. Schedules 11-28, box 120; 17-39, 17-55,17-112, 16-*57, 16-65, and 15-23; box 121 31-2, 31-7, 31-9, 31-70, 36-3, 36-37, 36-40, and 37-26, box 122; and 26-4, 24-39, 24-RT, 21-37, 41-1, 41-13, 46-30, 56-54, and 51-5, box 123.

Afterword, by David Montgomery

1. Susan Porter Benson, *Counter Cultures: Saleswomen, Managers, and Customers in American Department Stores, 1890–1940* (Urbana: University of Illinois Press, 1986).

2. E. P. Thompson, *The Making of the English Working Class* (New York: Vintage Books, 1967), 9.

3. Benson, *Counter Cultures,* 177–226. Benson elaborated her deconstruction of the "service sector" in "The 1920s through the Looking Glass of Gender: A Response to David Montgomery," *International Labor and Working-Class History* 32 (Fall 1987): 34–35.

4. Most notably Harry Braverman, *Labor and Monopoly Capital: The Degradation of Work in the Twentieth Century* (New York: Monthly Review Press, 1974).

5. This book, Introduction, 10–11.

6. Susan Porter Benson, "The 1920s through the Looking Glass of Gender," 32.

7. Dot Jones, "Serfdom and Slavery: Women's Work in Wales, 1890–1930," in *Class, Community, and the Labour Movement: Wales and Canada, 1850–1930,* edited by Deian R. Hopkin and Gregory S. Kealey (St. Johns, N.S.: Llafur and Canadian Committee on Labour History, 1989), 86–100.

8. Lawrence B. Glickman, *A Living Wage: American Workers and the Making of Consumer Society* (Ithaca: Cornell University Press, 1997), 158. For an examination of pre-1914 studies of the industrial earnings of women and men, see David Montgomery, *The Fall of the House of Labor: The Workplace, the State, and American Labor Activism, 1865–1925* (New York: Cambridge University Press, 1987), 135–43.

9. Peter Shergold, *Working-Class Life: The "American Standard" in Comparative Perspective, 1899–1913* (Pittsburgh: University of Pittsburgh Press, 1982). Katherine A. Harvey alerted us decades ago to the routine fluctuation between abundance and scarcity in the homes of even the most nearly prosperous coal miners. Harvey, *The Best-Dressed Miners: Life and Labor in the Maryland Coal Region, 1835–1910* (Ithaca: Cornell University Press, 1919). For an account of family survival in the

face of unemployment in the coal fields, as seen through the eyes of a little girl, see Sonya Jason, *Icon of Spring* (Pittsburgh: University of Pittsburgh Press, 1993).

10. Tensions surrounding children's economic roles are well analyzed in Stephen A. Lassonde, *Learning to Forget: Schooling and Family Life in New Haven's Working Class, 1870–1940* (New Haven: Yale University Press, 2005).

11. Ewa Morawska, *For Bread with Butter: Life-Worlds of East Central Europeans in Johnstown, Pennsylvania, 1890–1940* (New York: Cambridge University Press, 1985), 232–33.

Index

Children:
    as consumers, 14, 60, 68–71, 73–74, 75–76
    contributions by, to family support, 58–
      59, 64–71, 75–76
    education of, 41, 59–64
    gender differences in roles of, 14, 63, 65–
      66, 67, 69–70, 71, 75–76
    kin and neighbors' help with, 129–30 (*see
      also* Child care)
    parents' hopes for, 60–64
    see also Daughters; Sons
Cincinnati Consumers' League study, 68, 71,
    74
Clark, Gracia, 8, 78
Class differences
    in breadwinning ethic, 27
    in consumption, 8, 11, 12–13, 15, 75, 174
    and housework, 48, 106
Cleaning, 47
Clothing, 69–70, 137, 142–44
    gifts of, 126–29
    home-sewn, 142–44, 145
    and installment credit, 74, 164
    men's, 69–70, 143, 152
    secondhand, 126–29, 150–53, 158
College, 62
"Companionate marriage," 17
Conflict, 95–100, 137–38
    "cooperative," 10
    intergenerational, 59, 96–99, 152–53
    marital: *see* Marital conflict
    in shared housing, 95–100, 137–38
Consumerism, 179n17
Consumption, 6–8, 10–11, 40, 58, 75–76
    class differences in, 8, 11, 12–13, 15, 75, 174
    constraints on, 31, 75
    defined, 179n17
    and ethnicity, 6–7
    and family strategies, 7–8, 10–11, 31–32
    gender differences in, 14, 31–32, 69–70,
      71, 75–76
    and intergenerational issues, 69–76
    see also Credit
Cooking, 45, 47, 102, 142
"Cooperative conflict," 10
Corley, Mary Lou, 69
Counter Cultures (Benson), 171, 172–73
Cowan, Ruth Schwartz, 149
Credit, 14–15, 164–67
    attitudes toward, 165–67
    with local merchants (buying "on the
      book"), 14, 73
    see also Installment credit
Crowding, 95–96

Daughters, 61–62, 67–71, 152–53
    as consumers, 14, 69–71, 73, 75–76
    different roles for, than for sons, 14, 63,
      65–66, 67, 69–70, 71, 75–76
    wage earning by, 65–66, 67–68, 72, 75
Day nurseries, 22, 110–12, 113, 209n41
Delacorte, Carmen and Frank, 47–48
Department stores, 12–13, 171, 172–73
Dependence, fear of, 39, 84, 87
Depression of 1930s (Great Depression), 72,
    133, 144, 154
    and pooling of family money, 24–25, 65,
      68
    and secondhand goods, 128–29, 131, 154
Desertion, 21–22, 25, 54–55, 85, 182n37
Dishwashing, 47
Domestic violence: networks of support for
    victims of, 86
Domus, 5, 6
Dorn, Vera, 68
Drinking, 49, 54

Education, 41, 59–64
    vocational, 71–72
Ehrenreich, Barbara, 27
*Employment of Women in Slaughtering and
    Meat Packing, The*, 45–46, 81
English immigrants, 45
Entitlement, sense of, 10, 72, 73, 97
Ethnicity, 4–7, 22, 42, 189–90n182
    and class, 7, 50
    and hopes for children, 61
    and male participation in housework, 45,
      46
Ewen, Elizabeth, 16

Family economy, working-class,
    as partnership, 17, 35, 37–38, 41, 42, 47–48,
      50–51
    women as managers of, 16, 27–33, 70–71,
      105
    see also Consumption; Family fund; Men's
      wage earning; Mutuality, working-
      class; Reciprocity, working-class;
      Women's wage earning
Family enterprises, 51
Family fund, 22–25
    allocation of, 23–24
    control of, 25
    withholding of some wages from, 24–25,
      31
Family wage, 18, 58, 174
Female breadwinning ethic, 33–42. *See also*
    Women's wage earning

Food, 42, 168–69
  gifts of, 130–31
Fostering of children. *See* Child fostering
Furniture, 41, 131, 154–56
  secondhand, 153–56, 158

Gender differences:
  in daughters' and sons' roles, 14, 63, 65–66, 67, 69–70, 71, 75–76
  in roles in family economy, 16, 27–33, 70–71, 105
  in shared housing, 84–87, 103, 107
  in working-class reciprocity, 104–10, 121–22, 128–29, 137, 138
Gender equity, 17–18, 48–49
German immigrants, 45, 46
Glenn, Susan, 51
Glickman, Lawrence, 174
Glove making, 39, 132, 156, 157, 165
Great Depression. *See* Depression of 1930s
Griger, Helen, 73

Health, poor, 26–27, 88–90, 112. *See also* Medical bills
Heller Committee for Research in Social Economics, 60, 145
Hennings, Alice, 70
High schools, 153
Hobsbawm, Eric, 78
Hochschild, Arlie, 47–48, 50
Home ownership, 41, 81–82, 83–84, 159–63
Homework, industrial, 39, 48, 52, 132–33, 157, 158. *See also* Glove making
Houghteling, Leila, 140
Household appliances, 140–41
House-sharing. *See* Shared housing
Housework, 71, 122–23
  men's role in, 17, 44–49, 109
  partial alleviation of, through purchases, 141–50
  payment for, 123
  in shared housing, 105–10
Housing stock, 81
Hughes, Gwendolyn, "Mothers in Industry" study by, 80, 108, 110, 113, 116, 122, 145

Illness and injuries, 26–27, 35, 88–90, 112. *See also* Medical bills
Immigrants:
  and child care, 111, 113–14, 116
  European, 36, 38, 46, 60–61, 62–64, 111, 113–14, 116, 134
  and help for extended families, 38, 134

  and hopes for children, 60–61, 62–64
  and housework, 46
  Mexican, 38, 60, 134, 145–46, 151, 154
  and women's wage earning, 36, 38
Immigrant Woman and Her Job, The, 19, 21–22, 26, 45, 46, 60–61
Immigrant Women in Industry, 34
Independence
  assertion of, by working-class men, 19, 25, 57
  loss of, 96
  as motive of some women wage earners, 38–39
  see also Dependence, fear of
Individualism, 79, 173
Industrial accidents, 26, 46, 69, 89
Industrial homework, 39, 48, 52, 132–33, 157, 158. *See also* Glove making
Infidelity, 54
Injuries and illness, 26–27, 88–90, 112. *See also* Medical bills
In-law relationships, 102–3
Installment credit, 73–75, 149, 159–62
  working-class avoidance of, 14–15
Intergenerational conflict, 59, 96–99, 152–53
Irons, 140, 149
Italian immigrants, 45, 61

Jewish immigrants, 21–22, 45, 51, 61, 94–95
Jones, Dot, 173–74

Komarovsky, Mirra, 23–34, 24, 66, 126, 137

Ladurie, LeRoy, 6
Lamphere, Louise, 47, 50
Laundry, 145–47, 219n49
Levine, Susan, 16
Like a Family (Hall et al.), 20
Linker, Mollie, 51
"Little mother" role, fading of, 61–62
Loans, 133, 134–35

Madonna of 115th Street, The (Orsi), 5–6
Male breadwinning ethic, 16–17
  rebellion against, 19–22, 26–27
Manning, Caroline, 33, 45, 52, 101
Marchand, Roland, 13
Marital conflict, 52–57
  over family finances, 25, 31–32, 40, 41–42, 53
  over support for relatives, 38, 97–98
Marriages, working-class:
  bending of gender roles in, 16–17, 47–48, 50–51
  breakup of, 54–57 (*see also* Desertion)